What they're saying about *Bring In the Peacocks*...

"Brilliant and talented Hank Moonjean's autobiography is much more than an insider's look at major moviemaking from the 1950s on. It's a thoroughly entertaining page turner that will keep the reader mesmerized. This is, without a doubt, the funniest memoir I have ever read, filled with startling stories and wild times. The author's tone is light, his sense of humor keen and his devotion to the fine art of motion pictures infectious. You could no better than *Bring On the Peacocks*."

– Laura Wagner, *Classic Images*

"Bravo, Hank. It's a wonderful experience. Listen...Bette Davis washed dishes with his Mother. Please join the fun."

– Dom deLuise

"The best book I've read about Hollywood, Hollywood directors, and the making of movies—and I've read most of them...also the funniest."

– Jeffrey Hayden, film & stage director

I had the great pleasure of working with Hank at MGM when we were both kids. I nicknamed him Hankala and he called me Selma. We lived a rich full life and you'll find his book rich as well as enjoyable...and very funny."

– Debbie Reynolds

Bring in the Peacocks

Memoirs of a Hollywood Producer

by Hank Moonjean

BearManor Media
2009

Bring In the Peacocks
or
Memoirs of a Hollywood Producer

© 2009 Hank Moonjean
All rights reserved.

For information, address:

BearManor Media
P. O. Box 71426
Albany, GA 31708

bearmanormedia.com

Cover design by Carla Asmus

Typesetting and layout by John Teehan

Published in the USA by BearManor Media

ISBN—1-59393-465-3

Table of Contents

Prologue 1
Chapter 1 3
    The Early Years
Chapter 2 13
    More of the Beginning
Chapter 3 29
    Raintree County
Chapter 4 51
    More MGM Movies
Chapter 5 63
    Many More MGM Movies
Chapter 6 75
    And Yet More MGM Movies
Chapter 7 91
    Tall Story to *BUtterfield 8*
Chapter 8 107
    Onward
Chapter 9 121
    Cleopatra – Again
Chapter 10 135
    Back to MGM and *Mutiny*
Chapter 11 151
    The Prize
Chapter 12 165
    Molly Brown and Me
Chapter 13 173
    Peach and Beyond
Chapter 14 199
    Cool Hand Luke
Chapter 15 209
    Three More Comedies
Chapter 16 219
    Rosenberg – Three More Times

Chapter 17 227
  The David Merrick Saga

Chapter 18 235
  The Great Gatsby – Stateside

Chapter 19 245
  The Great Gatsby – London

Chapter 20 255
  Another Disappointment

Chapter 21 259
  Finally, Nichols

Chapter 22 265
  Beauty and the Beast – 1976

Chapter 23 271
  The End

Chapter 24 277
  Hooper

Chapter 25 271
  The Next Two

Chapter 26 301
  Paternity and Other Memories

Chapter 27 299
  Sharky's Machine

Chapter 28 305
  Another Major Disappointment

Chapter 29 309
  More Disappointment's : 1981–1982

Chapter 30 317
  Stealing Home – 1987

Chapter 31 321
  Dangerous Liaisons – 1988

Chapter 32 335
  The Wind Down

Postscript 343
Filmography 345
Index 369

To Brad Bennett

(Who has listened to these stories for over 45 years.)

Acknowledgements

To Brad Bennett for giving me continual encouragement.

To Angie Dickinson for being Angie Dickinson.

To Tom Erhardt for his literary wisdom.

To Lesley Logan for her literary expertise.

To Eddie Mensore who kindly tried to help me solve "the mystery of the computer."

To Larry "Blue" Markes for his legal expertise.

And a very special thanks to Maggie Arrington for her time, tireless effort, and continuing encouragement.

Prologue

"I love Americans. I just returned from New York City. They were so nice to me."

I said, "On behalf of the American people I am inviting you back." The princess smiled and purred, "Thank you very much."

Here I was inviting the future Queen of England to the United States. Here I was being presented to Princess Diana at the London premiere of *Dangerous Liaisons*, a film that I had produced. The year was 1988.

As I was being presented to her, I said, looking up at her magnificent eyes, "I'm the only American who worked on this film—with the exception of the actors." She said to me that she had just returned from New York City and that she loved America. I said, "On behalf of the American people, I invite you back." She smiled and thanked me, and moved graciously and beautifully along the reception line to charm Christopher Hampton.

It has been over forty years since I first dreamed of a career in the motion picture industry. It has been over forty years of meeting some of the most exciting personalities in the world…Presidents, royals, writers, statesmen, artists, politicians and all the talented producers, directors, actors and all the other equally talented people who are responsible for making movies.

And now a Princess.

For years, friends and colleagues have asked me, over and over, to write my memoirs of my forty-plus years in the motion picture industry.

2 Bring In the Peacocks

And for years I've refused on the theory that no one would be interested in reading about my career as a movie producer. Producers stay behind the scenes, we make the movies happen; we provide the material and the space for actors, cameramen, directors to create their magic. Not so long ago, Keanu Reeves asked me in all seriousness, "What does a producer do?" Considering the source, I wasn't surprised. But I realized that if Reeves didn't know, it's probable that the civilians are also clueless about the job of the people whose names appear on screen usually above the title with the names of the actors. It occurred to me that my adventures in the movie business might just be of interest to film-lovers. Certainly, every person in the motion picture industry has their own experiences, disappointments, and private laughs, and I would reckon that each of them has a story to tell, if for no other reason than that the stories about making movies are so often pretty damn funny.

Laughs. That's what made me reconsider writing my memoirs. I've seen some outrageous things that no one has ever read about and I've known some sad secrets that will remain with me forever. But I do remember the laughs. We all have the God-given gift of forgetting the bad times and remembering the good. I would like to share my good times with you, times that have stretched from the twilight of the studio system to the present day of independent producers and global corporation-owned studios; from the black-and-white days of chaste kisses and censored language to the anything-goes heyday of R-rated and beyond. I realized when writing this book that it was difficult to separate the good times from the sad. Hollywood is a tough place, a dream factory that can flip to nightmare in a matter of minutes for too many of its citizens. But like so many of those great old movies from the '30s and '40s that inspired me to chase the career, there's a happy ending and a lot of laughs.

– Hank Moonjean

Chapter 1
The Early Years

When I was a teenager in the late 1940s, my parents and I lived very near Paramount Studios in Hollywood. We had moved to California for my parents' health. They were older than my friends' parents: I had been what was then called their "love child," or as we joked in my house, "the tumor." While other kids my age were out playing sports with their fathers, I was given a dime and allowed to spend Saturday at the movies. Movies became the favorite part of my week, my childhood, my life. To be able to stroll up the street to the gates of Paramount was like a dream to me. I would see Marlene Dietrich and all the other Paramount stars enter the studio: Bob Hope, Bing Crosby, Paulette Goddard, Betty Hutton, and Ray Milland. I loved watching actors going to work, hoping that one day I would be working with them. Marlene had seen me often at the Paramount gate and one day she said in her husky, slightly accented voice, "I suppose you'd like to come into the studio." Are you kidding? Marlene was doing a picture called *Golden Earrings*, playing a gypsy. Marlene took me into the studio on a few unforgettable occasions and I would sit in the back observing everything. That was my first taste of moviemaking, and it was very heady stuff for a teenage boy. Thanks in large part to Marlene Dietrich; I knew exactly what I wanted to be when I grew up.

In 1954, I became an assistant director at MGM Studios. MGM was the greatest studio of all, a city within a city. In addition to the soundstages and all the creative and administrative departments that produce movies, it had its own fire department, police department and hospital. It had the best producers, directors, writers, cameramen, designers, art directors, makeup and hair, *and* the best production department. The production department consisted of unit managers, first assistant directors, second assistant directors, and script supervisors. The unit manager was the producer's link to the stage and the assistant director did whatever the director wanted or needed and a good assistant director knew what the director wanted or needed even before the director did. To me, the first assistant director was the force that could make or break a film. I always said that the best position on a film was the First Assistant Director. You were there during the creation of the film, often able to interject ideas and suggestions, yet you never had to make the nerve-wracking major decisions. That was the job of the producer.

How I got inside MGM was a minor miracle. I had graduated from the University of Southern California with a degree in Cinema, and I was immediately drafted into the Korean conflict. My brothers and I were all Army men. We were all drafted.

After I serving a twenty-four-month sentence, during which I never left the United States, I returned to California eager to get into the film business, as I had dreamed of since childhood. I wrote *one* letter to MGM in care of the production department, determined to start at the biggest and best studio in the world. I mailed my letter on a Monday morning. I received a call from MGM the following Thursday morning, asking me to come to the studio the next morning at ten o'clock. On Friday I was on the MGM payroll. Simple as that.

The letter that I had written was a typical letter from someone seeking a job—my educational background, my Army service record and various vital statistics. I mentioned that I spoke fluent Armenian and fluent Turkish. My parents were Armenians born in Turkey.

The Friday I went to MGM for my ten o'clock interview must have been a day filled with crises. I came to learn that every day at a motion picture studio was filled with crises. People were running around from office to office, taking no notice of me. I sat in the outer office of the head production manager, a man named Walter Strohm. Strohm's secretary apologized for the delay. Ten o'clock came and went. Eleven o'clock came and went. Finally, about noon, the secretary said that I should go to lunch and come back at two o'clock.

I discovered the commissary. I was in a whole new world. I was shown to a small table. I was in awe. Everywhere I looked, I recognized the stars and directors of the period, which was the end of the studio star system and the Golden Era of Hollywood. George Cukor, Ava Gardner, Stewart Granger, James Cagney, Jane Powell, Lauren Bacall. I wanted to be a part of this world, to sit at the table talking shop with these people. After lunch, I walked around the soundstages soaking up everything. I looked in the soundstages that had open doors. Everything was hustle and bustle, the busy behind-the-scenes controlled chaos that is moviemaking. I returned to the production office a little before two o'clock. Two o'clock came and went. Three o'clock came and went. The dew was beginning to fall off the lily. I had a suit and tie on—the first and last time I wore a suit to a studio. I was getting restless and nervous. I was beginning to wonder if I was ever going to see the production head. Finally, near four o'clock, the secretary ushered me into Walter Strohm's office. There was Strohm, a large man sitting behind a huge glass-topped desk. As I shook Strohm's hand, I could see my letter on his desk. Strohm introduced me to his assistant, a man named Joe Cook, who was sitting alongside Strohm's desk. (Months later Joe Cook took out a cigar box and showed me a box full of dried skin, which had fallen off his body from a disease he had contracted in Africa during the making of *Trader Horn*. Some people save everything.) Strohm got right to the point. "How come you speak Turkish? Are you a Turk? Can you read and write Turkish?" I replied, "No, I'm not a Turk. I'm an American born in Evanston, Illinois. My parents are Armenian. I speak fluent Turkish, but I can't write in Turkish. I can, however, read Turkish, if it's in print."

Strohm asked if I had ever heard of George Cukor. George Cukor was one of MGM's star directors, a very well-respected director. He had a tremendous flair for sophisticated comedy as well as drama. To start my career with the likes of Cukor was a miracle in itself. Of course I had heard of him. Strohm said the studio was going to produce a film in Istanbul to be directed by Cukor and to star Ava Gardner. "Are you sure you can speak Turkish?" The film was called *The Wilder Shores of Love*, from the book written by Lesley Blanch. Strohm said he was looking for someone to coordinate the production between Istanbul and Culver City. He said I wouldn't be going to Istanbul. Would I accept a salary of $50 a week? Absolutely, yes. Strohm said that I went on salary that day and for me to report to his office on Monday morning at ten o'clock. He would take me to Cukor's office and introduce me to the great director. I was on cloud nine. Strohm's parting words to me were, "Don't wear a suit and don't bring your lunch to work. You may not be here to eat it." That statement puzzled me but I later discovered that Strohm had a strange sense of humor. Thus began my career at MGM and Hollywood.

Monday morning Strohm took me to the Thalberg building (known by the employees for some reason as the "Iron Lung"), to meet with George Cukor. Cukor had elaborate offices. They were a series of rooms with a secretarial office. The walls were paneled and decorated in elegant taste. There were several doors to his offices. Photographs of the famous were abundant in silver frames. Strohm introduced me to Cukor's secretary, Irene, a devoted woman who stayed with her boss until his death. Strohm left me with Irene to go to a meeting. He asked her to introduce me to Mr. Cukor. Irene offered me a cup of coffee. I still couldn't believe where I was and what I was doing. Only last week, I was dreaming of a future in films. And here I am sitting outside the offices of one of Hollywood's most successful directors. After a few minutes, the door to Cukor's office opened and out stepped Greta Garbo! Garbo acknowledged Irene and passed by me with a smile. No one would believe that on my first day at MGM I had received a smile from the mysterious Greta Garbo. Irene now took me in and introduced me to Cukor. I was impressed by his friendly manner and his interest in my background and schooling. He said the first thing he wanted me to do is to read the book and then read the script of *The Wilder Shores of Love*. After my two years in the Army, where a good job was anything that didn't injure or bore you to death, this assignment was something on the order of winning the lottery. And I was being paid for the pleasure.

The next three months went smoothly. I had spent a great deal of time researching at the downtown Los Angeles library. But I also did many personal things for Cukor, like picking up packages or delivering gifts to friends. I didn't mind being a gopher. I was gophering for George Cukor. Cukor had a brilliant mind and was extremely intuitive. He had a tongue like a razor blade that could eviscerate a person in one sentence. Luckily for me, I wasn't Cukor's type. He preferred strong athletic types. But I was pleased because I knew Cukor liked me; if he hadn't, I wouldn't have lasted an hour. Luckily for me, Cukor wasn't my type either, and so we were able to remain friends until his death.

After the first three months, I was called into Strohm's office. Strohm said he had some bad news for me. *The Wilder Shores of Love* had been shelved. I was not privy to the inner workings of the Thalberg building so I never knew why the film was cancelled—it could have been money, contracts, or the whim of a highly-placed studio executive. All of a sudden my world was collapsing. And there was no going back to that other world. My dismay was short-lived.

Strohm asked if I would like to be an assistant director. Would I?? In 1954, each major studio was entitled to name one man a year to become an assistant director member of the Directors Guild of America. I was MGM's nominee for 1954. (Years later, this method was eliminated because of lawsuits brought against the DGA for having a "closed shop.") Strohm asked me if I had $500. I said I had. He said to take the $500 to the Directors Guild and see Joe Youngerman on Monday morning and not to tell anyone. Strohm said he wanted to hire someone that he selected and not a relative of a studio executive. Hence, the secrecy.

In life, being in the right place at the right time is so important. In my case, three months either way and I would have missed my golden opportunity. Timing is everything.

My first film as an assistant director was *Bhowani Junction*. This film replaced *The Wilder Shores of Love*. George Cukor was the director and Ava Gardner was the star. The story was set in India, but the Indian government refused MGM permission to shoot in their country. The company then decided to film in Lahore and Karachi, and the interiors were to be shot in London. I remained in the States, much as I would have when the other film was to be made in Istanbul. Ava's co-star was Stewart Granger. Prior to the company's departure for Pakistan, many tests were made of Ava's makeup, as she was to depict a half-caste Indian. We also tested hundreds of saris. I got to watch Cukor in action. In a short time, the company left for Pakistan. And I was their man in Culver City.

During the making of *Bhowani Junction*, extensive cablegrams went back and forth between Karachi and me over Ava Gardner's toilet seat. It seemed (difficult to comprehend in today's economy) that Miss Gardner had requested a new toilet seat as she was getting slivers on her ass. And the unit manager had to ask permission to purchase one. He could have bought 100 of them for what all the cablegrams cost. He wanted an American toilet seat. It seems that all Pakistani toilet seats come with slivers. I am happy we sent not only one toilet seat to Pakistan but three.

During this period, I was only a second assistant director (the Directors Guild required that you must be a second assistant for one year before becoming a first). The second assistant director assisted the first assistant director (paperwork, gophering, etc.), but was in a great position to learn the principles of making a film. The main duty of a second assistant director is to make sure the crew is on the set and the actors are in the makeup department being prepared. More importantly, the second assistant director is responsible for giving the actors their makeup calls and advises them as to what scenes are scheduled to be filmed that day.

At MGM, second assistant directors worked on the various films in production, at the time, sometimes for a day or two, sometimes for a week or more. Between 1954 and 1956, I worked at one time or another on every MGM film being shot. I even worked on the dance unit of *Oklahoma!*, which was not an MGM film, but they were using the studio's facilities. I admired the choreographer, the great and gifted Agnes DeMille. Some of the films I worked on during that period were *Hit the Deck, Love Me or Leave Me, The Cobweb, It's Always Fair Weather, Home from the Hill*, and *Moonfleet*, which starred Stewart Granger, Joan Greenwood and Liliane Montevecchi. During *Moonfleet*, I was asked by the production department to question Liliane Montevecchi about a recent driving ticket she had received. I asked her why she had been driving on the sidewalk. She said, "I drove down the sidewalk because there was no room on the street." History doesn't record what the judge thought of her defense.

Home from the Hill featured Eleanor Parker, Robert Mitchum, George Hamilton, and George Peppard in his first major role. Vincente Minnelli, one of MGM's busiest directors in those days, directed it. I worked on these films sporadically for several days. I was in a position to study the various styles of running a set, directing, dealing with the actors and the crew, and staying on schedule and within the budget. Those were great days for learning the ropes.

MGM decided to fight the threat of television by producing low-budget films in the million-dollar bracket. The first person hired under this new scheme was a director from New York City named Alex Segal. Dore Schary, the head of MGM, would always send a bottle of sherry to the director and stars on the first day of shooting. (Schary – Sherry.) When Segal received his bottle of sherry, he sent Schary a dead seagull. (Segal – Seagull.) Not the smartest move, just a smart-ass move whose humor—if indeed that was Segal's motive—was not appreciated. The guy was off to a lousy start in Hollywood.

Segal's movie was entitled *Ransom!*, and starred Glenn Ford and Donna Reed. The film was about a kidnapping of a child of wealthy parents. Within a few days, Segal had alienated everyone on the company with his autocratic and disagreeable ways. I don't think any director was so immediately disliked. Everyone was counting the remaining days of shooting. On one occasion at a Bel-Air estate used for the set of the kidnapped boy's home, Segal was staging a scene near a swimming pool. He was looking in his viewfinder and slowly walking backwards—directly in line with the pool. Although there were approximately fifty crew members standing by watching Segal's impending watery pratfall, not one of them said a word. Slowly, ever so slowly, Segal approached the pool and fell in with a resounding splash. Unfortunately, Segal could swim. I have never heard of Segal since. He certainly wasn't at MGM any longer, despite the fact that *Ransom!* was well received by the critics. The movie was remade in 1996 starring Mel Gibson and Rene Russo, but I don't think the later version came close to the quality of the simple black-and-white MGM version.

I worked on *Designing Woman* for about two weeks. Vincente Minnelli was the director and the cast included Gregory Peck, Lauren Bacall and Dolores Gray. The script was based on an idea submitted by Helen Rose, MGM's top costume designer. We were scheduled to do a scene in a fashionable nightclub on a soundstage. When putting in a call for extras, I got very creative and asked the casting office to call UCLA and get an authentic East Indian couple in their native costume. The local colleges were always happy to accommodate such requests. There were approximately eighty extras called for this scene. The Indian couple arrived and I placed them at a table toward the back of the nightclub. The man had a yellow turban and the lady was in a sari. The man's name was Bupesh, a name I'll never forget. As we were about to roll the cameras, Minnelli spotted Bupesh and asked, "Whose idea was that?" pointing to the Indian couple.

Now, I'm in deep trouble. Nervously, I said, "It was mine, Mr. Minnelli."

"It's a good touch. Have the man in the yellow turban come up to the camera."

I called Bupesh. Minnelli asked Bupesh if he hand-wrapped his turban. Bupesh said he didn't, that he didn't even know how to wrap a turban, and he lifted the turban off his head like a hat. Minnelli said he wanted an authentic hand-wrapped turban on Bupesh. Minnelli called the wardrobe man and asked him to get a real turban from the wardrobe department. The wardrobe man went to the stage phone and called the department. There were no real turbans in the studio. Panic. Minnelli said he wouldn't do the scene until we got a real turban. The first assistant director glared daggers at me. I eventually learned that many directors will use a similar ploy to gain time in preparing the scene and Minnelli was notorious for this ruse.

Casting called UCLA and asked to have an Indian who was able to hand-wrap a turban come to the studio as soon as possible. I was sweating bullets. It seemed like everyone on the set was looking at me. Forty-five minutes later, a student arrived wearing a white turban. The first assistant director brought the young man up to Minnelli. Minnelli asked the man to remove his turban. He did. Minnelli asked the man to unravel the turban and start from the beginning. The student wasn't quite sure what was going on, but he followed the instructions, and he unraveled the turban. The cloth was about six feet long. He held one end of the cloth in one hand and threw the cloth across a table with his other hand. He placed the cloth against his head, and swiftly wrapped it around his head. It was a turban in a few minutes. Minnelli was satisfied. The replacement sat where Bupesh had been and I sent Bupesh home. The scene resumed.

Two days later in the projection room we were reviewing the rushes of that day. I saw the white turban in the distance. Minnelli turned to me and said, "Small details make great pictures." I said, "It's so far away, it could have been my mother in a hoop skirt." That was my last day on *Designing Woman* but not my last day with Minnelli. Much more was to come.

I worked on *The Swan* with Grace Kelly, Louis Jourdan and Alec Guinness. It was during this film that Ridgeway (Reggie) Callow, a top assistant director, gave Grace Kelly the nickname of "Lollipop," which was okay by her until she started preparing for her life role as Her Serene Highness of Monaco.

Interrupted Melody was another film I worked on during this period. It starred Eleanor Parker, Glenn Ford and Roger Moore, in one of his early roles. It was the true story of a famous Australian opera singer, Marjorie Lawrence, who at the height of her career contracted polio, and the film depicts her struggle to overcome her handicap. During one memorable scene, Eleanor, playing Marjorie Lawrence, attempts suicide.

Eleanor had heavy weights strapped to her legs so that there would be no lower body movement. The scene called for her to slip off a sofa and drag herself to the bathroom cabinet and reach for sleeping pills. Just as she is about to swallow them, her husband (Glenn Ford) enters and knocks the bottle out of her hand. When the take ended, Eleanor, in her pink negligee, was helped up. She had blood all over her legs. The weights against the hemp rug cut her legs, but she did the scene without a word of complaint. She was very serious about her work.

The studio treated *Interrupted Melody* as a musical. Usually on a musical, you film the "book" first and then go into the song and dance numbers, which are endlessly rehearsed during the shooting. After the "book" was shot, everyone except Eleanor expected to go immediately into the many aria sequences from the various operas. Eleanor Parker rebelled; she was not ready. I remember her going up to the Iron Lung in a rage—and in costume, and ever so beautiful. She went to Dore Schary's office. The result was that the production was temporarily shut down.

From what I understood, Eleanor had protested that she was not a trained opera singer, and she needed instruction in how to move, how to breathe, and so on in order to make the role believable. Apparently, she convinced Dore Schary, and the studio got Mary Garden to teach her. Mary Garden was a famous retired Scottish soprano. She must have been in her seventies. Although there were volumes of Marjorie Lawrence's actual recordings, it was determined that Eileen Farrell would dub in the various Lawrence/Parker arias. More than likely, Marjorie Lawrence's recordings were not up to par to meet all the technical requirements. Each opera sequence was shot when Eleanor was ready. This wasn't a great expenditure as none of the principal actors were involved in these scenes—only opera singers and opera supers.

The only aria that was filmed during principal photography was from *Tristan and Isolde*—the reason being that there were actors involved and they had to get off the payroll before the company shut down. This aria was the final scene in the movie and it was the final day of principal photography. Seldom is the last scene of the film shot on the last day of photography. This sequence was shot on Stage 5—the theater stage. Stage 5 was virtually one-half of a theater, consisting of balconies, loges and a full backstage area. The storyline was that Marjorie Lawrence was doing a benefit performance, having at last come to grips with her handicap, which left her unable to walk. The reason *Tristan and Isolde* was selected was that Isolde is seated during this particular aria and not required to move along the stage.

The stage was now set. Eleanor is seated on rocks against a spectacular setting. The playback is ready and the camera starts to roll. The camera slowly moved toward Eleanor as she begins singing to playback. Suddenly, as happened in Marjorie Lawrence's life, she feels movement in her legs. As she continues singing, she stands up and ever so slowly walks along the rocks, taking one step and then another. I shall never forget this moment. Everyone on the entire crew were either crying or wiping their eyes. I never saw that moment in filmmaking again. Eleanor Parker deservedly was nominated for the Academy Award as Best Actress.

Chapter 2
More of the Beginning

In mid-1955, I worked for several days on a film entitled *The Tender Trap*, starring Frank Sinatra, Debbie Reynolds and Celeste Holm. It was during this film that I got to know Debbie Reynolds. Debbie was—and remains—a very special woman, warm and gutsy and just as unsinkable as Molly Brown, her great role from the '60s. I knew that we would be life-long friends. Debbie was 23 years old. I was 25.

But it wasn't until *The Catered Affair* that Debbie and I really became close. This was one of the first films I worked on in its entirety. The stars of the film were Bette Davis, Ernest Borgnine, Barry Fitzgerald and Debbie. Richard Brooks, an ex-marine who acted like he was still on duty, directed the film. In many ways, Brooks was a madman, but I liked him. There was something about Brooks that was different. Beneath his gruff exterior was a very sensitive man. He was the perfect example of someone whose bark was worst than his bite, although his bite could be pretty bad. Often, the extras would not accept calls to his set because they were terrified of him or they refused to accept his abuse.

The story of *The Catered Affair* was based on a television film written by Paddy Chayefsky, who wrote *Marty* and *Network*. The screen adaptation was done by the patrician Gore Vidal, who was making an artistic stretch in writing about a lower-middle-class family in Brooklyn. Davis and Borgnine play Debbie's parents.

On the first day of rehearsal, I went up to Miss Davis and introduced myself as the second assistant director. She turned away from me, saying, in her inimitably emphatic way, "I hate assistant directors." Great start! In the film, she had to wear a terrible full wig, having recently shaved her head for a role as Elizabeth I in *The Virgin Queen*. Davis was not only a big star; she was also a complete professional. She automatically assumed that whatever part you had on the making of the film, you were the absolute best—and God help you if you weren't. Davis could spot a phony, and when she did, she made it known. During the production, Ernest Borgnine and Anna Magnani won Oscars for that year. Bette, then, had a huge sign hung at the stage entrance, "Italians Go Home."

Prior to the start of *The Catered Affair*, Debbie and Eddie Fisher got engaged. They were very popular; the movie magazines dubbed them "America's Sweethearts." For some reason, Brooks resented Debbie's popularity. She spent a lot of time on the phone, probably speaking to Eddie. One day, while I was standing near Debbie on the set, Brooks came up to her and slapped her across her face. He was about to hit her again and I stepped in front of Debbie and said, "Once was enough." (God, I was brave!) Brooks just glared at me, but stopped. I think Debbie was more humiliated than hurt as this happened in front of the entire company, who were as shocked as she was.

I've never seen a director hit a star before or since. I don't know what the repercussions would be today if a director hit someone, certainly a lot of publicity and a possible lawsuit. In Debbie's case, the show went on. She was a trouper. The incident was never brought up again on the set. Interestingly, *The Catered Affair* was one of Debbie's greatest

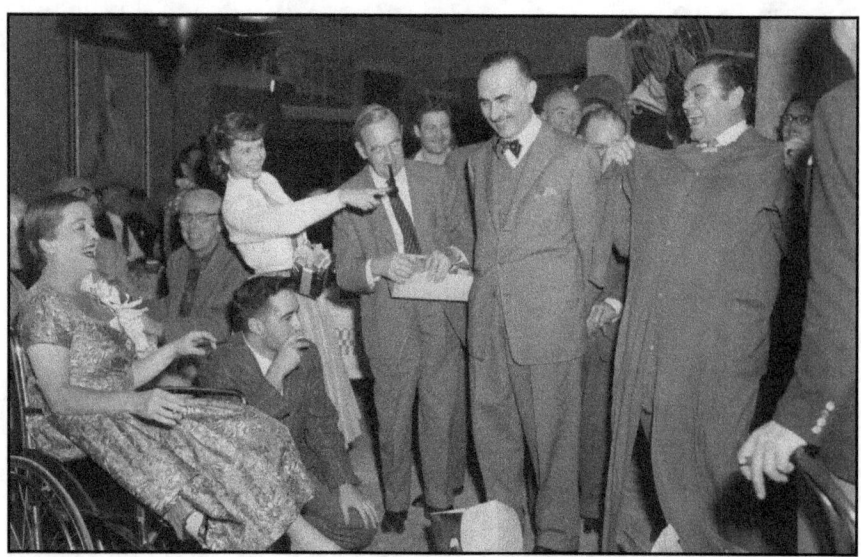

Wrap party on the set of *The Catered Affair*.

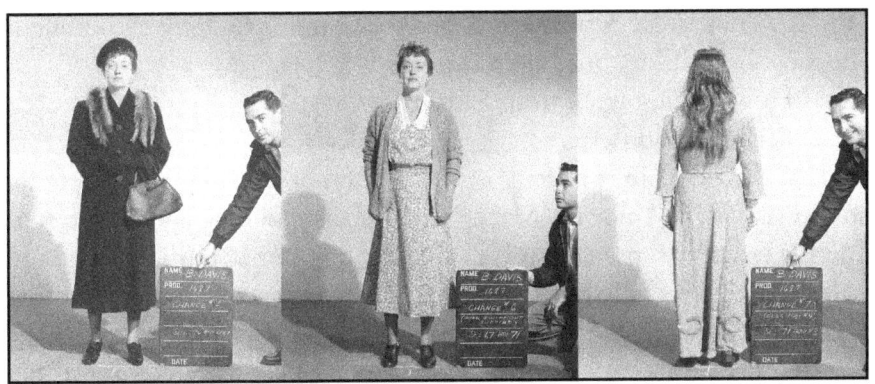
Bette Davis's wardrobe tests for *The Catered Affair*.

performances. By this time, Bette had become friendly with me. I asked her why, on our initial meeting, she said she hated assistant directors. Bette smiled and said, "Many years ago, when I was very new in movies, the assistant directors would give me the first makeup call of the day."

(As mentioned earlier, one of the duties of an assistant director is to tell the actors what time they are due in makeup and what time they are due on the set. A good assistant director must be able to calculate when an actor is due in makeup, particularly when the actor is not required for the first hours of filming.)

"The assistant director didn't care that I wasn't in the first shot, but to protect himself, he would have me on the set ready at all times. I was a nobody and the assistant director didn't care. Often, I would sit for hours. On occasions, I never even got before the camera. So I decided, then and there, that if I ever make it, I'd get even with them. Hence, my hatred."

In one sequence of *The Catered Affair*, we were filming a mom-and-pop grocery store on the stage. As always, when such a scene is completed, the prop men ask the crew to take home whatever fruit and vegetables they want. Otherwise, they are thrown away. So everybody got a bag and began filling it up with oranges, potatoes, etc. I was checking out the eggplants, looking for the best ones. Bette Davis came up behind me and said, "What do you do with those?" I turned and said that my mother makes wonderful Armenian dishes from eggplant. She said, "You're Armenian?"

"Yes."

Bette said, "Please invite Gary and me to dinner. We love Armenian food." Gary Merrill, the actor, was Bette's husband at the time.

I smiled and said, "Sure." Bette Davis to dinner? I doubt that.

A week passed. Bette said, "When am I coming to dinner?" I thought she must be kidding, but I played along.

"How about a week from Saturday?"

"Perfect," said Bette.

At this point in my life, I was doing a lot of traveling for the studio, so I lived with my mother, Mary. My brothers had long ago moved out, and my father had passed away. I saved a lot of money in those days, and I like to think I made my mother happy by being around. My mother was an old-fashioned Armenian lady who spoke very little English. She didn't really understand the star system or the celebrity culture of her adopted country, and when I told her that Bette Davis and her husband were coming to dinner on Saturday, and would she cook a meal, she merely said, "Of course, son." She did understand that she was to pull out all the stops for this dinner party and so she did. Armenian cooking is an all-day job. In this case, it was an all-week job. My mother outdid herself. She had enough food for twenty. I had asked my brothers, John and Cary, and my sisters-in-law, Peris and Ruth, to come to dinner at 7 p.m. sharp. They were not as excited about the event as I was, or at least they pretended not to be. One thing about my brothers was that they always kept a level head about the movie business, never having been as star-struck as I was, and they didn't want to swell my head by admiring those stars I knew or what I did.

I helped Mother set the table, and I was running back and forth from the kitchen to the dining room to the living room trying to make sure everything was perfect. Naturally, I was terribly nervous. Bette Davis at my house for dinner! I kept seeing in my mind glamorous photos of her dining at 21, or Chasen's or the Brown Derby—to which I could now add a mental snapshot of her sitting at my mother's table, eating eggplant.

At the stroke of seven, the doorbell rang and it was Bette and Gary. No brothers yet to help me make conversation. I introduced my mother to them, and then she returned to her work in the kitchen. They sat down. Bette took her shoes off and coiled herself on the sofa, considerably more relaxed than I was. I made drinks and Bette lit a cigarette, and another, and another. After idle conversation about whom I should marry—a favorite subject that married people like to trot out around young singles—my brothers and their wives finally arrived. It helped to have others around. After much talk and much drink, the food was served.

The food was amazing, and Bette was clearly impressed by the sheer number of dishes. We all sat down and ate and ate and ate. After dessert, Mother served Turkish coffee and Bette had her umpteenth cigarette. She and Gary were good sports. You'd think we all knew each other for years. They were down-to-earth, warm, friendly, amusing and most appreciative of my mother's work. But I doubt, for all their "just-folks" ways, they were prepared for what happened next.

Mother got up and said to Bette, "Come into the kitchen and help me with the dishes." I nearly choked! My sisters-in-law nearly choked! In unison, we said we would help later.   My mother said, "I've been cooking all week for her. Now she can help me clean up." After more protesting, Bette got up and walked into the kitchen, smiling. Still in shock, I looked into the kitchen. Bette was putting on an apron. There seemed to be 10,000 dishes to be washed. My mother shooed me away from the kitchen door and said, "Please, we'll come out when we're ready." They were in the kitchen for more than an hour. As my mother spoke very little English, who could say what they talked about and who understood what? But, eventually, they came out. More cigarettes and eventually the end of a very long, nervous, and slightly surreal evening.

The next Monday, Bette sent my mother a huge orchid plant with a touching card, which my mother adored. She was probably more impressed by the orchid and the card than by Bette's stature as a movie star. Bette said to me that she hadn't enjoyed herself so much in a long time.

Good for Mom...

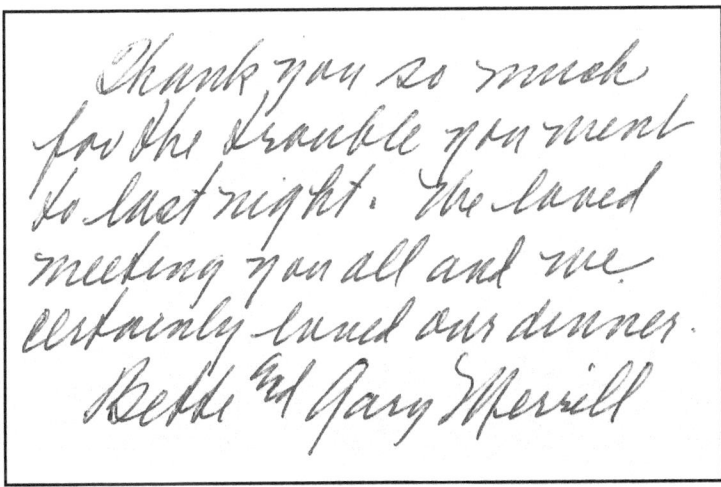

Thank you card from the Merrill's.

Often, I would be invited to "Hollywood" parties. One party particularly stands out. Eddie Fisher, Debbie and I went to George Burns and Gracie Allen's home. I had never met them, and was happy to be invited. Gracie was one of my favorite comediennes. But I learned that most comedians are only amusing when they're performing, as I've seen proven by Jerry Lewis, Milton Berle (occasionally funny off-stage) and Lily Tomlin, among others. The Burns' home was filled with celebrities, mostly comics, celebrating someone's birthday. Several people were gathered around Groucho Marx, who was holding court. The subject of Desilu Studios came up and how successful it had been for Lucille

My sister-in-law Peris, my Aunt Mary, and between them, Ann Blyth, on *The Kings Thief* set.

Ball and Desi Arnaz. Desilu used to be RKO Studios where the Marx Brothers made films. I asked Groucho how it was working with Lucy. Without batting an eyelash, Groucho said, "It was Zeppo who fucked her."

One of the films I worked on during this period was George Cukor's *Les Girls,* starring Mitzi Gaynor, Kay Kendall, Gene Kelly and Taina Elg. I was asked by the front office to tell the beautiful Kay Kendall she was not allowed to park her car inside the studio, which was an honor only for the holiest of the holy. I went to the makeup department to see her.

I said, "Miss Kendall, I've been asked by the front office to tell you that you are not allowed to park your car on the lot." She grabbed me by the arm and started pulling me out of the makeup department.

"You brown-eyed bastard. You come with me." Pulling me along the row of parked cars, she pointed to one and said, "Whose car is that?" "Deborah Kerr's."

"And whose car is that?" I said, "Robert Taylor's."

"And whose car is that?" "Elizabeth Taylor's."

Kendall said, "If they can fucking well park there, then I can fucking well park there." End of story. She parked her car on the lot thereafter. *High Society* was MGM's biggest film during this period. It starred Frank Sinatra, Bing Crosby, Celeste Holm and Grace Kelly, newly engaged to Prince Rainier. How Grace had changed since *The Swan*. On *The Swan* she was fun and warm, and fully lived up to her reputation as one of the most cheerfully promiscuous actresses in Hollywood. I did admire how democratic she was about whom she went to bed with. She slept with "above-the-line" (meaning executives, stars, producers) and she slept with "below-the-line" (the cameramen, electricians—all the people who make the films). Maestro Chepparo was the vocal coach at the studio. He had a small office above the alleyway next to Stage 5. That's where he would teach once a week or whenever he was required. When he wasn't using his office, that's where Grace often did her "vocalizing."

On *The Swan* we had called her "Lollipop." Now, we barely were allowed to speak to her. She was deep into her role of Princess Grace of Monaco, preparing to become Her Very Serene Highness. We were asked not to call her Lollipop anymore. It wasn't dignified. Grace was, reputation and all, a class act and a beautiful woman. She was destined to be a Princess. My final memory of her in Hollywood was watching Cole Porter on the stage piano teaching Grace to sing "True Love."

It was shortly after working with Bing on *High Society* that I was on a flight from London to Los Angeles (in the days before jets). As I sat down, I noticed a "Mr. Crosby" name plate on the back of the seat next to me. He was the last to board. Never making the assumption that he would remember me, I extended my hand and said, "Hank Moonjean. I was one of the assistant directors on *High Society*." He said, "Oh sure." Those were the last words he uttered for the entire sixteen hours of the flight. When I disembarked, after many drinks, I said, "It's been good talking to you again, Bing."

Years later, my nephew Dr. Richard Moonjean and his wife, Patricia, bought a home next door to the Crosby estate in Hillsborough, California. They said that Bing never entertained. Occasionally, my nephew would see him walking in the neighborhood—seldom acknowledging anyone. After Crosby died, he did not leave the estate to his wife. She was just given a monthly allowance. He probably moved to Hillsborough far from Hollywood so that he wouldn't have to entertain. The ten-million-plus estate still remains with a full staff. He must have been a sad and lonely man. And, obviously, a very private person, who enjoyed his seclusion.

Somebody Up There Likes Me was originally cast with James Dean in the lead. One Friday, I met Dean at the main gate to take him to wardrobe for fittings and then to makeup. He appeared to be quite shy, not saying much as he went about the business of fittings and makeup tests. After spending several hours with him, he thanked me. The next night, there was a Makeup and Hairdressers dance at the Hollywood Palladium. During the course of the evening, someone stepped up to the microphone and announced that James Dean had been killed in an automobile accident early that day. All of us realized what a terrible loss this was to the movies. It was Saturday, September 30, 1955.

During this same period, *Green Mansions* was a film that MGM planned to produce. Vincente Minnelli was set to direct and Pier Angeli was to star as "Rima the Bird Girl." An elaborate set was built on Stage 15, the longest stage at MGM. It was unusual to build an elaborate set just for a test. The flowers, the trees, the birds, and the undergrowth made a great tropical setting. Pier Angeli had a costume made of an angel-hair material—white and sparkling. She put it on and immediately started itching and breaking out. That was the end of Minnelli and Pier Angeli. Several years later, in 1959, *Green Mansions* was eventually made starring Audrey Hepburn and Anthony Perkins and directed by Hepburn's then-husband,

With Jean Simmons on the set of *Until They Sail*.

Mel Ferrer. I worked on that film for two weeks. It was my first with Perkins. I wasn't particularly impressed with Mel Ferrer's direction. But I must admit it wasn't an easy subject. It was about a bird girl fluttering around a South American jungle full of symbolism.

In 1957, I worked on *Until They Sail* in its entirety. This was a Robert Wise film and starred Paul Newman, Jean Simmons, Joan Fontaine, Piper Laurie, and Sandra Dee in her first film. *Until They Sail* was a story of four New Zealander sisters living in Christchurch during World War II. It wasn't a very successful movie. This was my first film with Paul Newman, the first of many. Jean Simmons was wonderful—she had a different dirty limerick daily. Joan Fontaine became a special friend and we are still great friends to this day. Piper Laurie went to the same high school as I did. Her name at the time was Rosetta Jacobs. Sandra Dee had been a child model in New York City. She was thirteen or fourteen at the time. Under labor laws, children, have strict rules and guidelines, i.e., number of hours in front of the camera, time spent in school, time spent resting, etc. A schoolteacher with a stopwatch times every minute. Sandra would arrive at the studio in full makeup. Makeup time is considered work time. The makeup man spent more time removing her makeup than applying it. After all, she was playing a teenager. She had the works—eyelashes, rouge, and lipstick. I told Sandra to come to work with a scrubbed face. She refused. I went to her mother, a charming woman named Douvan, and said Sandra could not come to work made up. Mrs. Douvan said there was nothing she could do. Finally, we got the agents involved and reluctantly Sandra came to work freshly scrubbed.

That summer I went to Europe for the first time—the greatest summer of my life. I stayed with Joan Fontaine in her rented villa in Mougins, France, the estate owned by Jacques Fath, the famous couturier. Joan Fontaine—there's a woman and a half. Beautiful, talented, extremely intelligent, great fun, very sexy, and, generally, the epitome of a grand lady. She was never much of a Hollywood person. Most of her friends were authors, politicians, artists—rarely actors. Through Joan I was introduced to many of the world's most famous people. Joan knew everybody. Through Joan I met the Duke and Duchess of Windsor, Somerset Maugham, and Pablo Picasso. (Over luncheon in Mougins, Picasso looked at me and said, "I'm fascinated with your right eye." I still don't know why.) Others I met were Aristotle Onassis, Lunt & Fontanne, the Aga Khan, Aly Khan, Jacques Fath, Elsa Maxwell and the entire international film colony. We spent months on the French Riviera.

While living in Mougins with Joan Fontaine, I would go to the Casino in Monte Carlo as well as the Summer Casino in Cannes to gamble. What elegance; in the evenings, everyone would be dressed in formal attire, with the women in furs and jewels. One night at the Summer Casino, I saw Jack Warner lose over half a million dollars playing baccarat in about an hour. He didn't bat an eyelash as he got up from the gaming table. Someone next to me said, "He won a lot more than that last night." Recently, I was in Monaco and visited the casino. All the elegance was gone. They were selling T-shirts and popcorn in the streets, and people in the casino were wearing Levis. Those days of glamour are as vanished as the Belle Epoch. That summer, Joan and I went to Eden Roc in Juan Les Pins to swim at the pool. We were lying by our cabana playing gin, when a very lovely girl slinked into the cabana next to us. She was slim and had a great body. Joan recognized her and whispered, "That's a man. That's Coccinelle." I looked over at "her" again. No way was she a man.

Joan said, "I'll bet you a thousand dollars I'm right."

"You're on." But how do you find out? You obviously can't go up to "her" and ask if she's a man. I lost the bet. Coccinelle was as famous in France as Marilyn Monroe was in the United States. They even looked alike. I would subsequently see billboards along the roads with Coccinelle's image advertising various products. She was one of the first men to have a sex-change operation. His real name was Jacques Dufresnoy. I believe she appeared in films and French cabaret as well.

One day Joan asked me to baby-sit for her two daughters, Debbie and Martita. Martita was her adopted Peruvian daughter. They were going to have a guest join them. I thought I would take them to the perfume factories in Grasse. A limousine pulled up to the estate and out stepped Princess Yasmin Aga Khan with two bodyguards. The Princess was the daughter of Aly Khan and Rita Hayworth. Yasmin was very polite and looked like her mother. I took the three girls to Grasse. A car with two bodyguards followed. Later I took them to lunch in Cannes. They were well behaved, and seemed to have enjoyed themselves. I enjoyed the afternoon myself even though it was a bit bizarre babysitting while bodyguards were within whispering distance at all times.

When Joan and I returned to Paris, Joan was invited to a black tie dinner at the Paris apartment of the Duke and Duchess of Windsor. I was Joan's escort. Although I had recently met them, we were not yet bosom buddies. We arrived at their lavish apartment, which was crawling with servants. Joan reintroduced me to the Windsors. I was very surprised to hear them referred to as "Your Majesty" and "Your Royal Highness" by the servants. I felt uncomfortable. I was the youngest person there. Most of the conversations were in French and I didn't know any of the other guests. The Duke had cornered Joan who looked very regal in

This is to remind you that
The Duke and Duchess of Windsor
expect you
on *Wednesday September 17th*
for *dinner*
at *8.45* o'clock

Black Tie

17 Sept 1958

DINER

Crème de Laitues

Homards à la Nage
Sauce Indienne
Riz à l'Andalouse

Perdreaux Rôtis sur Canapé
Bread Crumb Sauce
Haricots verts au Beurre
Céleris Raves Étuvées
Salade Endives Betteraves

Bombe Orientale
Petits Gâteaux

Rissoles au Parmesan

Above: The Windsor's invitation.
Left: The Windsor's menu.

her gown. I spent my time looking at all the photographs of the world's most famous people. (Very much like George Cukor's office.)

Finally, dinner was announced. Just like in the movies. The Duke escorted Joan into the dining room. The Duchess followed with some dignified-looking man. The rest of us entered the magnificent dining room. All in all, there were twelve guests. I think there were twice as many servants. Joan sat at the Duke's right, and I sat at the center of the table. On the table in front of me was a silver scroll holding a handwritten menu.

The place setting was enormous. I never saw so many silver utensils. There were six various-sized stemmed wine glasses. I was seated between two elderly French women who kept speaking to me in French. I would just smile and nod occasionally, saying "Oui." Never having been entertained by royalty before, I wasn't familiar with protocol. Usually when entertaining you ask your guest if he or she would prefer red or white wine. That is a no-no at the Windsors. It's considered rude. The butlers pour both and you choose one or the other. I drank both. I was still very uncomfortable. I could hardly see the Duchess or the Duke at the long table. I was way out of my element. I just kept drinking and eating and was anxious to go home.

After a long dinner, again just like in the movies, it was announced that the gentlemen would retire to the drawing room and the ladies would go somewhere else. I don't remember where; I was feeling no pain. The Duke was much friendlier than the Duchess. His fame must have gone to her head.

On the way home in our limousine, I asked Joan, "How did I do?" She said, "You did fine but I did notice you were still having your soup when the Duke had finished his."

"Joan, I was so far away, I didn't know what the Duke was eating. I didn't see the butler remove his plate." *And* I didn't know that when the Duke finished one course, everybody had to stop eating that particular course. "Besides, the soup was magnificent."

Several years later, my mother called me at my furnished apartment in Los Angeles, to tell me that she saw that my "friends" were staying at the Beverly Hills Hotel. She said she saw them on television. I said, "What friends, Mom?" She said, "The Duke and Duchess of Windsor." My mother didn't understand. She automatically assumed since I was a guest in their home, that we were the very best of friends.

With the ultra-glamorous Joan Fontaine—one of my most favorite women in the world.

Today, Joan lives in retirement in Carmel, California. We see little of each other, but we speak and correspond regularly. Joan is still a beautiful person. She never speaks of her sister, Olivia de Havilland. When she rarely does, she never says Olivia, it's always "Sister." Two sisters couldn't be more opposite. Joan is spice and Olivia is sugar. Joan is to-the-point. Olivia is terribly sweet. I once asked Olivia about a scene in *Gone With The Wind* when Hattie McDaniel (Mammy) is walking up the stairs with Melanie (Olivia) in tears because of Bonnie's death and Rhett's seclusion. Mammy leads Melanie to Rhett's room and Melanie pleads to be let in. The door opens and Melanie enters. The next shot is Melanie coming out of the room—spent and ill. I asked Olivia, "Was there a scene missing between Melanie entering the room and her immediately coming out?" Olivia, in all her sweetness, said, "Oh dear, I'll have to go home and check my script—I'll let you know." I am still waiting. You can get diabetes talking to Olivia.

Both sisters were brilliant actors. Olivia's *The Heiress* is one of the greatest films ever made, as well as *The Snake Pit* and *To Each His Own*. Joan's *Rebecca*, *A Letter from an Unknown Woman* and *The Constant Nymph* are memorable. Mrs. de Havilland-Fontaine had two formidable daughters.

Of all the glamorous actresses I worked with, I think the one actress I really loved was Joan, although we never had an affair. Our relationship was purely platonic.

Chapter 3
Raintree County

Back from Europe, *Raintree County* was my first film that was shot in part on a distant location. *Raintree County* was supposed to be the answer to *Gone With The Wind*. It starred Elizabeth Taylor, Montgomery Clift, Eva Marie Saint, Agnes Moorehead and dozens of other well-known actors. The director was Edward Dmytryk. We started filming in the studio, after which we were to go on location to Danville, Kentucky. This was MGM's biggest production at the time. I

On MGM soundstage going over *Raintree County* shooting schedule.

knew Elizabeth, but this was the first time I worked with her. It was Elizabeth who wanted Montgomery Clift on the film. Clift was the most intelligent actor I had ever met. It was no secret in Hollywood that Clift was a homosexual. It didn't matter. Anyone who knew Clift liked and respected him. Sadly, he was an alcoholic with a low tolerance. Clift would take one drink and he could barely stand up. Somehow, he would manage to get through each day. The film started at the studio on interior sets as well as on Lot 3, where we filmed the "Race" and other exteriors. *Raintree County* was the first film to use the new Panavision Camera, which took six grips to move the monstrosity around.

Elizabeth was always late to the set. As for Elizabeth's lateness, it was no surprise. She just couldn't help it. It didn't matter if she was due on the set at 9 a.m. or 10 a.m. or 11 a.m. Always late. But in her own way, she often made up for it. She was always letter-perfect and very professional when working. If there were one or two shots at the end of the day, and if you ask her to stay to complete the scene, she would.

One of the menial tasks of the Second Assistant Director was to call in late reports to the Iron Lung. There must have been volumes of Elizabeth Taylor late notes. Whenever Elizabeth would arrive on the set, I would go to the phone to call in the late report. Elizabeth knew what I was doing. She knew it was part of my job. However, occasionally she would come to the phone and listen. On the phone I would say, "Miss Elizabeth Taylor had a 7 a.m. call in makeup to be ready on Stage 12 at 9 a.m." "Miss Taylor arrived in makeup at 7:50 a.m. and arrived on Stage 12 at 10 a.m." "Miss Taylor kept the company waiting one hour, no explanation for the delay." Often, Elizabeth would take the phone from me and add "and fuck you too!"

There were many mornings when Elizabeth had her phone turned off at home. When she failed to show up on the set, I would take a limousine to her house in Beverly Hills, where she lived with her, at the time husband, Michael Wilding. What a job! This is work? I had a key to the back entrance to her house. I would go into her bedroom and switch on the coffeemaker the maid had prepared the evening before. I would shake Elizabeth awake. She would roll over with a smile knowing it would be me. You have never seen anything so breathtakingly beautiful. Her long black hair flowing over her face and neck. And those magnificent eyes. No photograph, no camera has ever captured that beauty. Often she would ask me to crawl in bed with her. Often I would, with my clothes on. She'd giggle and tease. I would say, "We've got to get to work. I'll get fired if we don't get to the studio." Elizabeth would say they couldn't fire me because she would quit the picture. On a couple of occasions, the studio sent a car to get me.

Eva Marie Saint was, and is, a terrific lady. She was fun—a real pro. We liked to jitterbug together. Eva Marie was happily married to director Jeffrey Hayden, and still is. I believe this was Eva Marie's first film since receiving the Academy Award for *On the Waterfront*. Often, it was difficult for her to act with Clift because of his drinking. But, being a pro, she was able to handle the situation. Eva Marie was as beautiful as Elizabeth, but a complete opposite, which is probably one reason she was cast. Eva Marie Saint had a great sense of humor. Once on the set, I knocked on her dressing room door to speak to her about something. I understood her to say, "Come in." I opened the door and saw that she was in her scanty underclothes. Embarrassed, I turned away. Eva Marie said, "Of course this means we're engaged." Another time, again in her dressing room, she passed wind. I must have looked embarrassed. She said, "What did you expect, *chimes?*"

"Swinging" Eva Marie Saint

Agnes Moorehead was a great and versatile actress. We became fast friends. She had made dozens of films, rarely playing the same type of role. She could play royalty down to a servant and always stole the scene. Her part in *Raintree County* wasn't that big, but it ran throughout the entire film.

Agnes seldom entertained, but she was invited to all the parties. She was always in demand because of her wit. The first Saturday after Thanksgiving, she'd give her annual Christmas party returning all the hospitality of the year in one fell swoop. It was always the first Christmas party of the season. Agnes had a fantastic home on Roxbury Drive, next door to Ira and Leonore Gershwin. The composer Sigmund Romberg previously owned her house. Her party would start at 6 p.m., sharp. In front of her home were dozens of attendants taking away the cars. (In Beverly Hills, you aren't allowed to park cars in the street at night unless you've gotten permission from the City.) There would be a Santa Claus standing on the lawn in the hot California sun wishing everybody a "Merry Christmas." As you approached the house, the huge door would open and there would stand Agnes at the inner entrance in a gorgeous gown wearing the tiara she sported at all fancy dress evenings. Alongside and in back of her would be a line of butlers. As you entered, Agnes would greet you, probably with a hug and a kiss. She would wish you a Merry Christmas and turn to the first butler. "Would you please see that Mr. and Mrs. So and So are being taken care of?" Everybody in Hollywood would be at the party—many drifting in after midnight. Everyone who was someone was there. It was *the* place to be. Ethel Merman took a fancy to my partner, Brad Bennett (who I was living with at this time), at one of these parties. He was, at the time, half her age. Of course, being a fan, he was terribly flattered. Agnes never left the front entrance. She never mingled with the hundreds of guests. Toward the end of the evening, she would be sitting on a high stool in the foyer- still greeting guests and bidding goodnight to others.

I once asked Agnes if she preferred film or stage work. Despite how completely different they are, she said she enjoyed both equally. However, like so many actors, she loved the immediate response from an audience in the theater. I have seen her one-woman stage show several times. It was called *The Fabulous Redhead*. It was a simple setting, with a spotlight on a stool in center stage. Alongside was a small oval table with a delicate covering, lit candelabra, three or four books with colorful ribbon bookmarkers (one ribbon definitely lavender). She entered stage right, dressed in an exquisite gown and wearing her trademark tiara. After the applause died down, she reached for the top book. It was the Bible. She opened the Bible to the ribbon marker and would begin reading. She would read a passage or two, then gently close it and start quoting the ensuing passages by memory. (Agnes was a daughter of a Presbyterian minister.) It was all very dramatic. She was very dramatic. She told me she did this show hundreds of times everywhere in the country—sometimes for ladies groups of twenty, sometimes for a theater full of admirers. But her greatest moment was when she performed in Scotland before an audience of twenty thousand. She said to me, "I had twenty thousand people in the palm of my hand. You could have heard a pin drop. That was one of the greatest moments of my career."

Before I entered the movie business, I used to play poker with Nicky Hilton, the oldest heir to the Hilton Hotel empire. My best friend in college, Bob Kelley, introduced me to the Hilton family. Bob grew up with Marilyn Hawley who eventually became Mrs. Barron Hilton. Barron was Nicky's younger brother. Nicky was a playboy and lived like a playboy. Nick was Elizabeth Taylor's first husband. That marriage didn't last very long. But he never got over his marriage to Elizabeth Taylor, and who would? For years, he always asked me how Elizabeth was or what she was doing.

At one poker session at Barron's house, Nicky brought an actress named Marilyn Novak to play poker with us. She was breathtakingly beautiful. She had a miniature dachshund draped on her shoulder like a fur piece. Marilyn wasn't a very good poker player, but she kept taking money from Nicky.

I asked her the name of the dog. She said, "Bang Bang. Nicky gave it to me." I always wondered why the dog was named Bang Bang. During the game, Bang Bang made a dump—not a serious one. Marilyn Hilton, Nicky's sister-in-law, was furious. She told Nicky never to bring Bang Bang or Bang Bang's mistress into her home again. Bang Bang's mistress soon became known as Kim Novak.

Back to *Raintree County*. After filming for many weeks at the studio, the company began preparations to move to Danville, Kentucky. Crews had already gone ahead weeks before to prepare sets and locations. We were to start filming the following Monday in Danville. Many crew members left for Kentucky on the Friday night so that they would have their cars on location. Some crew members, with Edward Dmytryk, the director, flew to Kentucky the next day, Saturday. The cast and I were to fly out Sunday morning.

That Saturday night, Elizabeth had a sort of "going away" party. I was not there, but her guests were Mike Todd, Roddy McDowall, Millard Kaufman, the screenwriter of *Raintree County*, several others *and* Montgomery Clift. Through the years many people would later claim that they were at that party. The lists get longer. As usual, Monty was drinking. I was never quite sure as to what exactly happened but the story goes that Monty ran out of Elizabeth's house, jumped into his car and raced down the narrow, winding road. Monty crashed into a telephone pole head on. The impact was so loud that they heard it at Elizabeth's house. Everybody knew instinctively that it was Monty.

Elizabeth was the first to get to the car. She was hysterical. Someone called an ambulance. It was there in minutes. Monty was put in the ambulance and Elizabeth climbed in. No one was sure whether or not Monty was dead or alive. The ambulance raced down to the hospital. As the ambulance backed up to the emergency entrance, the attendant got out. Elizabeth stepped out with blood all over her. The driver asked Elizabeth for $10 before they would bring Monty into the hospital's emergency room. Elizabeth, obviously, hadn't brought her handbag and she couldn't believe what was happening. She attempted to search Monty's pockets. There was no money to be found; like royalty, actors rarely carry money. She became hysterical. She had a huge diamond ring (probably from Mike Todd) which she took off and tried to hand to the attendant. He refused to take it. He wanted $10—refusing a ring that probably cost $50,000. Luckily, by that time, Mike Todd and Roddy McDowall arrived on a motorcycle. Mike gave the attendant the money. Monty was whisked into the hospital. Still, no one knew whether or not Monty was alive. This was the way this tragic story was relayed to me. I'm not sure if the ambulance business was true, although I believe Elizabeth told me that part. The outcome was that Monty was alive, but nearly every bone in his handsome face was smashed.

Needless to say, the company was shut down. There was talk of recasting Monty, but Elizabeth would not hear of it. Besides, nearly half of the film was shot and the costs to shoot everything over again would be astronomical. The studio asked all the cast members to take a fifty-percent salary cut while Monty was recuperating. Every actor agreed except Agnes Moorehead. Agnes was a shrewd businesswoman. She said the studio was rich enough to continue paying her "meager" salary, and stood steadfast. I collected money from the crew to send Monty flowers. The crew liked Monty; he was their "doctor." Monty was a floating drugstore. He had two suitcases; one for clothes and one for medications. He always tried to prescribe medication to the crew even though we had a doctor and nurse in attendance.

During Monty's recuperation, I saw a great deal of Elizabeth. Her marriage with Michael Wilding was virtually over. One evening, I picked up Elizabeth to go somewhere in Beverly Hills. Elizabeth kept waving her left hand and arm as she and I spoke in the car. I could see that she was wearing a *huge* diamond ring. The diamond was so big that Helen Keller would have noticed it. I made no comment. I just kept driving. She continued waving her hand and I continued to not react. She saw a paperboy on the corner of Beverly Drive. (They had newsboys in those days.) Elizabeth said, "Stop the car. I want a newspaper." I never saw Elizabeth read a newspaper. As I lowered the window, she continued waving her left hand. She bought the paper. I drove on—still not reacting to the ring. But, you can't get the best of Elizabeth. I looked over and saw her putting on some lipstick, using her diamond ring as a mirror, and I couldn't keep up the pretence anymore, I had to laugh. Mike Todd had given her the ring the day before and she wanted all her friends to see it.

In many ways, we were growing up together. We were only in our early 20s and we did crazy juvenile things. One Halloween, Elizabeth and I went trick or treating in Bel-Air. For those of you who don't know Bel-Air, it is one of the most affluent areas in America. Every block is the estate of some billionaire. If you're going trick or tricking, you may as well start at the top. Elizabeth put a nylon stocking over her head and would ring the doorbell of the outer gate of an estate. Sometimes we were ignored. Sometimes we were asked to come around the servants' entrance. We were let into the kitchens and given cake or cookies. We would have preferred a drink. Elizabeth was always ready for fun. She was very special to me in those days.

During the film's hiatus, I was having lunch with my mother, and for some reason I said to my mother, in jest, that I was going to marry Elizabeth Taylor, if she would have me. I don't know what possessed me to tell such a lie. I never had to impress my mother. My mother's eyes began to well up and her chin began to tremble. She said to me in Armenian, "Son, she has three children. I want you to marry someone who hasn't been 'used.'" (The word "virgin" in Armenian translates to "unused." If you aren't a virgin, you are considered "used.") I didn't think my mother would react the way she did. She thought I was telling the truth.

I said, "Mom, if you don't want me to marry Elizabeth, I won't. I wouldn't hurt you for the world." Mother calmed down. Several days passed. My remarks about marrying Elizabeth must have preyed on Mother's mind.

Shortly after, Elizabeth called me at my mother's house. I wasn't home. Mother, said, "Hank's not here. But I'm glad you called. I want you to leave my Hank alone. You're used." Elizabeth must have thought my mother had lost it. She hung up the phone, baffled. A few days later, I was with Elizabeth. She said, "I've got a bone to pick with you. I spoke to your mother the other day and she told me to leave you alone because I was 'used.' What the fuck was she talking about?" I was absolutely embarrassed. My mother never even told me that Elizabeth had called. Reluctantly, I said to Elizabeth, "I told my mother that I intended marrying you. But she didn't want me to because you aren't a virgin. You're a 'used' woman. She wants me to marry a virgin." Elizabeth smiled and said, "Good fucking luck if you can find one."

Montgomery Clift got to know my mother. He would call her occasionally just to speak with her. He had never met her but he absolutely adored her. But on the very first time he called my home, he asked for me and my mother said I wasn't home, "Was there any message?" Monty said, "Tell Hank that Montgomery Clift called." My mother said, "Please spell it." Why wasn't his first name Joe? Anyway, after several minutes of Monty spelling out his name, my mother asked him if he was an assistant director who worked with me. Monty began to laugh. After mother got to know Monty, through me, she would tell him to cut down on his drinking. "It isn't good for you." Often, he would call my house and not even speak with me. He was searching for some kind of love and my mother provided Monty with something that no one else could, I guess. Often, he would send her a large bottle of scotch, not knowing that she never drank liquor. She said he was a very lonely man who wanted to be loved. My mother was so right.

I believe it was well over two months before the company resumed production on *Raintree County*. We had lost several of our crew members. They would go on to other productions. Fortunately, there were no weather problems because of the delay. For instance, if we were to have done the movie in Montana, there would have been a definite change in the scenery and weather. Luckily, the novel was set in Kentucky and much of the movie was filmed in a swamp near Tarzan's Lagoon on Lot 3 in Culver City, which was constructed by the Art Department.

I had seen Monty several times during his recuperation period. He just didn't look the same. Why should he, after that near-fatal accident? It looked as if his youth had been taken away from him. He had had a horrible ordeal and he knew it. And it showed.

Danville, Kentucky – Elizabeth and me after a water fight on the set.

Finally, the day came to fly the company to Danville, Kentucky for location shooting. Most of the crew had left a few days before. I remained in Los Angeles to accompany the actors to the airport. Limousines were ordered to pick up the stars and get them to the Los Angeles Airport. It was the old airport: no security, just a wire fence. You'd show your ticket to a gate man and walk on the tarmac to the plane. I was waiting at the curb for Elizabeth and Monty to arrive in their separate limousines. Everybody else was there. I was getting nervous. The airplane attendants were getting nervous. The plane was ready to depart. I kept running from the curb, to the wire fence, to the plane stalling for time. Finally, in the distance, I saw a limousine winding slowly along the circular entrance eventually pulling up to the departure gate. Good, one of them has arrived. Which one? As the limousine approached, I saw no one in the back seat. The car stopped, I opened the door and there was Monty dead drunk on the car floor. I picked him up. He wasn't heavy but his body was like rubber. He sort of "melted." Someone helped me get Monty to the plane. All the passengers were disgruntled. One of the first-class passengers was Liberace. He was furious with me. "Who does she think she is?" referring to Elizabeth. I kept asking the airline personnel to please wait a few minutes more; assuring them Elizabeth would eventually be here. She eventually did arrive and we took off—not a minute before a mutiny.

Danville is a small town. The townspeople were excited about having a major motion picture shot in their town. We had secured every hotel and motel. The location manager found private homes for the principal actors. We had two African-American actresses playing Elizabeth's "mammies" in the film—Rosalind Hayes and Isabel Cooley. (Isabel was also one of Elizabeth's handmaidens in *Cleopatra* years later.) Being black in the still-segregated Deep South meant that no hotel or motel would accept them. Finally, the local minister took them in. Elizabeth was furious but there was nothing she could do about it.

Working on locations is much harder than in the studio. In Kentucky, we had to fight all the elements—mosquitoes, chiggers, rain and heat and more heat. The stars' dressing rooms were air-conditioned. Lucky for them. Tents were erected to house the wardrobe and makeup for the extras. Tents were set up for serving meals. It was almost like a circus moving into town. Finally, production resumed after many weeks of delay. Reggie Callow, the first assistant director, was in full charge. Shooting started out with the usual problems—Elizabeth late and Monty drunk.

The company had hired Marguerite Lamkin, sister of Speed Lamkin, the writer, to teach Elizabeth to speak "Southern." Marguerite was the most Southern woman I ever knew; her speech dripped with "you'alls." She was fun to be around and she seemed to know everyone.

She arranged marvelous parties. Marguerite knew Tennessee Williams and always claimed that Williams used her as a prototype for "Maggie

Helping Eva Marie Saint.

the Cat" in *Cat on a Hot Tin Roof*. Marguerite now lives in London, married to one of the Queen's barrister.

Another visitor who spent time with us was Libby Holman, the great blues singer of the 1920s. She was a dear friend of Monty's. She was bright and witty and I adored her. Her life story would make a sensational movie. She offered me the rights to her life story. Unfortunately, she didn't put it in writing; I had no proof and her life story was purchased and now lies in some studio's archives. Someday, hopefully, it will make a brilliant and fascinating film. As heir to the Reynolds tobacco fortune, Libby was a very wealthy woman. She had an incredible estate in Connecticut called "Treetops." She once told me she only loved three men in her life, and all three died a tragic death: her husband, her son in a skiing accident, and Montgomery Clift.

During the making of *Raintree County*, Mike Todd, who was wooing Elizabeth at this time, called and said he was sending his private plane to Danville to bring Elizabeth and me to New York City for the opening of *My Fair Lady*. It was on a Saturday—on location, you work on Saturdays. Elizabeth wasn't working that Saturday so she wanted me to go with her. I said I couldn't go, as I had to work. She said she would speak to the producer and he would let me go. I asked Elizabeth not to speak to David Lewis, the producer, because I didn't want to jeopardize my work. I didn't care about *My Fair Lady*. My work was more important. Elizabeth refused to go alone and I sent the plane back to New York empty.

For the most part, we all had a good time making *Raintree County*. We had regular spaghetti fights at Elizabeth's rented house. Spaghetti fights are like pie-throwing fights; you just can't help yourself. I don't know who would start it (certainly not me), but Elizabeth would have a ball, giggling and laughing and throwing pasta. A sit-down dinner at Elizabeth's was always interesting. Never a dull moment. Only Elizabeth knew how to handle Monty in a social setting. Monty craved attention. He would do something shocking such as putting out his cigarette on an untouched filet mignon, just to see the reactions of those around him. Elizabeth would ignore him and insisted that everyone else ignore him as well. Many a time he would "melt" off his chair at the dinner table, boneless, and lie under the table for the rest of the evening. One day we were filming a sequence at a small-town train station complete with a period train. The set was designed near a train trestle that had a drop off at least forty feet. I don't remember too much about the scene except it involved

Raintree County 41

First Assistant Reggie Callow in the middle.

My all-time favorite photograph. Agnes Moorehead and me at the Danville railroad station.

Monty, Agnes Moorehead, and Walter Abel. Monty was high as usual. The camera was set on the opposite side of the trestle, facing the train and station. There were huge black barrels set near the tracks on the train trestle. I told Reggie that I was worried about Monty's condition.

I said I would hide behind one of the barrels, out of camera range, in case Monty fell. Sure enough, when the scene ended and Director

Dmytryk yelled, "Cut, print!" Monty yelled "whoopee" and jumped in the air falling against the railing near the barrel I was hiding behind. I grabbed his wide belt and he nearly took me over with him. I felt as if I had saved the movie and even possibly saved Monty's life. I was beaming. Dmytryk came up to me and said, "You should have let the bastard drop." In reality, Dmytryk was the bastard. I never heard Monty say an unkind word about anybody. He was his own worst enemy.

Walter Plunkett, who designed the clothes for *Gone With The Wind*, designed the costumes that Elizabeth and Eva Marie wore in *Raintree County*. He was a brilliant designer and a very gentle man. Walter told me some of his experiences with Mae West. In the early '30s, Plunkett, then a young man, was *the* costume designer in Hollywood. When Mae West heard about him, she made Paramount Pictures arrange a meeting. Mae was the "Queen" of Paramount. The date was set for Plunkett to go to Mae's apartment. It was called Ravenswood and was on Rossmore Boulevard, in Hollywood, very close to the Paramount Studios. She owned the building and lived there her entire life. Plunkett arrived on time, a bit nervous. After all, this was the legendary Mae West, reigning queen of Hollywood. A maid opened the door. She asked Plunkett to remove his shoes, not to smoke, and she offered him a soda. He entered an all-white palace. Everything was white, except the maid. The maid ushered Plunkett into the living room and he sat in the center of a white sofa, getting more nervous by the second. There was absolute silence. Suddenly, a double door swung open and Mae made her entrance. All she was wearing was a pair of white slippers. Plunkett gasped. This was probably the first naked woman he had ever seen. She said in her most seductive drawl, "I thought you'd like to see what you have to work with." She sat across from him. He didn't know where to look. As he was attempting to discuss the script of Mae's forthcoming movie, she reached over to a very large white jar on the white table next to her. She stuck her hand into the jar and pulled out a glob of something. As she massaged the one breast, she said, "Cocoa butter is good for your tits." She then, proceeded to work on the other breast. Plunkett was hired and provided us with one of his funniest Hollywood stories.

For the most part, Plunkett's period dresses were sheer hell for Elizabeth and Eva Marie. Not only were they heavy, but the women had to be virtually sewn into the costumes, shrinking their bodies until they could hardly breathe. I resorted to wearing a pair of scissors around my neck and whenever Elizabeth and Eva Marie felt ill or about to faint, I would

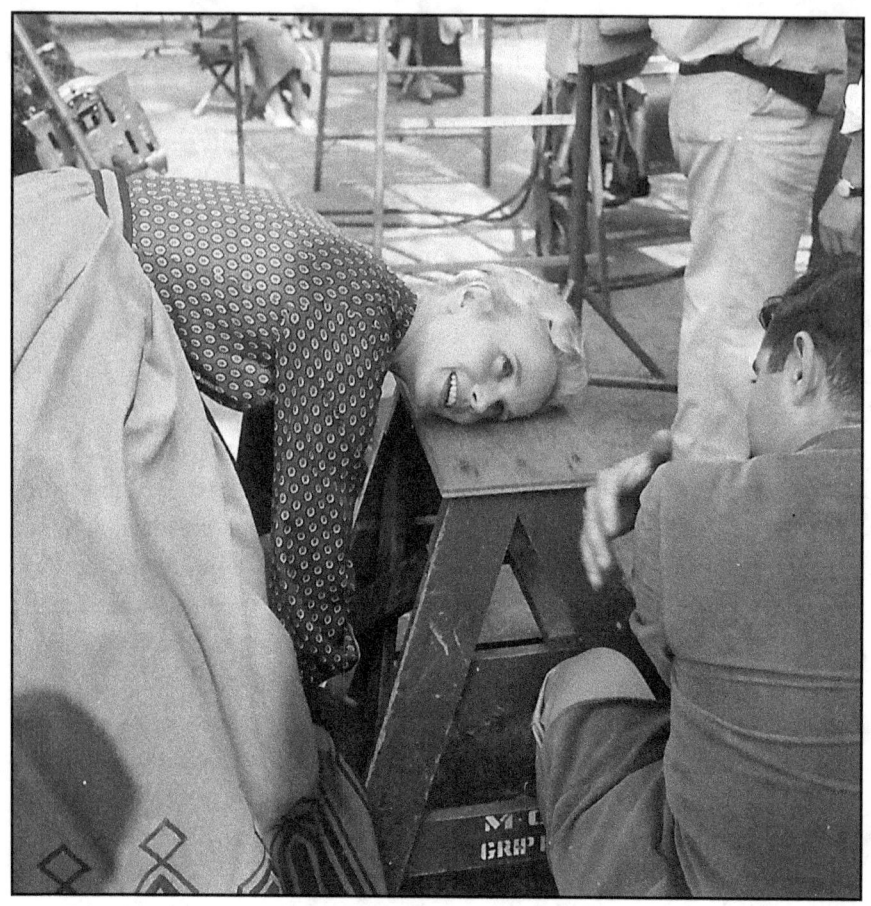

Eva Marie telling me a funny joke.

cut the corset ties so they could catch their breath. The chiggers were also a problem. Elizabeth and I would take turns putting clear finger nail polish on the chiggers to suffocate them.

Occasionally, I would drive far out of town, maybe forty or fifty miles, to get away from the crowd to have a quiet dinner with Elizabeth in some small out-of-the-way restaurant. With Elizabeth, there was nowhere to hide. We'd find someplace to eat and within minutes, there would be literally one hundred or two hundred people gawking at her. The price of fame. On one occasion, I heard someone say, "Look, look, she's eating!!"

Lee Marvin was also a member of the cast. This hulking actor, with a great face, was fun to work with. He had a great sense of humor. I was to work with him years later on *Pocket Money*. In *Raintree County*, Lee played a rebel soldier. In one of his scenes, where he runs through the fields dodging Union fire and jumping over "dead" bodies, Lee zigged instead of zagging. He ran over an explosive device and he detonated it. The explosion was so intense it blew his fake beard off. Luckily, he wasn't hurt.

We eventually returned to the studio to complete the filming. Everyone was glad to be home. At the studio, Elizabeth played her most dramatic scenes as well as her final scene in which she dies under the Raintree. Elizabeth received an Academy Award nomination for Best Actress. It was the first of her five nominations.

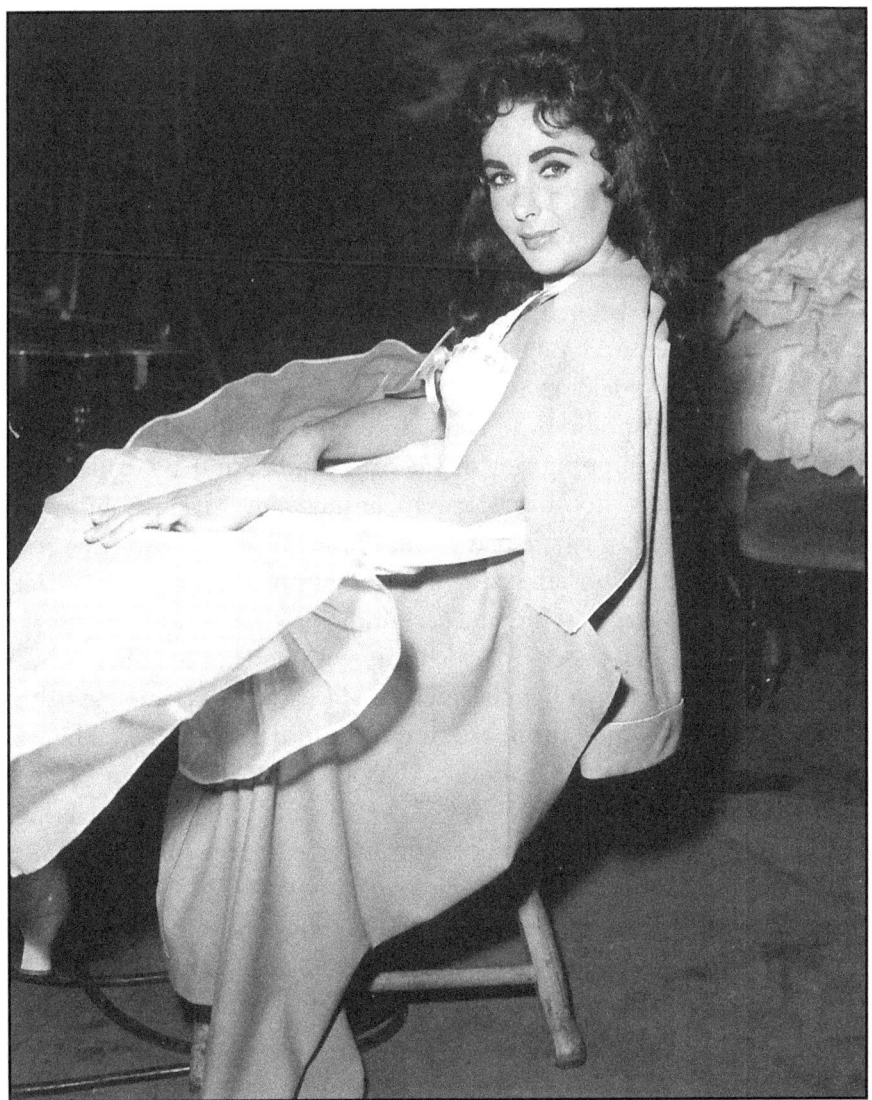

Elizabeth between takes.

Eva Marie, whose scenes were mostly with Monty, wasn't particularly happy with the entire production. Her husband, Jeffrey Hayden, was filming *The Vintage* in France with Michele Morgan, the role that Eva Marie was scheduled to play. But because of all the delays on *Raintree County*, Jeffrey had to start filming while the grapes were still on the vines. Actors can wait, but grapes won't.

The last scenes we shot were on the process stage called rear projection. The process stage was guarded. No one was allowed to enter. It was a barren stage with double projectors. One background projector shows moving shots, which are called plates. In the case in question, Monty and Eva are "riding" in an open horse carriage in the countryside. The background plate shows what the carriage is passing. This plate was shot on location. In the foreground, Monty and Eva are sitting in the carriage and the main cameras now photographs the actors against the moving background plate. The illusion is that the scene was shot on location. The carriage is jiggled to give it movement and occasionally a tree branch is passed in front of an arc as though the carriage has passed under a tree.

This system is seldom used today. Per usual, Monty was high. He kept giggling and spoiling the takes. In one take, Monty, who was extremely thin, was slipping out of his own clothes and his collar kept moving up. Process shooting is extremely slow and extremely boring. I think by this time Eva Marie had it and she snapped. She had been putting up with Monty for almost a year. She jumped out of the carriage, ran off the soundstage crying and screaming, "Get me Kurt Frings, get me Kurt Frings." (Her agent.) I caught up with her and held her tightly. Tears were flowing down her cheeks. Eva Marie, when crying, looks like she's smiling. All I could think of was how beautiful she looked. She was glowing even as she was screaming, "Get me Kurt Frings," and I kept saying, "You're beautiful." She calmed down, still asking for Kurt Frings and I was still telling her how beautiful she was. Someone had called Dore Schary, the head of the studio, to the set. Eva Marie was in her dressing room. Schary entered and walked straight toward Monty. I was standing near Monty and Schary. Schary said to Monty, "Mr. Clift, I understand you've been drinking." I couldn't believe what I was hearing. Monty was drunk or at least drinking every day of the entire production. And the studio was privy to his drinking from the very beginning. There are absolutely no secrets in Hollywood. Maybe if Schary had said some-

Montgomery Clift conferring with director Dmytryk.

thing to Monty at the beginning instead of the end, things might have been better—especially for Monty. We will never know.

The following year, 1958, I returned to Paris after *Raintree County*. I saw Monty several times. He was about to start *The Young Lions*. Marlon Brando was in the film as well as Dean Martin. Monty had made himself more unattractive by pushing out his ears. I think the deep reasoning behind making himself more unattractive was that he knew his looks were gone, so it wouldn't matter how grotesque he looked. According to Monty, Brando's favorite actor was Montgomery Clift and Clift's favorite actor was Marlon Brando. We were all staying at the Raphael Hotel on the Avenue Kleber. One afternoon, Brando phoned Monty to have him come up to his rooms on the top floor of the hotel. Since I knew Brando, Monty asked if I would join them. Why not. We entered Brando's suite. There were several attractive women hovering near Brando. Brando asked Monty to come out to the balcony. Bear in mind that Clift had been drinking. The three of us stepped out on the balcony overlooking the Avenue. Clift immediately tried to impress Brando by climbing on top of the balustrade. We were on the fifth or sixth floor. Marlon didn't react. (He must have known about Elizabeth's edict about ignoring Clift's desire for attention.) I was getting nervous and became poised to grab him by the belt, once again. Monty started to walk along the balustrade as if he were walking a tightrope. Brando never flinched and only continued their conversation. My only thought was to get Clift off before he fell. Monty finally stepped off. I could see that they both had a great deal of respect for each other. Unfortunately, Brando and Clift never had a scene together in the entire film. (Toward the end of the film, you see Clift passing by Brando's dead body.) What a treat it would have been to see two of the greatest actors in Hollywood acting with one another. Monty died several years later at a young age. He was a kind, unhappy soul who loved all his friends. My one regret is that the last time I saw Monty was an unhappy experience for me.

Just before I was leaving Paris, Monty asked me to go to dinner with him—sort of a goodbye dinner. He wanted to go to L'Escargot, a restaurant in the heart of Les Halles, the produce market for all of Paris. (The market has long since moved to the outskirts of the city.) This restaurant was world famous—especially for escargots. And it was fashionable to go very late at night. Monty and I arrived just after midnight. The hotel had made the reservations. Of course, Monty was really stewed. We sat in a corner table with Monty facing the wall. I could see the entire room filled with the high society of Paris who had come there after a night at the opera or the theater. It was all very elegant and from the menu, I could see that it was a very expensive restaurant. We ordered escargot and wine. Monty was getting boisterous. I asked him to keep his voice down. Monty was happy to be with a friend and he was sorry that I was leaving early in the morning. The snails finally arrived. They reeked with garlic but they were so good. I looked at Monty as he ate his first snail. He took the empty shell and threw it over his shoulder. I watched it land on the floor. I don't think anyone noticed. I said nothing. He did the same thing again and it landed on someone's table. The patrons started looking at us. Monty began giggling and again, I said nothing. He did it a third time and this time I could see the patrons call for the maitre d'. I can't tell you how embarrassed I was. Everyone in the restaurant was looking at me and the back of Monty's head. I said to Monty, "If you do that one more time, I will get up and leave." Of course he did and I got up and left.

I never saw him again. In looking back, I thought what an uncaring friend I was to him that night. I should have realized he was hurting and craving attention. After all, it wasn't a crime. I should have paid the bill and forced him out of the restaurant and taken him back to the hotel. That evening will remain a very sad memory of that gifted, wonderful, exasperating man, Montgomery Clift.

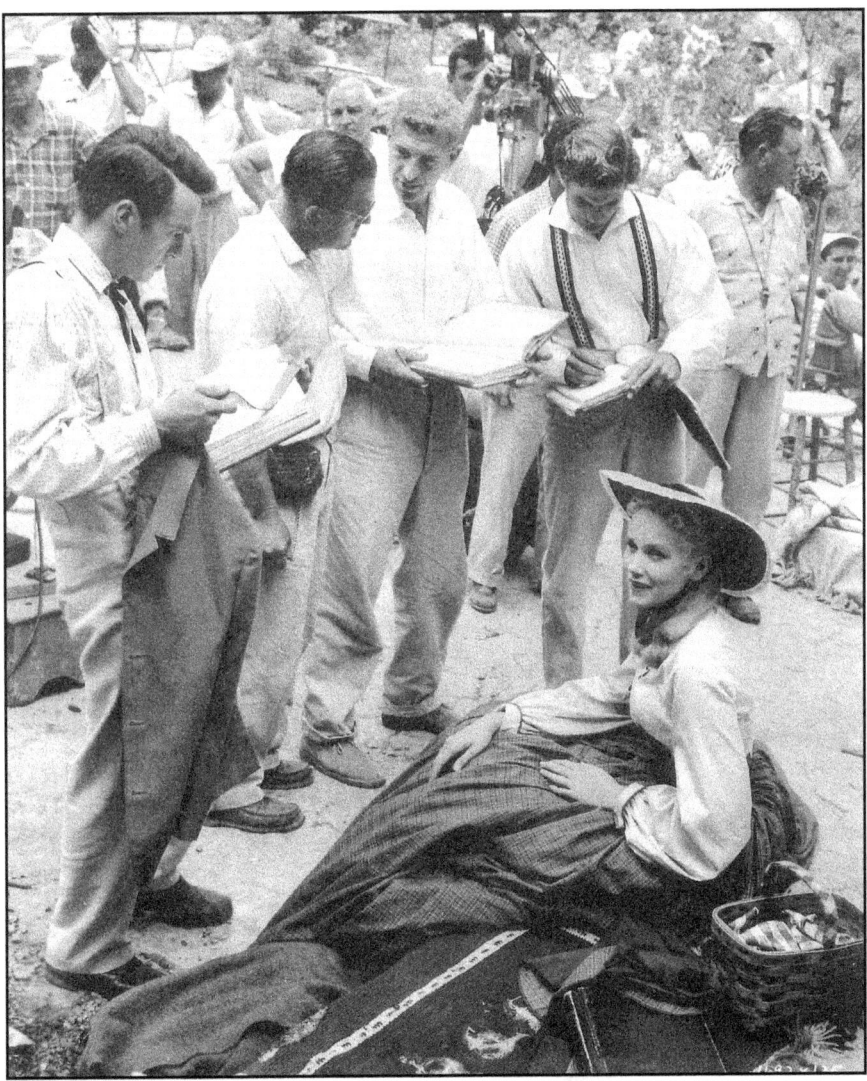

Script conference with Montgomery Clift, Eddie Dmytryk, Millard Kaufman, Rod Taylor, and Eva Marie Saint.

Chapter 4
More MGM Movies

Sometime during 1955, I worked several days on *I'll Cry Tomorrow* starring Susan Hayward. This was the autobiography of Lillian Roth, the famous singer of the '30s who became an alcoholic. Very early one morning, while waiting for Ms. Hayward to arrive in the makeup department, a chauffeur came into the department and asked me to give him a hand. We went out to his limousine. He opened the door. Susan Hayward was lying on the back seat muttering. She was drunk. I said something stupid like, "You're drunk." She looked up at me, never having seen me, and said, "What do you expect? I'm supposed to be a drunk." It was the only time in my career when I saw an actor who was playing a drunk, actually drunk.

The MGM makeup department was something to marvel over. Around 7 a.m. on any given day, it was teeming with stars. Sydney Guilaroff, the chief hair designer, oversaw his domain like a queen. His domain consisted of ten to twelve barber chairs. In each chair sat a star, usually actresses (the men, if wearing period wigs, were usually prepared in a private room). At each chair was a female hairdresser following Guilaroff's specific instructions. Guilaroff was never a member of the hairdressers union. Guilaroff had an arrogance that alienated many union hairdressers. And each time Guilaroff attempted to become a member, he was rejected. He was not allowed on any shooting set—the only exception was on test days when makeup and various hairstyles were tested and photographed prior to principal photography. This man was a genius at creating hairstyles, especially with woman's wigs. Guilaroff designed

Norma Shearer's wigs for *Marie Antoinette*. He was always dressed in an expensive suit looking like he stepped out of *Esquire Magazine*. Except he always wore slippers. In the many years I knew Sydney, I never saw him without a tie. He would go from chair to chair, making corrections and helping the hairdressers, and moving things along quickly and efficiently. Every chair's occupant had to be ready and out by at least 8:30 a.m. Most films started shooting at 9 a.m.

Guilaroff was brought to MGM in the '30s by the then-reigning queen of MGM, Joan Crawford. He had been credited for many films. He was certainly the most famous hairdresser in films. Guilaroff also was a direct link to all the executives in the Thalberg building. It was common knowledge that after everyone had gone to the set, he would make his morning phone call. After all, if your hairdresser doesn't know, who should? All the set gossip and intrigue and problems were reported. Even in a studio salon, the stars would let their hair down.

In 1996, Guilaroff wrote his autobiography entitled *Crowning Glory; Reflections of Hollywood's Favorite Confidant*. It was the best fiction of that year.

Guilaroff's friendly enemy at MGM was the dress designer Helen Rose. Helen was the epitome of grace, femininity and class. Always impeccably dressed, she was well loved by everybody and a good friend of mine. She won several Oscars, designed Elizabeth Taylor's first wedding gown and also designed Grace Kelly's royal wedding gown. Helen never liked Guilaroff's hairstyles and Guilaroff never liked Helen's creations. During makeup, hair and wardrobe tests, Helen and Sydney Guilaroff would be working with the various stars on the set, each protecting their own domain. Once during a wardrobe and hair test, while Guilaroff and Helen were in their respective departments, the company was preparing to test gowns on French actress Danielle Darrieux for a film entitled *Rich, Young and Pretty*. As the women costumers were fitting a strapless gown on Miss Darrieux, they noticed that she had a fistful of hair under her armpits. The costumers were embarrassed and they called Helen in her office and asked what they should do. Helen said, "Call Guilaroff, this is a hair problem."

So it went, film after film. Sydney Guilaroff was a very wealthy man but through the years he squandered all of it. In his last few years, Debbie Reynolds, among others, paid his rent and helped support him. Helen Rose won the Academy Award for Best Costumer Designer for *Rich, Young and Pretty*.

Back to *I'll Cry Tomorrow*. During shooting one afternoon, I was asked to inform Jo Van Fleet that they were ready for her on the set. I went to her dressing room and knocked on her door. No response. I knew she was inside. I knocked again and entered. She was standing in front of a full-length mirror trembling. "I'm only three years older than her and I'm playing her mother. I'm only three years older…," repeating it over and over. I said, "Nevertheless, they want you on the set."

Susan Hayward was nominated for an Academy Award that year for Best Actress for *I'll Cry Tomorrow*; Jo Van Fleet won the Academy Award for Best Supporting Actress, but not for *I'll Cry Tomorrow*. She won it for *East of Eden*, playing James Dean's mother.

Another film that I worked on during this period was *The Prodigal*. One morning around 5 a.m., my phone rang and it was Arvid (Griff) Griffen, another top first assistant. Griff asked me if I would come to Stage 12 and give him a hand, as his assistant was ill. He said it wasn't a complicated day, just Lana Turner (*just* Lana Turner!) and Edmond Purdom. I quickly showered and got to the studio and went to Stage 12. The director was the underrated Richard Thorpe. Griff said to me that Thorpe wanted to have a quiet rehearsal and that when the two actors were in costume I was to clear the set of unessential crew members. I said to Griff that I had never met Lana and Purdom. He said, "You will soon." I went to the makeup department and saw that both actors were getting made up. I, then, went back to the stage and told the costumers to get them dressed immediately when they arrive on the set and let me know when they were ready.

The scene that was to be shot was being lit with stand-ins. The set was a huge four-poster period bed. *The Prodigal* was based on a biblical story from the Old Testament. Exactly what this film is about is still a mystery to film buffs. Purdom's stand-in was lying on his back bolstered with some pillows. Lana's stand-in was leaning over him, one knee on the bed alongside his body and her other leg on the floor.

Eventually, Lana arrived. Unbelievably beautiful! She immediately went to her dressing room to get dressed. Purdom did the same. A few minutes later, the wardrobe lady said that Lana was ready. I cleared the stage of the entire crew with the exception of Thorpe, the camera crew, script girl, Griff and myself. Purdom came to the set first followed by Lana. Lana had hardly anything on—just beads and some colorful material on the essential areas. Stunningly gorgeous. I stood about twenty feet away as Griff got things into motion.

They began to rehearse. I couldn't hear a word from where I was standing, staring in awe at Lana. I had seen her many times in the commissary, but never in front of a camera. As the rehearsal continued, I saw Lana push Purdom flat on the bed. She screamed out, "This God-damned fucking Englishman has a hard-on and I'm going home." I was stunned. Lana Turner using words like that! She stormed past me and went into her dressing room.

Griff came to me and said, "Go get her!"

I said, "*Me?* She doesn't even know who I am."

"You're an assistant director now, *go* get her."

I walked to Lana's dressing room uncertain as to how to handle this very delicate situation. I gently knocked on the dressing room door. No response. I knocked a little harder. Still no response. Finally, on the third knock, she yelled, "Who is it?" I stupidly said, "Miss Turner, you don't know me, but they want you on the set." She yelled back, "Tell them to go fuck themselves."

I went to Griff and he asked, "What did she say?"

"She's not coming out."

"What did she say?"

I reluctantly said, "She said go fuck yourselves."

Griff said, "Go get her! This is part of your job."

I took this trip two more times and each time she screamed out the same epitaph. Unbeknownst to me, Thorpe and Griff were getting ready to shoot something else. I'd become the brunt of a joke. They all knew Lana and when Lana said she's going home, nothing would stop her. However, I made a fourth attempt. This time, her dressing room door swung open nearly hitting me in my face. She glowered at me. She said, "Didn't I tell you three times to tell them to go fuck themselves?"

I said, "Yes."

"Well, TELL them!"

I took three steps toward the set and Lana said, "You...do you have any family?"

I turned. Finally, recognition. I said, "Yes."

"Fuck them too!" she said storming off the stage. Through the years, Lana and I became friends. We often laughed about that day.

On April 4, 1958, Lana Turner became involved in the murder of her boyfriend, Johnny Stompanato. The publicity department of the studio was going to have a hard time with this scandal. Lana's first line of defense was led, as always, by the marvelous Emily Torchia. Emily was one of MGM's top publicists. Her entire life was devoted to the studio and the stars she handled in a career that lasted for over forty years. Everyone loved Emily. Emily was what was then called a spinster, and really was the epitome of an old maid. If you were to cast a librarian or a schoolteacher, you would look for someone like Emily. She was always immaculately dressed with matching hat, shoes and gloves. Always gloves. Emily was a devout Catholic, and she stopped in the cathedral across from the studio daily. When the teenaged Lana Turner was put under contract at MGM, Emily was assigned to her. No two more opposite creatures existed. If you said "shit" in front of Emily, she would turn beet red and possibly not speak to you for several days. "Shit" to Lana was nothing—child's play. Lana adored Emily. Emily adored Lana. Emily arranged Lana's dances, dates, parties, personal appearances, and was even a bridesmaid several times for Lana. She had a drip-dry bridesmaid dress. Whenever Lana was loaned out to another studio, Emily was sure to go. Lana's involvement in a murder was serious business and a publicity nightmare for MGM who regarded Lana as a valuable MGM investment. Howard Strickling, the publicity chief since MGM's inception, had his hands full. He should have written a book about MGM. Strickling knew every scandal and where all the bodies were buried, but, unfortunately, he took it all to his grave. Strickling was an admirable soft-spoken gentleman who was loyal to the end.

Strickling sent out telegrams to all the senior and junior publicists telling them to report to his office tomorrow at 10 a.m. sharp to discuss the Lana Turner situation. No excuses. The next morning, all the publicists started filing solemnly into Strickling's office. Stanley Brossette, my publicist, told me that Emily was the last to arrive. Emily, always bubbly and strangely bubbly that morning, entered the large room. She delicately began removing her gloves—finger by finger. She said, "I understand Lana was naughty again last night."

The first full musical film I worked on almost to completion was *Kismet*. Although I had worked on several Vincente Minnelli films before *Kismet* they were very early on while I was just learning. *Kismet* starred Howard Keel, Ann Blyth, Vic Damone, Dolores Gray (in her first film) and Monty Woolley. Although this film was made over forty years ago, it remains crystal clear in my memory and probably will forever. Musicals are treated very differently from "straight" films. You have scoring sessions. You have dance rehearsals and more dance rehearsals. It's a completely different approach to filmmaking.

Early on, we were testing Ann Blyth's and Dolores Gray's wardrobe. Ann and Dolores were complete opposites in every respect. First, we would test one of Ann's costumes and then one of Dolores'. Dolores played Lalume, a seductress. Dolores Gray could really belt out a song, very much like Ethel Merman. Dolores put on a particular costume and the cameraman turned to me and said, "Call Bob Vogel."

Bob Vogel was MGM's censorship head. I called Vogel and he rushed to the set. Dolores was wearing a flesh-colored costume of the period with lots of bangles. From a distance, it looked like all Dolores was wearing were bangles. Vogel said the dress would never get by the censors. The dress was designed by Tony Duquette. The problem was discussed in detail with Duquette, Minnelli, and Vogel. Suddenly, Duquette went into action. There were bolts of material on the set. He had his assistant select a bolt of contrasting silk material. The assistant, with great flair, threw the bolt across the stage and began bunching up the material. He, then, placed his hand on Dolores' crotch, and began sewing the new material to the existing costume. The assistant worked diligently as though this was his daily routine. The crew standing by was laughing. Dolores Gray, with her intricate hairstyle and high-heeled shoes, looked about seven feet tall. She looked down at the short assistant sewing away and said, "That's all right, honey; I'm just waiting for you to bite off the knot." Minnelli, through all this, was oblivious to what was going on. He was always in his own world.

During filming, Dolores Gray's mother would visit the set. She was a typical stage mother. Dolores was no child at this time. She must have been in her mid-30s. After each shot with Dolores, Minnelli would say, "Cut, print it," and Dolores would look at her mother. Her mother, looking down at her knitting, never glancing at Dolores, would move her head left to right, and back again. Dolores would say, "Oh, Vincente, let me do it again, I can do it better." We'd do another take and the same thing would happen. It got so that the entire crew, instead of looking at Minnelli, would look at Dolores' mother in hopes that she'd like it, so we could move on. Minnelli, apparently, wasn't aware of this, although on her next film, *Designing Woman*, her contract barred her mother from the set. Vincente Minnelli directed that film, too.

It was during *Kismet* that Minnelli said to me, "When I'm looking up at the ceiling, you're not to speak to me." Minnelli was a fascinating man, extremely difficult, extremely demanding. He had sort of a twitch with his mouth—like fish out of water, rolling his huge dark eyes. He would also hum the musical scales. He must have consumed at least forty cups of coffee a day. He was the most feminine man I ever met. Yet, I don't think he was a homosexual. In several recent publications however, it's been stated Minnelli was a bisexual, but I never saw any signs of active bisexuality or homosexuality in the years I worked with him.

He was married several times, once to Judy Garland, and fathered several children; the most famous of them is, of course, Liza Minnelli. He worshiped Liza as Liza worshiped him. Minnelli could hear a pin drop but he never would hear Liza stomping on the stage making herself known. Liza, with the huge brown eyes, with long dark hair down her back, often visited her father's set. I would go up to Liza with my finger to my lip trying to quiet her down. She would just glare at me.

Standing in awe on the set of my first musical, *Kismet*.

The best gift I received by working with Minnelli was that I got to know Judy Garland. What a lady! What a talent! I am sorry that I never got to make a film with her. Judy would often call the shooting stage. I would answer the telephone. Judy would say, "This is Judy Garland. May I speak to Mr. Minnelli if he's not too busy?" I'd say, "Hi, Judy, it's Hank." Judy would say, "Honey, I'm glad you answered the phone. How are you? Is he driving you crazy?" We'd laugh. Judy remained a friend until her death many years later.

Jack Cole, the famous choreographer, rehearsed *Kismet* for months with dozens of Hollywood's top gypsies. (Dancers are referred to as "gypsies.") The only principal actor involved in a dance routine was Dolores Gray. She'd bring donuts to the dancers. Julie Robinson was one of the key dancers. She later became Mrs. Harry Belafonte. Ross Bagdasarian, who wrote "The Chipmunk Song," had a small part. Two of the three Princesses of Ababu, Reiko Sato and Pat Dunn, were in the original Broadway play. Reiko, a beautiful Japanese girl, was going around with Marlon Brando at the time. One of the harem girls married one of Bing Crosby's sons. Dancers, whether in Hollywood or on Broadway, are the hardest workers. Cole wore bells on his ankles. The bells gave him the beat and the rhythm. He was extremely cross-eyed and I never knew who he was looking at. Often, I would look over my shoulder to see if he was speaking to me or to someone behind me.

I was so green in the musical business, that I was able to be brave. I had read all the union requirements concerning dancers. Dancers had to have a break every so often. Cole was a tyrant and strict taskmaster. The dancers feared him. All Cole dancers eventually suffered leg and knee problems. I would interrupt him to say that it was time for a break. He would look at me (I think it was me), not very happy that I interrupted him, but he always went along. I also made sure there was ice available in the rehearsal halls, another union rule, and given Cole's punishing rehearsals, quite necessary on this movie. Often, on Friday afternoons, the dancers would come up to me and ask me to tell Cole, "It's Friday, they've had a tough week. How about a short day?" Again, he would look at me (I think) and say, "Okay, just ten minutes more." The dancers loved me.

Stage 15 was then and maybe still is the longest soundstage in the world. A set for *Kismet* was built from one end of the stage almost to the opposite end. It was a mystical garden with a gazebo at the top of the set with a winding path surrounded by weeping willow trees, flowers and all sorts of flora. The set was high at the gazebo but gradually tapered down to the cement floor at the other end. It was built for the "Stranger in Paradise" musical number to be sung by Ann Blyth and Vic Damone. The entire set was covered with green sod over a wooden piling. It all looked very real.

The night before the shooting of this sequence, as is traditional, all the key crew accompanied Minnelli to Stage 15 to discuss the first shot of the morning. The cameraman, art director, set decorator, prop men and the production crew and me, at the tail end of the line, followed Minnelli. Minnelli started at the top near the gazebo and worked his way down the set, asking for more flowers here, fewer flowers there, etc. As he backed down near the winding path, Minnelli said he wanted the first live peacock to be placed there, pointing to the spot. This was the first time I had of any peacocks. A grip got a wooden peg and hammered it into the soft sod so we'd know the exact mark in the morning. The second of the two peacocks would be at the other end of the stage by the camera. Other minor changes were made and the first shot for the morning was planned. It was an establishing shot of the entire set with Ann and Damone walking and singing along the path heading toward the camera at the very end of the stage. For some reason, I was delegated to be in charge of the peacocks.

The morning arrived. The wind machines were placed to give movement to the trees. A playback was set up with the pre-recorded song sung by Ann and Damone. There are "click" tracks on the recording to cue the actors when to start singing. The first click is to cue the performer to be ready. The second click means to commence singing. They will actually sing, but the pre-recorded music will be used in the final film. There are people from the music department to make sure Ann and Damone are in sync with the music. The massive set is lighted. Minnelli has finished instructing the actors. The camera is in position. The choreographer, Jack Cole, is fluttering around. We are nearly ready.

Then someone yelled, "BRING IN THE PEACOCKS!" It was relayed again, "BRING IN THE PEACOCKS!" I relayed it." BRING IN THE PEACOCKS!" Suddenly, two of the most beautiful white peacocks were led in. The first peacock was ushered up to the peg that was placed in the sod the night before. I said to Don Vanni, the prop man, "Mr. Minnelli wants the peacock placed here with its feathers fanned out." Vanni said, "This is a male peacock. They don't 'fan out' unless there is a female peacock nearby." I said, "Well, bring in the female." Vanni said no female peacock was ordered. (I wondered if that was a mistake on my part. Are assistant directors in charge of peacocks?) What to do? Vanni realized we had a problem. He asked if the peacock moved or stood still. I said it didn't move. So, Vanni tied the feet of the peacock in the sod. He, then, stretched the peacock's tail and wired each side somehow to the earth. Success! Minnelli, in the meantime, was unaware of what was happening.

Now for the second peacock. Minnelli wanted the second peacock alongside the camera at the opposite end of the set so that the camera would reveal and frame some of the peacock's white feathers. A very artistic shot. I explained this to Vanni. Vanni said it was impossible as we were now on solid cement. No place to nail the peacock down. Another problem—a major problem. I didn't know what to do. Everyone was waiting. Minnelli was sitting to the left of the camera. Vanni said to me, "I'll save your ass. Tell me when you're ready."

"We've been ready for ten minutes," I said. The actors were in position. The playback was ready, the trees were blowing gently, and the camera was ready. Vanni's assistant brought in the second peacock and

Howard Keel on *Kismet* set.

pulled it to the right of the camera. The assistant got on his stomach and held the peacock's feet. Vanni layed on the other side of the camera, pulling the peacock under the camera very carefully. He said for me to roll the cameras. I rolled the camera. The soundman yelled, "SPEED." Minnelli said "ACTION" and Vanni shoved his finger up the peacock's ass. The feathers fanned out on cue.

The shot continued perfectly. The singers were on cue. However, no one was looking at the shot. Everyone was looking at Vanni on the floor. After Minnelli said, "CUT," Vanni pulled his finger out and, like clockwork, the feathers closed up like a fan. With Minnelli, you have many takes. Before each take, Vanni shoved his finger up the peacock and after each "cut" Vanni pulled his finger out. This went on all morning. Everyone at MGM had heard that there was someone on Stage 15 who was laying on the floor with a finger up a peacock's ass. Executives visited the set. Lana Turner, still shooting *The Prodigal* next door, said, "There's a man on Stage 15 with his finger up a peacock's ass." Lana brought her entire crew to observe the proceedings. I honestly don't think Minnelli ever knew what was happening. After all this, the peacock shot was never in the final film but was the most talked about shot in *Kismet*.

Chapter 5
Many More MGM Movies

Lust for Life, the biography of artist Vincent Van Gogh, was the film that immediately followed *Kismet*. This was a film that Vincente Minnelli was anxious to make. The story was that the studio forced Minnelli to direct *Kismet* first before he could undertake the making of *Lust for Life*.

Most of the film was made in Europe and I was the Culver City contact. My main responsibility was obtaining releases on the Van Gogh and Gauguin paintings that were to be used in the production. The producer was John Houseman. We borrowed paintings from all over the world. Van Gogh's nephew Theo, who owned a great many of his uncle's paintings, was the only person who refused to cooperate. The insurance costs involved in the movie were exorbitant. Every painting that was going to be reproduced, either completely or in various stages of completion, had government agents watching over it. Artists came from France to copy the paintings. There were dozens of paintings. The understanding was that when the reproduced painting was no longer needed, it had to be destroyed. At the time, MGM had a huge incinerator. Each painting was thrown into the fire with a secret service man overseeing the destruction, and taking notes. By the time the film was completed, every reproduced painting was destroyed.

Forty percent of the film was made at the studio and sixty percent in France and Belgium. The shooting began in Europe and finished at the studio. The film starred Kirk Douglas as Van Gogh and Anthony Quinn as Paul Gauguin. Quinn won the Best Supporting Actor for the film. He was magnificent.

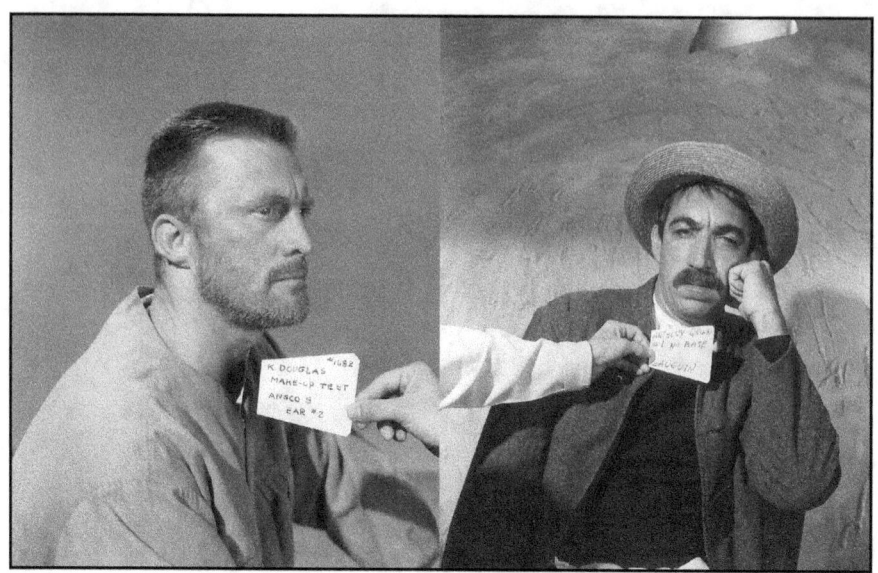

Studio makeup test for *Lust for Life*.

Kirk Douglas is the only actor that I ever worked with that I disliked. Talk about ego…I saw him recently. He's an old man who has mellowed through the years. On this film, I became friends with three British actresses—Pamela Brown and Jill Bennett, both of whom have since died, and Jeannette Sterke, who soon after married Keith Michel, a well-known London West End performer.

A classic Minnelli moment was when we were filming a short scene on MGM's Back Lot 3 at night. The shot was a midget playing Toulouse-Lautrec crossing from a small building from camera right—up a cobblestoned street, walking about twenty yards and entering another building—camera left. Minnelli shot sixty-three takes of this very simple scene. I thought the night would never end.

On another occasion, Minnelli wanted a shot of the sun rising up over the ocean. He wanted to send a second unit camera crew to the east coast to get this transition shot. The studio refused. Minnelli was way over budget. They suggested that he look at dozens of sunrise shots that were in the MGM film library. They were all available to him. Minnelli and his editor viewed them and none were acceptable.

Minnelli got the bright idea to shoot the sun setting off Santa Monica, and then reverse the film. Brilliant idea. I should have thought of that myself. It would save the cost of sending a crew to the east coast

With Noel Purcell, Kirk Douglas and Pamela Brown at Santa Monica Beach location.

and would cost a mere pittance. A second unit was dispatched to Santa Monica late one afternoon. Many shots were filmed at various times of day with the sun setting along the seashore. Several days later, we ran the second unit sunset shots. The film was reversed. The sunset, now a sunrise, looked perfect. Then, we noticed that the waves were going away from the shore. Not such a good idea, after all.

There was a scene in *Lust for Life* that took place in a small French café on the soundstage with Douglas and Quinn. The actors were sitting against a window in a bay area of the café drinking. Through the window, you could see large sunflowers. The sunflowers were just set dressing. It had nothing to do with the story. They were "planted" along the outside of the window. Minnelli sent for the set decorator, who rushed to the set. "Are the sunflowers real?" Minnelli could have taken 10 steps and seen for himself.

"No, Mr. Minnelli. They are expensive fakes." Minnelli said he wanted to have real sunflowers instead. The decorator called the studio's florist. Sorry, the only real sunflowers available at this time of the year

With the famous British actress, Pamela Brown.

Minnelli and Kirk Douglas discussing script. Walter Plunkett standing in the background.

were in Australia. Minnelli said to order them. That scene was postponed until the real sunflowers arrived. Again, it was another Minnelli ploy to stall for time. This would happen many more times with Minnelli. It always amazed me that the studio allowed it to happen.

The Opposite Sex was a remake of *The Women* that starred June Allyson, Dolores Gray, Joan Collins, Agnes Moorehead, the fabulous Ann Sheridan and the ageless Ann Miller. During production, Ann Sheridan asked me to order a birthday cake from the studio commissary, as the coming Friday was Ann Miller's birthday. Sheridan said she would tend to the details. Come Friday, at the end of the day's filming, the chef wheeled in a three-layer cake with sparklers as the crew sang "Happy Birthday" to Ann Miller. As the cake was wheeled in we could see the inscription: "39 MY ASS." It has been many years since Ann Miller was 39 years old. Ann Sheridan was a terrific, sexy lady with a great sense of humor.

Speaking of Ann Miller, I heard a very funny story from Eve Arden about her. In 1937, at RKO Studios, they were making a film called *Stage Door*. This was a very successful film starring Katharine Hepburn, Lucille Ball, Ginger Rogers, Andrea Leeds and dozens of other actresses, including Miller and Arden, produced by Pandro S. Berman. The story was about a theatrical boarding house for budding actresses in New York City. During an afternoon shooting on the soundstage, someone brought in a newspaper and handed it to Hepburn. The headlines read: JEAN HARLOW DIES. A pall fell over the entire set. Filming ceased. Some of the actresses were crying. Katharine Hepburn, stunned by the news, had the newspaper spread open on her lap. Everyone was in shock, everyone except Ann Miller. Ann was in one corner of the stage practicing her dance steps. She slowly tapped herself toward the center of the stage where some of the actresses had gathered. "A one and a two and a one and a two." Ann was tapping herself toward Hepburn. She looked over Hepburn's shoulder. "A one and a two and a one and a two. Oh, my God, Jean Harlow's dead, Jean Harlow's dead, and a one and a two and a one and a two." And off she continued tapping, never missing a beat. Moral: the show must go on.

In 1956, after working a short time on *The Opposite Sex*, I went to England for the first time. While there, a Welsh friend of mine, living in London, asked me if I would go to Spain with him on a short holiday. Steven had recently divorced.

I agreed. We flew to Barcelona and took a bus to our final destination—Benidorm. The bus trip from Barcelona to Benidorm took longer than the flight from London. Benidorm was a small sleepy seaside town with one decent hotel. Today, Benidorm looks like Miami Beach.

Our small hotel reminded me of the hotel in the film *Separate Tables* (set in a small seaside English hotel). We checked in, unpacked and went downstairs for a look-see. It was off-season so the hotel was not crowded.

After dinner, we sat around watching the "waxworks." I felt this trip was a mistake. However, I did notice some card tables in the "social" room. Being a fanatical bridge player, I looked around for some players. I spotted Sir Michael Redgrave, the splendid British actor, with a male companion. (Redgrave had not yet been knighted.)

We played for several hours and days. Redgrave was a superb player. They returned to London on the third day. Many years later I played bridge with Redgrave's son-in-law, Tony Richardson, a well-known film director who was also an exceptional bridge player.

There was very little to do in Benidorm. The sea was too cold and very little opportunity to go shopping. So back to the bridge table, we had met a charming elderly English couple who were interested in playing. He was a botanist and lecturer at the University of Aberystwyth in Wales. He and his wife reminded us of Mr. and Mrs. Chips. The Chips were excellent players and we spent the remaining evenings playing cards. The four of us were scheduled to fly to London on the same flight.

A few days before our departure, I got the worst case of dysentery—the absolute worst. It was either from the Spanish cuisine or the Spanish wine. In any case I could clear out a room in a minute. Luckily, that didn't happen. I'm sure if I broke wind near a thriving plant, I'm positive the leaves would wither. If I broke wind along the seashore, I'm sure the waves would reserves. It lasted for days. Lucky for me (and anyone else) they were not "sneaky" farts. I was always forewarned by the rumbling and able to get away. This condition tapered off toward the end of our stay.

The day of our departure, Mr. and Mrs. Chips, Steven and myself and a few others boarded the bus for the Barcelona airport. All was well along the long drive along the Costa Brava. We finally reached the airport. This was before all the tight security of today. After going through passport control, we all boarded the plane. The airline was called *The Hunting Clan* and had only 24 seats.

I sat next to the window in the first row. Steven sat next to me. The Chips sat across from us. Mrs. Chips sat next to the window, and Mr. Chips sat across from Steven. The plane's engines began to rev up. We were ready to take off. Suddenly, the engines started to rumble and so did my stomach. I let loose my final and most lethal fart. I was so embarrassed. Steven, I'm sure, was getting nauseated. I heard Mrs. Chips say, "Dear, what is that *dreadful* smell?" Mr. Chips said, without a beat, "Dear, I told you before, the Spanish use a very cheap grade of petrol in their planes."

Who would expect a Welsh botanist to be so knowledgeable about Spanish gasoline?

Meanwhile, back in Hollywood, the Pantages Theater in Los Angeles was the setting for the 1957 Academy Awards. In those days, assistant directors would be asked to help and I was one of the assistants selected. Since the presenters are part of the audience, just before the presenter is required on stage, an assistant director would go to escort him or her backstage. I had the privilege of escorting Sophia Loren. Sophia is tall and beautiful.

Backstage, they were getting ready to begin a medley of Oscar-winning songs. Mae West and Rock Hudson were going to do a duet of "Baby, It's Cold Outside" from MGM's *Neptune's Daughter*. A chaise lounge on casters was rolled in. Mae West was supposed to be draped over the chaise with Rock Hudson sitting next to her. Each time Mae started to sit down, the chaise it would move or slide from underneath her. The show was being televised. The television technicians were getting nervous as that number was coming up next. Each time Mae made an attempt, the chaise would pull away. Rock started to laugh. We all laughed. This wasn't the time to laugh. The entire world was waiting to see Mae and Rock sing. I and several other assistants wedged the chaise so that when Mae would sit down, we would keep it from moving. Rock still couldn't stop laughing. Finally, Mae sort of threw herself on the chaise and the prop men pushed the chaise on stage. Not a minute too soon. Rock jumped on it as it got in range of the television cameras. On television, you could see Rock laughing. It was the highlight of the evening.

In 1957 I went to Europe for a short trip. While I was in Paris, William Kaplan, the unit manager, asked me to give him, or rather, Minnelli, a hand, with the filming of *Gigi*. Kaplan said that Minnelli would appreciate seeing a familiar face. I would never really know what

Minnelli thought about me. He never said a kind word or gave a compliment to me in all the years I worked on his films. I guess the fact that I was on his films at all was adequate recognition.

Doing a period costume film in Paris in the summer is difficult. The ice palace along the park off the Champs-Elysées still existed. MGM took over the entire complex which was used for the dressing of the extras. The ice palace was also used for an ice-skating sequence in the film. That sequence was filmed twice. Minnelli did not like the performance of the original actor. So Jacques Bergerac, Ginger Rogers' husband at the time, was brought in and the entire scene was reshot. To prepare a scene involving hundreds of extras that require hair, makeup and costumes takes considerable time. We started filming in the Bois de Boulogne with Maurice Chevalier singing "Thank Heaven for Little Girls," a scene that required extras, horses, children, carriages and a playback.

When filming in the States, lunchtime is either one half hour or forty-two minutes or one hour. In France, lunch is officially one hour. But by the time lunch has ended, everybody has pulled themselves together, it's been two hours and, of course, everyone gets a bottle of wine with lunch. Minnelli's best work was always after lunch. So the shooting took forever. Arthur Freed, the producer, was most anxious to return to the studio. He fought daily with Minnelli. One luncheon, I saw Freed, angry with Minnelli, push all the dishes off their table. The Ugly American. Cecil Beaton, the costume designer, thought the movie was all about his designs and costumes. Beaton, too, would argue daily with Minnelli. Another difficult day/night was filming at Maxim's. That sequence was extremely difficult because of the lack of space and the lack of air. Much tension, many nerves, much drama. I thought someone would be murdered before the end of the night. It was the end of a difficult schedule and everyone was tired and anxious to get home. Luckily, it ended without incident.

After *Gigi* returned to the studio, I remained in Paris. The first preview of *Gigi* was in Santa Barbara, California. It was considered a disaster, or at least, not what the studio was expecting. Another director, Charles Walters, was brought in to "doctor up" the film, unbeknownst to Minnelli. Walters cut, recut, shot some new scenes and generally made the film that became a huge success. The rest is history.

I was asked if I would work in Amsterdam on the second unit of *The Diary of Anne Frank*. Never having been to the Netherlands, I jumped at the opportunity. George Stevens, Jr., son of the director, George Stevens,

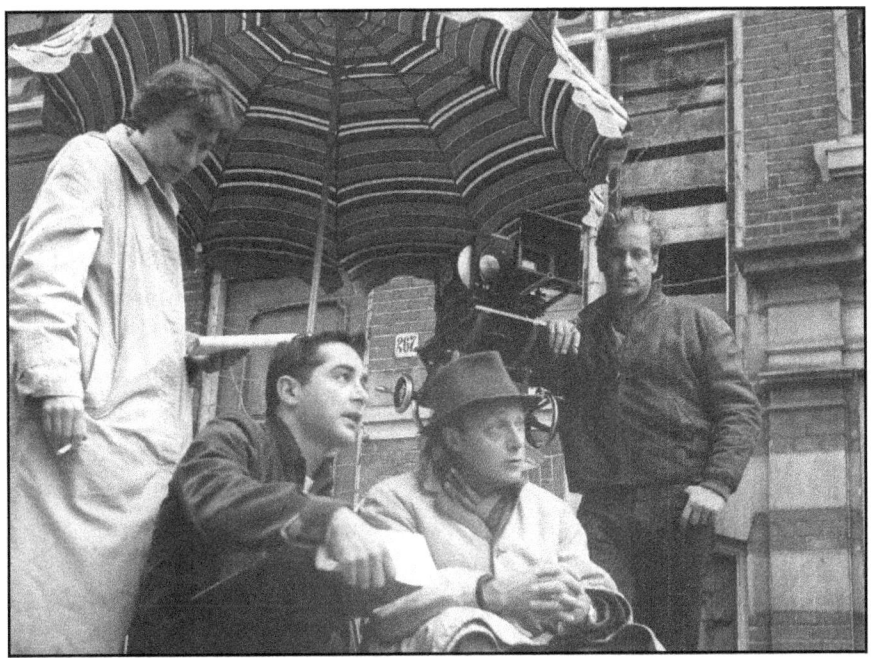

Amsterdam Holland with cameraman Jack Cardiff in front of Anne Frank House.

who was in Hollywood directing the main unit, was in charge of the second unit. I spent six weeks on the project. This was an experience I would never forget.

The cameraman was the distinguished Englishman, Jack Cardiff. It was the first film that I worked on which depicted actual events. We filmed in the attic where the Franks had spent years in hiding. We filmed the streets where the Dutch Jews were rounded up and sent to concentration camps. The entire experience was so vivid.

None of the actors were on location—just doubles. However, Otto Frank, who was living in Switzerland, visited the set. He was an interesting man. The "Diary" had made him very wealthy. The Dutch Jews did not like Otto Frank. They said he used his daughter and her diary for commercial gain. In the meantime, he had married a Christian woman and lived in splendor in Switzerland. Today, the Anne Frank house is a museum.

Ben Kadish was the Unit Manager on *Anne Frank*. We were old friends. One evening in Amsterdam, we went to a bar/nightclub to have drinks. At the next table sat two lovely Dutch women alone. They were all smiles. Ben got into a conversation with them and he asked them if they would like to join us. They jumped at the suggestion. The four of us clicked. Like all the Dutch, they spoke perfect English. They were charming. We were charmed. After a couple of drinks, Ben asked the ladies if they would like to go to another club. They said they would love to but they wanted to check with their husbands. The two ladies got up and crossed the bar to a table where two men sat alone. The men turned and looked at Ben and me. We were both flabbergasted. The ladies returned to our table all smiles. Their husbands approved. I said something like this never happens in our country. We didn't understand. I was uncomfortable. The ladies were giggling. One of them said, "Oh, it's perfectly okay. We do it all the time. There is no problem. Our husbands want us to have a good time."

I said, "But not with us." Ben, although disappointed, concurred. We missed our "Dutch Treat."

I quickly discovered that the Dutch had a very liberal attitude toward sex. Everything and anything goes. The red light district in Amsterdam is something to behold. For blocks, prostitutes sit in dramatically lit windows selling their wares. Whatever sexual pleasures you want, you can find it there. And all the prostitutes are examined monthly. In their rooms, a document is in evidence indicating that the lady is healthy. I soon discovered that such places exist all over Europe—particularly in Germany and most particularly in Hamburg. I guess we Americans are "backwards"—fortunately. After my Dutch experience, I returned to Paris.

One weekend, I went to St-Germain-Au-Les, just outside Paris, to visit friends. They had a spectacular "Moulin" in the country. Early one morning, I was walking along a beautiful tree-lined lane when I saw a woman approaching from the opposite direction. She was heavy-set and was wearing a floppy long coat. Just as she passed me, she said "Bon Jour" and kept on walking. I recognized her immediately. It was Deanna Durbin. Deanna was an actress who made many musical films at Universal Studios in the '30s and '40s. She worked with Henry Koster and Joe Pasternak. After several failed marriages, Deanna married a Frenchman and moved to France. She never made another film.

Thanks to the film industry I've met a myriad of celebrities, politicians, and European royalty, as well as actors, directors and producers. I have often been asked who impressed me the most. Without any hesitation, I say Eleanor Roosevelt. When I was leaving Paris on a flight to London after *Anne Frank* I had the pleasure of sitting next to Eleanor

Roosevelt. What charisma. As I sat down, I introduced myself and said, "Mrs. Roosevelt, I am an American." She had a big smile for me. Her entire face lit up. Mrs. Roosevelt asked me what I was doing in Europe. I told her that I was an assistant director in the motion picture field. She was genuinely interested in what I did. At this time, Mrs. Roosevelt worked for UNESCO. We spoke all the way to London. I was only sorry we weren't flying to Los Angeles. London is less than an hour from Paris. I felt cheated. I could have gone around the world listening to her.

We finally reached London. As I got up, I noticed she had two heavy-looking handbags. I offered to carry one of them. She smiled and said that she was use to carrying them—they balanced her. We inched along the unending corridors working our way to customs. It seemed like a dozen planes arrived at the same time. Several hundred travelers were waiting to be processed and it was taking forever. I asked the man behind me to hold my place and I worked my way to the immigration desks. I asked to see someone in charge. An official was pointed out to me. I went up to him and said, "Do you know that Mrs. Eleanor Roosevelt is standing back there in the queue? I would think that if your Queen Mother arrived in New York City she would not be standing in line and would get special consideration."

The official smiled at me and said, "Mrs. Roosevelt often takes that flight. The American Embassy in Paris always alerts us of her travel plans. She always refuses any VIP treatment." I should have guessed that. I went back to my place in line. We finally reached passport control. Mrs. Roosevelt shook my hand and said she enjoyed my company. I wanted to hug and kiss her. I didn't. I wish I had. I will never forget that flight or that memory.

Chapter 6
And Yet More MGM Movies

I returned to MGM (one always returns to their homeland) and I immediately went to work on a film entitled *The Seventh Sin* starring Eleanor Parker, Bill Travers, George Sanders, Jean-Pierre Aumont and that great French actress, Françoise Rosay. The initial director on this film was fired because he was always drunk. Vincente Minnelli replaced him but never received screen credit. The film was a remake of a Greta Garbo film called *The Painted Veil*. I got to know Eleanor on this film. I fell in love with her. She was a real pro and such a great beauty.

An extensive second unit in Hong Kong, directed by the initial director, had already filmed reels of footage. I would like to describe the story of *The Seventh Sin*, but I'm afraid I don't remember the details and frankly I didn't even understand it at the time. I remember that Eleanor played a "loose woman" who decided to work in Mother Superior Françoise Rosay's convent, probably as repentance. Eleanor would faint a great deal—especially if things were going badly. On this film, she fainted regularly. One day, the scene that Minnelli was staging involved Eleanor, Françoise, George Sanders and Jean-Pierre in the convent's sparse dining room. They were gathered around a long table. Eleanor had said to me earlier, "If he [Minnelli] touches me again, I'm going to faint." Most actors do not like to be touched or be moved about like furniture. They prefer "step two inches to the right or step back," etc. Eleanor was standing between the table and the camera. Sure enough, Minnelli pushed Eleanor's shoulder to shift her around. On cue, Eleanor fainted, falling between the table and the camera. Minnelli paid no attention or was oblivious to Eleanor on the floor.

Eleanor Parker with the original director of *The Seventh Sin*.

With his viewfinder, Minnelli would step over the prone Eleanor, setting and resetting things on the table. Minnelli always spent hours "dressing" the set and only minutes with his actors. He stepped back over Eleanor again, and again stepped over her to do more readjusting. I was on the floor with Bill McGarry, the First Assistant Director, trying to pull Eleanor. I said, "He's going to step on her, *pull*." We finally got Eleanor out of harm's way and took her to her dressing room. You may not believe this, but those that know and worked with Minnelli, will. Minnelli said, "Where is Eleanor?"

With George Sanders, Eleanor Parker and Françoise Rosay.
Vincent Minnelli discussing script.

On another occasion, Françoise said to me, "Henri, I'm beginning to twitch like him [Minnelli]. I can't look at him anymore."

The next year I met Mme. Rosay at her lovely Parisian apartment near the Eiffel Tower. We walked to the Eiffel Tower to have dinner on the premiere etage. For those who don't know Mme. Rosay, she was the Bette Davis of France. She had tremendous presence. As the elevator arrived at the restaurant level, she was immediately recognized. The four musicians, playing their violins, led Mme. Rosay to her table. Everyone in the restaurant stood up and applauded her. Françoise knew how to milk this moment. She walked ever so slowly, occasionally bowing her head or smiling at someone. She was royalty. And she made me feel like I was her consort.

I worked sporadically on other films during 1956-1959. Richard Brooks directed *The Last Hunt*. It starred Stewart Granger, Robert Taylor and Anne Bancroft. It was on this film that Anne Bancroft was thrown from her horse on the soundstage. I can still hear her back cracking. An arc light snapped on and spooked the horse. Mel Brooks, Anne's husband, told me many years later that by breaking her back, Anne became a formidable actress. After she recovered, she went to New York City to study with the Actors Studio. Until then, she only made mediocre, forgettable films. Debra Paget replaced Anne as the Indian Maiden. And Anne Bancroft later won the Oscar for *The Miracle Worker*.

Jailhouse Rock was Elvis' first MGM movie. The producer was Pandro S. Berman, a brilliant man and the person who single-handedly helped achieve my dreams in the film business. More on Elvis, and much more on Pandro, later. I only worked on the dance unit of this film. I considered Elvis a friend from the very beginning.

Around this time, Alfred Hitchcock was making *North By Northwest*, the only film I ever lobbied to get work on. Unfortunately for me, he had his own regular production staff. But I was asked to do one thing for the project, one that should have been easy.

The production department asked me to arrange for a studio limousine (driver must be in uniform) and go to Cary Grant's home in Bel-Air and take him to the Los Angeles Airport in the morning. He was flying to New York City for location shooting. The next day, the limousine picked me up and we drove to Mr. Grant's home. It was a very spacious home—worthy of Mr. Grant. As the car pulled up the drive, I stepped out and walked to the front door. I rang the doorbell. A butler (or major domo) opened the door.

"I've come to pick up Mr. Grant and take him to the airport," I said. The butler leaned out, looked to the left and then to the right. He said, "Where's the second limousine?"

"What second limousine? Isn't it just Mr. Grant?"

The butler, looking down his nose at me, said, "Mr. Grant *never* travels with his luggage."

I was dumbfounded. I said, "May I use your phone?"

"NO," he said and shut the door. Where do you find a public phone in Bel-Air? I told the driver to take me to the Bel-Air Hotel—the only public phone within miles. I called the studio and explained the situation. Meanwhile, Mr. Grant missed his plane. The next day two limousines were dispatched—but not with me. I never worked with Cary Grant.

However, I was immediately rewarded by being assigned to *Cat on a Hot Tin Roof*, the Tennessee Williams play, directed and adapted for the screen by Richard Brooks. This successful film starred Elizabeth Taylor, Paul Newman, Burl Ives, Judith Anderson, Jack Carson and Madeleine Sherwood. I was excited to be working with Elizabeth again. I would often "chaperone" Elizabeth and Mike Todd and newlyweds Eddie Fisher and Debbie Reynolds. I had kept my friendship alive with Elizabeth since the *Raintree County* days. As I mentioned before, Richard Brooks was a madman whom I respected and liked. Unfortunately, I only worked on *Cat* for two or three weeks.

During production, Mike Todd was killed in an airplane accident. Mike had become a close friend. Elizabeth had always badgered Mike to hire me for his company. Enough has been written about Mike's tragic death. Except, if all the people that said they were supposed to have been on that ill-fated flight had been telling the truth. Mike would have had to own a 747!

The production shut down for several days. Elizabeth went into deep mourning. The company eventually resumed shooting, but I was switched to another film.

One morning, while still on the film, I went to check on the cast in makeup. Naturally, Elizabeth was late. Madeleine was there. And in the first chair sat Judith Anderson. She was quite a character, a fine actress and had a tremendous sense of humor. No great beauty she, but this particular morning she looked like a bus had hit her. I said, "Judith, are you okay?" She said, "Darling, last night all my holes were violated."

Madeleine Sherwood was a big pain in the ass. No one particularly liked her. If crew members don't like an actor, there is something obviously wrong. Generally, everyone on a film roots for the director, the actors, and the success of the film. Maybe she was just nervous. Anyway, I was to find out in a couple of years.

Elizabeth eventually came back and gave a brilliant performance. I think she looked her most radiant in *Cat on a Hot Tin Roof*. She looked sad. She had reason to be. Elizabeth was nominated for Best Actress for the second time.

It was after *Cat* and the death of Mike Todd that Elizabeth fell in love with Eddie Fisher and Eddie fell out of love with Debbie Reynolds. Volumes were written about this "scandal." The outcome was that three people were involved in a sad, devastating situation. Debbie was certainly hurt the most and she now faced the reality of raising two small children by herself. America's sweethearts were no more.

The film I went on to next was titled *Never So Few*. The year was 1958. It was to star Frank Sinatra, Haya Harareet (Esther in *Ben-Hur*,) and Sammy Davis Jr. The director was John Sturges. John Sturges was filming a large second unit in the jungles of Cambodia using doubles for the three principal actors. As weeks passed, it was announced that Steve McQueen was going to replace Sammy Davis. A week later, it was announced that Gina Lollobrigida was to replace Haya Harareet. Thousands of feet of film were shot with a black double for Sammy. Luckily, Gina and Haya had the same coloring.

Meanwhile, as the second unit was still filming in Cambodia, sets were being built in the studio in preparation for studio filming. The day Gina Lollobrigida arrived at MGM was momentous. This was to be her first film to be shot in Hollywood. She arrived at the main gate with her husband, Milko, a doctor who became her agent, and a female companion whom I discovered, much later, was Gina's sister. I introduced myself and escorted them to Helen Rose's Salon in the ladies wardrobe department. Gina had a hat on. I discovered she always wore a wig. Helen's staff had all the dresses on mannequins, displayed beautifully. Introductions were made. Gina, not smiling, spouted off Italian intermittently. Helen asked me to conduct the meeting. "The first costume you wear in the film, scene, etc. etc. and the second outfit you wear is a, etc. etc." Gina paid no attention to me. The first thing she said, in English, was "I hate white." I was surrounded by white dresses. "But, Miss Lollobrigida, we have already established these white dresses on the second unit." Gina glared at me with a look that said, "Who is he to tell me what I can wear and what I can't wear!" After going through the entire script, Helen tried to be very diplomatic, but we were both nervous. Finally, Gina said, "Send all my costumes to Bungalow 4 at the Beverly Hills Hotel with a sewing machine."

"But, Miss Lollobrigida, we have all the seamstresses and equipment here," Helen said.

"Please, Bungalow 4, as soon as possible." What we didn't know but soon found out was that her sister was also a seamstress. Sister made whatever alterations were required.

With Frank Sinatra on the set of *Never So Few*.

Eventually, the second unit returned and the studio shooting began. Sinatra took an immediate dislike to Gina. I think it was mutual. I'd tell Frank that we were ready. Frank would say, "Has the wop come out of her dressing room yet?" Then, he would refuse to appear until he was told she was waiting for him. I'd go to Gina to tell her we were ready to shoot and she would ask if Sinatra was out on the set. I got myself a whistle and I told them that when I blew the whistle, come out charging.

One afternoon, word came down from the publicity office that the King of Belgium and his party wanted to visit the set the next day. Everyone got excited, except Sinatra. The publicity department was nervous, the secret service was nervous, the executives were nervous—but not Sinatra.

Howard Strickling, head of publicity, came to the set to talk to Sinatra, just before the royal party was scheduled to arrive, trying to impress upon Sinatra the need for protocol and respect. The local television station was going to cover the event. Gina had a very revealing dress showing her very famous breasts. The dress had a shawl to go with it. As

Quoting Gina, "Enrico, I want to paint your balls gold."

the royal party entered, with the cameras rolling, an executive kept throwing Gina's shawl over her shoulders, so her famous breasts weren't so obvious. She would immediately push the shawl off. Again, the shawl was thrown over her and she was getting more furious. The King was eventually introduced to Gina without her shawl. Sinatra was introduced next. As he shook the King's hand, Sinatra said, "You're skinnier than I am, Charlie!" The party left very quickly.

Gina is a very underrated actress. She has a terrific sense of humor and great timing. But she is a worrywart. She worries about everything. I said to her once, "Gina, we have hairdressers to watch your hair, we have makeup men to watch your makeup, we have cameramen to watch the shadows, why don't you just concentrate on your acting?" This wasn't meant to be insulting and Gina didn't take it as an insult.

"Enrico," she said (I was Henri last year), "what you say is right. I made Gina. I made Gina's clothes. I made Gina's hair. I made Gina's everything. I cannot change." It was shortly after that she came up to me and said, "Enrico, I want to paint your balls gold." I didn't know what it exactly meant, but I hope it was a compliment. And she never had the opportunity to paint my balls gold.

In those days, MGM was a great place to work. It was the studio to be reckoned with. I would walk around the main lot looking at all its glory. There was activity all over. Everybody was doing something, going somewhere. You passed dress extras, Indians, cowboys, dancers. Walter Pidgeon and Robert Taylor would be walking crisply taking their morning constitutional. Walter would always say "Lovely morning." You would walk by the Powell bungalow and hear Eleanor Powell tapping away. You would walk by the cutting rooms and hear the babble of different voices of different stars of films that were being edited. You could walk by Gertrude Fogler and Lillian Burns' bungalows and hear them give some starlet vocal and acting lessons. Dueling lessons were given to many of the actors. You'd walk by Esther Williams' diving double, Esther Williams' underwater double, Esther Williams' stand-in and, even occasionally, Esther Williams.

The MGM commissary was also fascinating. Like everything at MGM, it was very well organized. As you entered, there were three long tables about thirty feet long. The first table was for all the key staff currently shooting a film. Many times lunch was limited to only half an hour. The first table took top preference—for immediate service. The second table was for directors and producers, and the third table was for writers and various visiting VIPs. All three tables had a telephone. There were tables for two along the walls and tables for four filling out the restaurant. In one corner of the room, off to one side, was "The Lion's Den." That was for the very, very VIPs. During the Academy Award season, if an employee at MGM was nominated for an Oscar, everybody in the commissary would applaud as she or he entered. If that person won the Oscar months later, everyone would stand and applaud.

MGM had a fan mail department, with many desks, each bearing the name of one of MGM's stars. A fan mail employee would take care of a particular actor's fan mail. Tons of mail was delivered to this building daily.

If you have an autographed photo of Clark Gable or Robert Taylor, chances are a fan mail employee signed it. Joan Crawford was the only exception. She made it known that she and she alone would write her fans and autograph photos. Amazingly, money would be enclosed in some letters. That money would eventually go to a charity. Often, food, cookies, and cake would be mailed. That food was destroyed. Quite often, there would be threatening or suspicious letters, which were sent immediately to MGM's police department.

You would walk by the dance rehearsal halls and hear drums and music. Occasionally, you would hear an actor singing. This was MGM in all its glory. Sadly, those days are gone forever. As a matter of fact, there is no MGM Studios anymore. Sony Pictures purchased the main lot. Lot 2 and Lot 3 are now apartment complexes. The gated community where Lot 3 used to be is called "Raintree." Lot 2, at one time, had New York City's Third Avenue El. It had a tenement district, Andy Hardy's street, and *The Philadelphia Story* house, which was used hundreds of times with a little redressing. It had Esther Williams' outdoor pool, Hannibal's bridge and Cohn Park (named after executive Joe Cohn). It had the London *Gaslight* street. It had a small city town square. It had a Chinese street, a carryover from *The Good Earth*. At one time, it had a train station and a working train. I worked on all these sets dozens of times on various films. Lot 2 also had the animation department. Jack Nicholson, who worked there before he made it big as an actor, loved to ride his bicycle back and forth to the main lot delivering mail. Often, he would visit the sets and watch the filming.

Lot 3 had Tarzan's lagoon and jungle. It had a tremendous western town and street. It had a typical French village set and a set called "Portsmouth," an English village. It had parts of different European villages. When I worked on *Mutiny on the Bounty*, the Brando version, the entire top deck was built over water. There were parts of the *Bounty* all over the studio.

The main lot was where you'd find the buildings that housed various departments: camera, property, sound, wardrobe, makeup and production. It also had dozens of soundstages. The Thalberg building, which was just on the outside the main lot entrance, housed the MGM brass. This huge building was built after Irving Thalberg's death. It was three stories high. One could spend hours researching in the basement, which contained thousands of unproduced scripts and important documents stored under lock and key. I remember once, when they had their annual clean up, a janitor was pushing a huge wooden trash bin piled high with documents en route to the incinerator. As he passed, he asked if I wanted any of it. The very first thing I picked up was a twenty-page document written half in Swedish and half in English. It was a Greta Garbo contract, signed by Garbo in several places. I dug deeper and found a Wallace Beery and a Marie Dressler contract. All signed. Stupidly, I placed them back in the trash bin. I didn't want them. I had no room for them. A dealer in autographs recently told me, that the Garbo contract was worth $350,000.

There was a chef, always dressed in white with a chef's hat, who pushed a cart containing pound cake and cold milk or cream. He would go from office to office unannounced, and walk in with a slice of cake and milk. Ulcers, anyone?

The eastern wing of the Thalberg Building on the first floor was what was known as "The Freed Unit." Arthur Freed had his own domain and all his brilliant staff had offices next to him: Roger Edens, Lela Simone, Andre Previn, Kay Thompson and many other writers and musicians. At the opposite end of the building were the offices of Pandro S. Berman. At one time, I had an office next to him. Directly across from Berman's office was the office of Martin Ransohoff. Many a day, his secretary would run out hysterically. He had a serious case of flatulence that would resound down the halls. Often I could hear it in my office next to Pandro.

The remainder of the Thalberg building had other producers, directors and executives. There was an executive dining room, a gym, Dr. Mitchell's office (the MGM chiropractor) and in the basement, all the executive screening rooms. Margaret Booth, "the wicked witch of Culver City," was also there in the projection rooms.

Margaret Booth was the oldest employee at MGM. She began as an editor when it was called "Metro" and remained there through dozens of different regimes. She must have known where all the bodies were buried. She was loved and despised. Many directors would not work at MGM unless Booth was barred from touching their film. Booth was supervising film editor whose one specialty was knowing how to cut and re-cut scenes that contained African Americans. In those days, the Southern states did not want to see whites and blacks intermingling. It was easy with Lena Horne. She would do a specialty number and, for the South, it was just eliminated from the prints. It was more difficult when a black person was incorporated in a scene with dialogue. If anyone could cut the offending actor out of a scene, it was Booth.

On *High Society*, Louis Armstrong and his band were in the movie. Armstrong had an all-black orchestra with the exception of his drummer. Booth came to the set, very worried. She spoke to the director. She spoke to the cameraman. The drummer was relegated to a corner. You only see him once, very quickly with the entire band. Booth was given an honorary Academy Award in 1977 for her contribution to the film industry. What a mistake, what a travesty!

It was on *High Society* that Armstrong, who at one time was extremely heavy, told me how to lose weight. He said, "Eat as much as you want before 4 p.m. and nothing thereafter." I didn't try the diet. I prefer being chubby.

The policeman on duty at the main gate during the day was a wonderful man whose name really was Ken Hollywood. He was an institution. All the stars loved him. As a matter of fact, everyone loved him. He was the official MGM greeter.

I worked at MGM Studios exclusively for almost all of six years. I had been a first assistant director for a while, but never on my own film. That was still in the future. On one occasion, I went to 20th Century-Fox to work on the dance unit of *South Pacific*. I got to meet the very talented and brilliant director, Joshua Logan, who much later became an integral part of my career. I was on that project for about a month. The choreographer, Leroy Prinz, amused me. He did not look like a choreographer. He did not act like a choreographer. He looked more like a Las Vegas croupier. I never saw him show a dance step. He always had a cigarette in his mouth, with his head tilted sideways so the smoke would not go into his eyes. He had a walking stick. He would tap a dancer's leg or tap the floor. He must have been a success. He choreographed many a film.

The second time I worked away from MGM during this period was when I went to Desilu Studios to work on *I Love Lucy*. I loved Lucy! She was a hard-working lady who was very unhappy with Desi. Desi was unhappy with her. I enjoyed William Frawley, but I disliked Vivian Vance.

She wanted to be Lucy. Lucy took a great liking to me. She was friendly toward me from the very beginning. I was even allowed in her makeup room. I used to watch the torture she would go through every shooting day just to get ready for the camera. Lucy's makeup man had a contraption that reached the ceiling. He would wrap a thin gauze under Lucy's neck and chin and stretch the line that pulled Lucy's jaw and lower neck up. After getting to a certain point, he would cut the line, tying it to the top of Lucy's head. He would then put her wig on, covering the gauze with makeup. Who said the life of an actor was easy? She had the same makeup man and hairdresser for years. The *Lucy* set was a family affair. It had the same crew probably from the very first *I Love Lucy*.

I also worked on two Lucy one-hour shows, *The Lucy-Desi Comedy Hour*. The first was with Tallulah Bankhead. What a character! She spent most of the day chasing after Lucy's stand-in, Hazel. Hazel must have been sixty at the time. Hazel was terrified that Tallulah would catch her. Tallulah was notorious for her heavy drinking and passion for the same sex. The second show I did was with Betty Grable and Harry James. Betty Grable was the best. We would have lunch daily and she would tell me stories of her 20th Century-Fox days when she was their top star and she told me a very revealing story about her early days at that studio. When she got her contract at Fox, the reigning musical queen at the time was Alice Faye. Alice was getting older and when she heard that Betty was coming to Fox, Alice was smart enough to know her musical days were numbered. That's showbiz! Alice and Betty co-starred in a movie called *Tin Pan Alley*. They became great friends immediately.

One afternoon during a shooting day at Fox, an assistant director came up to Betty and said that Mr. Zanuck (Darryl) wanted to see her immediately. Alice overheard this and went to Betty, who was worried about what the boss wanted. Alice told her she knew exactly what was up. It happened to Alice often. Alice said she is pretty sure that when Betty went to Zanuck's office, Zanuck would be behind his desk with his pants off.

"Zanuck will chase you around the office until he catches you," Alice explained.

Betty, panic-stricken, said, "What should I do? What did you do?"

Alice had gone through this dozens of times.

"Tell Zanuck: Sorry, Darryl, I would love to, but it's that time of the month and he'll let you go."

Betty, fortified, went up to Zanuck's office. What happened was exactly as Alice described—with the same departure line. Alice Faye also told Betty that Zanuck should have kept a calendar handy.

Soon afterwards, Alice Faye retired and Betty Grable became the Queen of 20th Century-Fox musicals. She made dozens of musicals. She became the most famous pin-up girl during World War II. Years later, another young actress became a contract player at 20th Century-Fox. Her name was Marilyn Monroe. Another generation. When Betty, whose career was waning, and Marilyn were doing a film together, *How to Marry a Millionaire,* an assistant director came up to Marilyn and said that Mr. Zanuck wanted to see her immediately. Betty overheard this. Betty went to Marilyn and relayed Alice's story to Monroe, from a generation ago. Marilyn was grateful to Betty for her advice. Marilyn went up to Zanuck's office—but never came back to the set.

Zanuck must have caught her.

Betty also told me over lunch, "I'll never know how or why I made it. I was a lousy actress. I danced a little, I sang a little." It was a sad day when Betty Grable died of cancer.

Months later, after I returned to MGM, I was walking down the main street at the studio with Bill Tuttle, the head of makeup. He asked where had I been. I said I had gone over to Desilu Studios for a few months to see what television was like. In my conversation with Bill, I mentioned that Lucy and I were "just like that," placing one finger over the other. Bill said, "Well, here she comes." I looked up and there was Lucy with someone walking toward us. I outstretched my arms and said, "Lucy." She walked right past me. Was I embarrassed! I forgot she was blind as a bat. She must have been preoccupied because I ran into her many, many times thereafter and I always got a hug and a kiss.

The best thing that happened to me while working at Desilu Studios was meeting Betty Crosby, the widow of Oscar-winning cameraman Floyd Crosby and stepmother to David Crosby of Crosby, Stills, Nash and Young. Betty was the script girl who would eventually work on many of my films. She's an extraordinary lady with a quick-wit and smiles. We've remained very close friends all these years. I've always loved her.

On all the films that I worked on during these years, I was never given screen credits. Screen credits for assistant directors at MGM didn't start until the late '50s and then only to the first assistant directors. Now every assistant is given credit, including the second assistant director and

Joe E. Brown visiting the set.

the second, second assistant director. I think this is a step forward. Everyone who works on a film should be given screen credit. They've worked hard for it and it's their only recognition.

Early in 1960, I worked on MGM's remake of *Cimarron* for a couple of weeks. The film starred Glenn Ford, Maria Schell and Anne Baxter. I was introduced to Anne many years ago at one of Agnes Moorehead's Christmas parties. I liked her. We became fast friends. Anne was a tough determined actress (much like her character *"Eve"* in *All About Eve*.) and usually got what she wanted. When I saw her on the set, she gave me a kiss. After some dishing, I said to her, "You know, you have the best part in this movie." She said, "Shh, don't tell anybody". As it happened, she needn't have worried. The film was a major flop.

Only a film buff would recognize the gum-chewing famous comedienne, Iris Adrian.

Chapter 7
Tall Story to *BUtterfield 8*

Early in 1960, I made my first film as a First Assistant Director. Ironically, it wasn't at MGM. It was at Warner Bros. Joshua Logan, whom I had worked for on *South Pacific*, remembered me and requested me. Since MGM didn't give me the chance to run my own production, I readily accepted the assignment. The film was *Tall Story*, starring Anthony Perkins, Ray Walston, Anne Jackson, and, in her first film, Jane Fonda. It was a thin story. A small college town invites a Russian basketball team to play at their school. Perkins is the star player. Jane is the cheerleader and is in love with the Perkins' character.

I rented a small apartment in West Hollywood. It was a four-apartment complex. The landlord was on the ground floor. I had the apartment next to him. By chance, Jane Fonda lived above me and a lady of the night was next to Jane above the landlord. Jane and I became quick friends. Most of the time, I drove her to the studio. Jane is not a morning person. I had a convertible at the time. Jane would come down the stairs, grumble a "Good Morning," get in the car and we would take off—usually just before 7 a.m., Jane would remove her shoes and put her feet on my dashboard. She would take out a container of yogurt and a spoon and commence to have her breakfast. As we drove over the Cahuenga Pass to Warner Bros., with my radio blasting, I would glance at Jane. She was a very attractive young lady who looked very much like her father, Henry Fonda. It was a quiet journey. I'd drop her off at makeup and go on to the stage.

The business at hand was lining up two basketball teams. I called both UCLA and the University of Southern California (my alma mater) and asked if their basketball teams would be interested in being in a

With cameraman Ellsworth Fredericks and Joshua Logan on the *Tall Story* set.

motion picture. They came in droves. I requested that they wear their basketball jerseys. I had a basketball hoop set up on the stage. We wanted to see how they played. I asked Perkins to put on his basketball jersey and come to the interview.

I had to select a basketball double for Perkins who didn't know how to play. Joshua and I began picking the players. Josh said for me to select

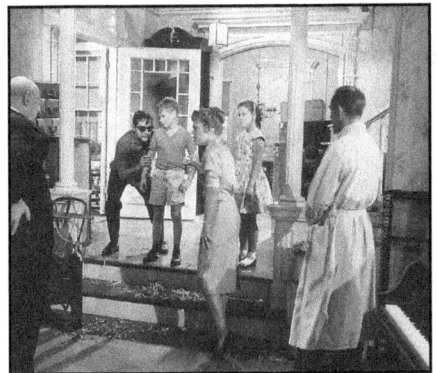

Helping the underrated actress
Anne Jackson on the set of
Tall Story.

a "Russian-looking" type to play the captain of the Russian team. I walked over to a young man who played excellent ball and who looked Slavic. Since the captain had lines, I had to make sure he could handle it. He was handsome and had an appealing smile and he said that lines were no problem. His name was Gary Yurosek, and we hired him. After *Tall Story* was completed, Josh put him under personal contract. Joshua Logan's middle name was Lockwood. He changed the young actor's name to Gary Lockwood and Gary, years later, starred in *2001: A Space Odyssey* directed by Stanley Kubrick. My first "Moonjean discovery."

There was a great deal of fanfare over Jane's first movie. Much was written about Logan being her Godfather and her being Hollywood royalty. Jane hated all the publicity. As a matter of fact, she hated the entire film. But she took to the camera like a seasoned pro. Anne Jackson and Ray Walston played a married couple. Walston was a college professor. Another professor in the film was Marc Connelly, the famed playwright. Anne Jackson (Eli Wallach's bride of many years) was a sweetheart; very professional, very warm and very talented and good fun.

With the great character actress, Elizabeth Patterson, on her last feature film, *Tall Story*.

The film broke no records. But Josh Logan and his wife, Nedda, and I became close friends until their deaths. Anne and Eli Wallach remain friends. And I would see Jane occasionally.

Joanne Woodward said to me once, "The worst thing about making a movie is you work very closely with the crew, you eat together, you laugh together, you're together ten to twelve hours a day for months. Suddenly the film is over and you may never see each other again." Sometimes, you are glad. Glenn Close told me she never missed anyone on a previous film. That was history. Onward and upward was her motto. She probably has very few friends in the film business.

On *Tall Story*, Perkins was a real trouper. I think Jane fell in love with him. He had eyes for someone else. Jane went on to win two Oscars. Tony died at a young age—leaving behind two handsome sons. His widow, Berry Berenson, was killed in the 9/11 terrorist attacks. She was on one of the ill-fated planes that hit the World Trade Center. Jane would always say to me, "You're a beautiful person," and I would, in return, say the same greeting to her. We seldom see each other, but when we do, we always say, "You're a beautiful person." At a recent Savannah Film Festival, Jane was honored. This was the first time I had seen her in years. She

With Jane Fonda.

has become a tough social and political activist—extremely attractive and extremely intelligent. She wasn't the same young girl I had met so many years ago.

It was about this time that I sold four half-hour television scripts to Four Star Theater, which was headed by Charles Boyer, David Niven, Ida Lupino and Dick Powell. It was my first venture into screenwriting, thanks to Eleanor Parker, who encouraged me. Unfortunately, only one of the scripts was produced, on Four Star's *The David Niven Show*. It was entitled "The Twist of the Key." Initially, that script was submitted to Alfred Hitchcock's television company, as it was a thriller. His producer, Joan Harrison, rejected the script. But in her rejection letter, she asked me to promise to give her first refusal on anything else I wrote, which was very flattering. The basic plot was simple. A very large villain locks the heroine, Anne Francis, in a room and places the key in the pocket of his trousers. There is a scuffle. He is shot and his huge body falls on top of Anne and, because of his huge frame, she cannot move. I don't remember how it ended. That was over forty years ago. But, I promise you it ended happily. That was the end of my writing career. I was too busy working on films. But I often made script suggestions on some of my projects that were accepted by the screenwriters.

It was already Elizabeth and Eddie's first wedding anniversary. They had planned on having an intimate party for two hundred of their closest friends at the La Scala in Beverly Hills, which was a very fashionable restaurant in those days. Elizabeth and Eddie asked me to sit at their table. As usual, I was on time. The restaurant was bulging with all the Hollywood elite. I hardly knew anyone but I recognized everyone. I sat at the bar. I noticed cigarettes were offered to guests in short whiskey glasses along the bar along with peanuts. Everyone appeared to be restless as Elizabeth and Eddie were late—no surprise there. The party really couldn't get started without them. I stayed at the bar getting higher and higher. More than an hour had passed. John Wayne came up to the bar and stood next to me. He was TALL. I smiled at him. He just looked down at me and walked away. I don't like Westerns anyway. Then Benny Thau, the MGM executive, sat on the bar stool next to me. We smiled at each other. I don't think he knew who I was. I continued drinking. Finally, I turned to Thau and said, "You know, technically, you are my boss. I work at MGM." Thau looked at me very strangely. I thought what a strange expression he has until I realized I had lifted the glass full of cigarettes to my mouth instead of my cocktail glass. As I tipped the glass, cigarettes fell over the bar and all over me. How smooth. From then on everything went downhill. I don't remember too much after that. I'm not much of a drinker.

At MGM, I was assigned to *BUtterfield 8*, a novel by John O'Hara. Pandro Berman was the producer. The director was Daniel Mann—a fine man who I had met earlier on *I'll Cry Tomorrow*. Elizabeth Taylor was to star. She did not want to be in it. She hated the script—hated everything about it. She had been offered *Two for the Seesaw* and *The*

With Anthony Perkins.

Children's Hour, both of which she wanted to do. Both roles subsequently went to Shirley MacLaine. Elizabeth begged MGM to be released from *BUtterfield 8*. This was the last film under her contract. She offered to do a second film just to be released from this film—two for the price of one. Pandro wouldn't budge. The studio wouldn't budge. Now, they had to reckon with Elizabeth Taylor—a walking time bomb. She did everything she could to get off the project. She said she would only make the film in New York City. She was surprised when they agreed. She said she wanted Eddie Fisher to have the secondary male role. She was surprised when they agreed to that as well. Eddie's only previous film was co-starring with his then-wife Debbie Reynolds—a film called *Bundle of Joy*. Second wife, second movie role. She made all sorts of demands and all were agreed upon (but really they were nothing compared to the demands of the current "stars"). Laurence Harvey, Dina Merrill, Kay Medford, Mildred Dunnock, Betty Field and Susan Oliver were contracted to appear in *BUtterfield 8*. One of Mildred Dunnock's first film roles was in *Kiss of Death*. She was the lady in the wheelchair that Richard Widmark shoved down the stairs. I suggested to Pandro to cast Jane Fonda for the

Between director Danny Mann and Laurence Harvey.

role Susan Oliver got. He said he didn't know her work and I couldn't talk him into it. I didn't know whether or not Jane would have even considered it. After all, in her first film, she had the leading female role. Later, Pandro was sorry he hadn't taken my suggestion. However, Susan Oliver handled the role professionally.

I arrived in New York City in the dead of winter. For a Hollywood assistant director, going to work in New York City was like entering a war zone. In those days, there was a great deal of animosity between the New York unions and the Hollywood unions. They had signs up reading "Keep 'Em in the East." I had to have a "standby" assistant director. In this case, he was a man by the name of John Bowman, who was relegated to the office. Fortunately for me, he was happy doing that (you can't have two chiefs running the set). Our cameraman, Joseph Ruttenberg, a sweet talented man, also had to have a "standby." Our sets were built on several Manhattan soundstages as well as the Gold Medal Studios in the Bronx. That studio was in the war zone. Extras had to be driven from the subway station, as they were afraid to walk to the studio. Elizabeth wouldn't enter the stage until we all stomped on the floor to scare the rats away (how we missed the luxury of the studios in Culver City). Helen Rose and Sydney Guilaroff arrived to start off the film. Helen returned but Guilaroff remained for the entire shoot. Pandro and his wife, Kathryn Hereford, who was the associate producer, had offices in their hotel.

Filming began with the opening scenes. Elizabeth, playing a high-class prostitute, wakes up in a hotel room. Her gentlemen caller, Laurence Harvey, has left her some cash on the mantle. The problem is that Elizabeth, naked, is lying under the sheets. Ordinarily, when you wake up naked in a hotel room and you are alone, you don't cover yourself. Who's to see? In this case, the camera. What to do? So, Elizabeth and Danny Mann draped a sheet around her body to her satisfaction. Problem solved. Although Elizabeth hated every minute of the film, she still was a pro. Letter perfect. Cooperative with the production department and me. But, as usual, she was compulsively, consistently late. Pandro said to me, "Hank, she likes you. She trusts you. Why don't you tell her to be ready at 8 a.m. instead of 9 a.m.? That way, we can remain on schedule."

I said to Pandro, Elizabeth is no fool. "She knows production as well as you. Right now, she trusts me. She knows I've never lied to her. If I give her that sort of call, I've lost her trust forever. If you want her to have an earlier call, you give it to her."

Mildred Dunnock, as Elizabeth Taylor's mother in *BUtterfield 8*.

The one-day that Elizabeth was on time was the day she forgot to bring Theresa, her dog. She had used Theresa in a scene the previous day. We had to send the limousine to pick up the dog. No late note.

Shooting went on without incident. All the cast got along. Laurence Harvey was a real character. He had a terrific sense of humor and was well liked by everybody. One of Harvey's many eccentricities was that before he applied his makeup he would lie completely naked in his makeup chair and a makeup man would pour witch hazel from his chest up to his face.

Elizabeth and Eddie were in love. She helped him with the scenes. Eddie was passable but certainly no great actor. He never professed to be. We filmed many scenes in Greenwich Village. The apartment that was used in the film that Elizabeth shared with her movie mother, Mildred Dunnock, was next to a women's prison. The movie apartment that Eddie had was on Gay Street around the corner. From the women's prison (which no longer exists) all the women would hang out the windows and yell all sorts of epitaphs to Elizabeth. Elizabeth would look up and yell, "Fuck you!" (You must realize by now that those are Elizabeth's favorite words.) Gloria, Elizabeth's film character, drove a small red car and there were many scenes of Elizabeth driving around that neighborhood. Often, I hid in the backseat to make sure she would be safe and secure.

One morning we had to shoot a scene in front of the Mark Cross store. I believe it was on Fifth Avenue. We got Elizabeth ready and had her hidden in a production vehicle, ready to step out at a moment's notice. We set up a dummy camera across the street to draw attention away from the actual camera. This is done often when you are working with stars as famous as Elizabeth. Everyone was working quietly and efficiently, trying very hard not to be conspicuous. The scene involved Elizabeth and Laurence walking arm-in-arm by the Mark Cross store, they pause, look in the window and enter. Everyone and everything is finally ready. We are set up. Who were we kidding? In minutes, after several takes, there were at least 100 people around the camera. In a short time there must have been 1,000 people around the Mark Cross store. We quickly got the actors in cars and they sped away. We eventually built and shot the interior of the Mark Cross store on a stage in the Gold Medal Studios in the Bronx.

During the production, we had heard of a "Dr. Feelgood," who had a lucrative practice in Manhattan. He was giving famous people "pep" shots. Elizabeth, Eddie and Harvey and I were interested. We decided we'd go every Friday after work. Elizabeth, Eddie and Harvey went. I couldn't go with them because I had too much paperwork that had to be sent to Culver City to report on the day's progress. God must have had His hand on my shoulder. I never got to go. Elizabeth, Eddie and Harvey went regularly. Months later, the pep shots that were given by Dr. Feelgood were determined to be amphetamine, "speed." Whoever heard of speed in 1960? Everyone who went to him became hooked, including President John F. Kennedy and Marilyn Monroe. That quack eventually lost his license after destroying, or nearly destroying, many lives.

We had several scenes to be shot in a small town north of New York City called Stony Point. We were to film in the local motel. It was in the freezing winter. Since we were scheduled to be there for several days, the company took over the entire motel. The actors (only Elizabeth, Larry and Kay Medford) had accommodations across the road in a bed and breakfast.

The first night after work, the New York crew had a major beer blast. The next morning, a key member of the crew was still hung over in his room asleep. (Remember, I still wasn't fully accepted by the New York crew, who were very reserved with me.) During the day's filming, Danny Mann said, "Where is so and so?" Without missing a beat, I said that I sent him to Manhattan to pick up something. The crew heard me. I wasn't being gallant. I just wasn't about to get someone in trouble. It was just a normal reaction. Of course, if it had been the sound mixer, that would have been a different story, because his presence was essential. No one said anything to me, but after that, and all the years later when I worked in New York, I was welcomed with open arms—well, nearly.

Midway during the production, there was an actors strike. We were allowed to shoot until midnight—not a second later on a Saturday. We were shooting in Manhattan on a second-floor bar/nightclub. It was the famous scene where Elizabeth digs her stiletto heel into Harvey's shoe. We had started on a normal day and it went on after dinner. Elizabeth, always the professional, agreed to work until midnight. Therefore, insuring the completion of the scene. Laurence Harvey, waiting in a local bar to be called to the set, saw a gun in a policeman's holster. The policeman was part of our security. Harvey asked if he could look at it. The officer reluctantly handed him his revolver. He said, eyeing the revolver, "Officer, I may as well try your gun. I've had everything else shoved up my ass." Hermione Baddeley once said to me, "I don't know why they call Larry Harvey queer, he's always fucked me."

The studio kept us in New York during the two-month strike. We had to be ready the moment the strike was over. During this period I was staying at the famous Astor Hotel, now gone, in the heart of the theater district. I remember walking to all the shows. I must have seen Ethel Merman in *Gypsy* a dozen times. I would go see Anthony Perkins in

Greenwillow, often watching from backstage. I loved that show! I thought Tony's singing was exceptional. Unfortunately, the play was not a success. I saw *Five Finger Exercise, West Side Story, Bells Are Ringing* and scores of other plays. It was really my introduction to the Broadway Theater.

    I spent many evenings with Josh and Nedda Logan. They had a magnificent penthouse apartment overlooking the East River. They always had fascinating guests. One afternoon, while on the Logan penthouse terrace, Josh saw Mary Martin standing on her penthouse terrace across the street. Josh introduced me to her. We were yelling back and forth. Josh was basically a warm and loving person who would fall into deep depressions. Often, he would have to be hospitalized. He would snap out of it, and months later, the condition would reappear. Nedda Logan was a snob. Josh was her second husband. She was the daughter of Ned Harrigan of Harrigan and Hart, an early New York theatrical team. "H-A-double R-I-G-A-N spells Harrigan." Nedda thrived on the rich and famous.

    During the strike, Dina Merrill would invite some of us to her "boat" anchored near her apartment on the East River. The "boat" looked like the *Queen Mary*. Dina was the daughter of Marjorie Merriweather Post, of the Post cereal fortune—one of America's wealthiest women. You would never know that Dina was an heiress. She was as regular as anyone else. Great personality and a very good, classy actress.

    The strike eventually was settled. Everyone was anxious to get back to work, especially Elizabeth. There was a rumor going around that she was going to get a million dollars for her next film. She was to be the highest-paid actress in movie history. Of course, the movie was *Cleopatra*.

    One day Elizabeth and Eddie went to the offices of Rodgers and Hammerstein in Manhattan. Eddie had been teaching Elizabeth to sing. She was being considered for the lead in the next Rodgers and Hammerstein musical. I don't remember if it was for a film or a play. According to Eddie, Elizabeth's singing voice was excellent and she probably could have managed the role. But when they got to Rodgers and Hammerstein's office, Elizabeth froze and wasn't able to perform. There went Elizabeth's musical career. Years later, she was able to prove she could manage a song. Remember, "Send in the Clowns" from *A Little Night Music*?

    In 1959, Ingemar Johansson had become the world's heavyweight boxing champion after he KO'd Floyd Patterson in the third round.

Elizabeth thought Ingemar was cute. Eddie was able to get ringside seats for three at Madison Square Garden for the return bout. Eddie and I waited and waited and waited for Elizabeth. She finally made her appearance, as beautiful as ever and as late as ever. We raced to the Garden in Elizabeth's limousine. We ran down the long corridors of the Garden and up the aisle to our seats just as the fight ended. Floyd Patterson had KO'd Ingemar in the fifth round. The three of us turned around to avoid the crowds. No luck. The crowds recognized Elizabeth. I thought there was going to be a stampede. But Elizabeth knows how to handle such a moment, with her years of experience. She would smile at the people and, barely audible, say, "Fuck you" and "Fuck you" and "You, up there. Fuck you, too." For years, Elizabeth had built up immunity toward crowds. Much of the time, people would yell obscene remarks or make obscene gestures just to get her goat, to get her off-guard. They would try to make her lose her cool. That's why she smiles during these episodes, tuning out everybody and everything, repeating her favorite expression.

Elizabeth always liked my windbreaker jackets. I had several made especially for me in Los Angeles. I wore them on the set all the time. In some scenes, Elizabeth borrowed my windbreaker. I had to give the ones she wore to the studio in case of retakes. In one scene with Eddie, Elizabeth was supposedly going to make breakfast for him, wearing one of my jackets. Elizabeth picked up an egg and turned to the camera and said, "What do you do with it?" She had never made eggs in her entire life. I showed her how.

BUtterfield 8 finally ended. Elizabeth won the Oscar as the Best Actress for her performance. She accepted the award graciously but never believed she was worthy of it. She did prove her worthiness by receiving a second Oscar for *Who's Afraid of Virginia Woolf?* years later. Joseph Ruttenberg, the cameraman was also nominated for an Oscar for best cinematography. Ironically, so was the New York standby cameraman. He never set foot on the soundstage and yet he received a nomination because his name was on the screen.

During the making of *BUtterfield 8* Jane Fonda was living in New York City. For the entire eleven months, I was in New York on the film; I never got to see her. We were on a five-day workweek, but for some reason or another, every time we had a dinner date, she'd cancel or I would cancel. She traveled a great deal of the time. It was becoming a joke. Finally, we were on the last week of the film. We arranged to have

The rewards of my bet with Elizabeth that she would get an Oscar nomination.

dinner the last Friday, before I left for London the next morning. I said, "Jane, come hell or high water, we are going to dinner this Friday." Friday was to be a "short day." The last scene to be shot was scheduled right after lunch, a scene of Elizabeth taking a shower. It would take an hour at the most.

It was a steamy August. As fate would have it, everything went wrong that Friday morning. The morning work lapped over into the afternoon. We still had the shower scene to do. I began to get nervous. Finally, we did get to the shower scene. Elizabeth was ready and we discovered that the water wasn't heated (a good assistant director would have seen to that earlier). It would take over an hour to heat. Elizabeth and Eddie, who by this time were bored with my "phantom" date with Jane Fonda, told me to go. Elizabeth said, "Take my limousine; I'll go back with Eddie." Danny Mann said to go. I refused. I wanted to be there until the last shot. Besides, I had to complete the paperwork. However, I said I would take Elizabeth's car, as it would be quicker to get to Manhattan. We were filming in the Bronx at the Gold Medal Studios, and it could take approximately one hour to my East 63rd Street apartment. I called Jane and said I might be late, but I would be there.

Finally, the filming was over. A lot of kisses and hugs and goodbyes. No tears. We had no cast and crew party—everyone was glad it was over. I quickly finished all the paperwork and jumped into Elizabeth's limo at about 5 p.m. I was to pick up Jane at 7 p.m. Friday evening traffic...7It was bumper to bumper all the way to Manhattan. I got to my apartment after six and I quickly showered and shaved. I was dead tired after an exhausting week but I was determined to make this date. I had bought a terrific dark summer suit months earlier. I put on my new suit. I called

Jane and said that I was on my way.

It took a while to hail a cab. Finally, I caught one and headed for Jane's apartment somewhere on the Eastside, not too far from my apartment. I was wringing wet. It must have been ninety degrees. The cab pulled up in front of Jane's apartment. I opened the taxi door and, with my right foot, stepped into the deepest pile of wet horseshit you have ever seen. My black shoe was yellow. The smell was staggering. The cabbie wanted his money. I paid him and he left quickly. There I stood alone with Jane's doorman observing the proceeding. I was frustrated, tired and angry. I noticed there was a tall wire city trash container piled high with newspapers at the corner with an attached sign reading, "Cast Your Vote for a Cleaner New York." I dragged my right leg over to the bin and took a discarded newspaper off the top and began wiping the horseshit off my shoe. I noticed a large puddle of water in the gutter near the trash bin. I placed the soiled newspaper back on top of the trash and took a step into the gutter to wash off the shit. Suddenly, a soft gentle August breeze, out of nowhere, picked up the newspaper and slapped me on the nape of my neck and slowly slithered down my back. They say if you step in shit, it's very lucky. What about if you get it in your hair, on your shirt collar, down your jacket and finally on your pant leg? I must be the luckiest man alive. All this time, the doorman was watching with relish. I hailed a cab. Jumped in. Took my soiled jacket off and rolled it up, opened the windows and gave the driver my address. The driver could smell the manure. Finally, I got to my apartment and I threw the jacket down the garbage chute. I called Jane. I said, "I won't be there. I can't explain. I'll call you later." Years later, I told Jane the story. I don't think she believed me and I didn't blame her. I found it hard to believe myself—but it did happen.

So ended *BUtterfield 8*. In spite of all the problems, it was a very successful film.

Chapter 8
Onward

On the next Saturday, Elizabeth and Eddie and I flew to London from New York City. Elizabeth was to meet Rouben Mamoulian, the initial director of *Cleopatra*. Her co-stars were to be Peter Finch (Caesar) and Stephen Boyd (Mark Anthony). Elizabeth and Eddie had the Oliver Messel Suite at the Dorchester Hotel. Richard Hanley, Elizabeth's secretary, met us at the airport. Dick Hanley was so much more than a secretary: he was Elizabeth's father, mother, adviser, psychiatrist, confidant, but, most of all, Elizabeth's best friend. Dick had only three jobs in his entire life. He started his career as a private secretary to Louis B. Mayer at MGM. Mike Todd took Dick away from Mayer and after Mike married Elizabeth, Dick became their secretary, and stayed with Elizabeth after Mike died. For the record, I had absolutely nothing to do with *Cleopatra*, neither the Mamoulian fiasco nor the Mankiewicz disaster. (*Cleopatra* eventually got out of the "Red.") I was in London to look for film projects that Eddie and I could produce together after *Cleopatra*.

The sets for *Cleopatra* were already built at the Pinewood Studios. Elizabeth had insisted that Sydney Guilaroff design her wigs. The British unions balked at Guilaroff working in England. The situation got very sticky. It was even discussed in the British Parliament. Guilaroff loved the notoriety. It was finally decided that Guilaroff would do Elizabeth's hair and wigs in the upstairs of a local inn very near Pinewood Studios. However, Guilaroff was not to enter the studio. That satisfied everyone.

London was cold and damp—certainly the wrong climate for a film set in Egypt. Occasionally, I would go with Elizabeth to the studio in her limousine. One day, I noticed a huge barge loaded with sand going up the Thames, to its final destination at Pinewood Studios. The driver said it was sand being brought in from Egypt. It seems English sand is different from Egyptian sand. Believe it! Only in the movies! When we got to the studios, Elizabeth was to test some of her costumes. Elizabeth's dressing room was on the outside of the soundstage. I said to the unit manager that her dressing room should be on the heated stage. He said there was no room there for her dressing room. I said she'd catch cold wearing her flimsy costumes. It was a prediction that unfortunately proved true. A few weeks later, Elizabeth got pneumonia. She had to have a tracheotomy and nearly died.

The *Cleopatra* company, predictably, closed down production. Everyone was dismissed. After spending months in the London Clinic, Elizabeth returned to the Dorchester Hotel to recuperate. Eddie spent most of his time in California recording songs. One of Elizabeth's monthly phone bills during this period was well over $30,000. Elizabeth loved to play Hearts, a card game. She loved to "dump the old lady" on anyone, giggling like a little girl. It was during this period that a photographer crawled down from the roof of the Dorchester Hotel to photograph Elizabeth with some unidentified men playing cards. The unidentified men were a friend of mine from Wales and myself. That photograph was circulated all over the world.

During Elizabeth's recuperation period, Dick Hanley made arrangements for Elizabeth and me to go shopping at Jaeger's on Regent Street on a Sunday afternoon. It was a form of therapy for Elizabeth. In those days all the stores in London were closed on Sundays. We arrived at the designated time. The manager unlocked the door. We entered and he locked the door behind us. Elizabeth began shopping. She would say, "I'd like that sweater in every color. I'd like those pedal pushers in every color." Elizabeth bought and bought. We were there for over an hour. She told the manager to have everything delivered to the Dorchester Hotel. This scene would be duplicated on a grander scale soon in Geneva, Switzerland.

After a long delay and recuperation time, 20th Century-Fox announced that *Cleopatra* would be filmed in Rome the next year. Another time, another place, another cast, except for Elizabeth. Producing a movie with Eddie, starring Elizabeth, was not in the immediate future. I decided to go to Paris to seek employment. Many American films were being shot in France and Germany, and I enjoyed working in Europe.

Ben Kadish was the unit manager on *Fanny*. This was a Joshua Logan film starring Leslie Caron, Charles Boyer, Maurice Chevalier and German actor Horst Buchholz. Ben had just returned to Paris after an extensive shoot in old Marseilles. Ben asked if I could work on *Fanny* for the balance of the film in Paris. I accepted gladly. I went to work right away, glad to see Josh Logan again.

Ben and I loved Mexican food, and I scoured Paris for a Mexican restaurant. No such restaurant existed. We even took the train to Brussels to go to the World's Fair and visit the Mexico Pavilion. It was the only country that did not have a restaurant in their pavilion.

One Saturday, I was looking around Fauchon's famous culinary store. The establishment had the greatest array of international foods. I happened to come upon a row of tin cans containing tamales. I had earlier passed by a display of huge avocados. A bright light went on. Why don't I prepare a Mexican dinner in my apartment? So I went back to the produce department and selected two avocados. I had never seen avocados so large. They were twice the size of California avocados. I picked up several cans of tamales, bought some dried beans, various cheeses, a bag of tortilla chips, and a bottle of tequila. Back at the studio, I told Ben of my dinner plans. I had a marvelous first-floor apartment on Rue Massenet. The date was set for the following Saturday. On Saturday I shopped at the local market where I purchased some "finger food." I was determined to have a perfect Mexican dinner. Ben and I were going to entertain two girls from the studio. Ben was going to bring the girls to my apartment around seven. During the afternoon, I started to prepare dinner. Incidentally, I never cooked a Mexican dinner. When I am alone and am cooking in the kitchen, I am usually in the nude (but never when I'm frying). That afternoon I was wearing jockey shorts. The first thing I did was to prepare the avocados for a guacamole dip. This I knew how to make. I cut the avocado, added the necessary spices and lemon and mashed the entire mixture. I added the two pits so that the dip wouldn't discolor. I still couldn't get over the size of the avocados. I placed the guacamole in the refrigerator. I put the dried beans in water to boil. Next, I opened the cans of tamales and neatly arranged them on a tray, sprinkling cheese over the top. I prepared the ingredients for the tossed salad. Each time I opened the refrigerator door a strong odor emerged from my guacamole. I took the dip out and skimmed the dark top off the guacamole and placed it back in the refrigerator. I put the tray of tamales in the oven on low. After taking a shower, I put my jockey shorts back on to check out the kitchen. The tamales were doing well. The beans were still like rocks. And the smell from the refrigerator was nauseating. I took the dip out and tasted it. It tasted like bananas. I must have used sugar instead of salt. No other explanation. I thought I'd better throw my dip away. Otherwise, we would all be sick. My trashcan was just outside of the kitchen door. I opened the kitchen door and stepped out to dump my guacamole in the bin. The kitchen door slowly swung shut, and the door locked from the inside. There I was in my jockey shorts (thank God I wasn't in the nude) on my knees attempting to push the key from the inside keyhole onto the newspaper I laid under the door. The dip was beginning to nauseate me as the odor was reeking from the trash bin. Suddenly, I heard footsteps coming down the back stairs. I heard a yelp and I looked up and saw a girl who looked like Brigitte Bardot turn around and run back up the stairs. The key finally fell on the newspaper but the key was too thick to pass underneath the door. Panic.

I had no alternative but to go outside to the front entrance. Maybe the concierge was home. It was still daylight. I rang the concierge's doorbell. No response. I rang the doorbell of one of my next-door neighbors. No answer. I rang every doorbell.

My apartment faced the street. I looked up. My balcony was only about 30 feet from the street and I could see that my balcony window was open. There wasn't a soul around. The facade of the building had deep indentations about two feet apart, like stepping-stones. I decided to climb up to the balcony. I reached about a fourth of the way, when I heard a shrill police car siren beeping on and off. Suddenly, I was not alone. Everybody poured out of my apartment house, including the concierge and the Brigitte Bardot lookalike. People came out from across the street. I barely spoke French; all I could understand from the police was the word "passport." I never carry my passport in my jockey shorts. I was trying to explain myself to the police when Ben and the girls arrived. Ben saw me and couldn't stop laughing. I asked one of the girls to explain to the police what had happened. Another crazy American. The concierge eventually unlocked my apartment and the four of us went in. I went immediately to the kitchen. The tamales were burning. The beans were still like rocks. (I did not know that beans had to soak for a week or a month or whatever.) I told Ben and the girls to help themselves to the drinks and "finger food" while I showered again. I also asked Ben to call his favorite restaurant and book a table for four at 9 p.m. There would be no Mexican food tonight or any other night while in Paris.

Thereafter, everyone in the apartment looked on me with suspicion, and "Brigitte Bardot" would cross the street when she would see me. The mystery of the avocado? What I bought were not avocados. They were a tropical fruit from Africa. Very rare and very expensive. But the fruit had all the makings of an avocado—the color, the rind, the pit and the texture. The next time I'm in Fauchon's, I will be sure to ask for something by name instead of pointing.

When I was living in Paris, William Kaplan heard I was there. He called and asked me if I could help him and Minnelli on *The Four Horsemen of the Apocalypse*. I jumped at the opportunity, even though Minnelli was as strange as ever. It was basically a glorified second unit. We were to shoot in various parts of Paris. The biggest challenge was to recreate the Germans marching into Paris during World War II. I think the Germans had it easier than we did. Kaplan was able to get permission to shoot that scene on a Sunday—just one day only. It involved the Champs-Elysées, a few blocks from the Place de la Concorde. It involved several hundred extras, many dozens of German tanks, jeeps and other infantry vehicles. Also, the streets had to be lined with Parisians watching this sad event. The extras dressed in the ice palace, which we had used on *Gigi*. Six cameras were placed at strategic spots along the boulevard. I had as many assistants.

The main camera was at the Place de la Concorde on a fifty-foot scaffold shooting down the boulevard toward the Arc de Triomphe. We were having trouble with the French extras. They weren't happy putting on German uniforms. We lined up the armor along the boulevard and placed the soldiers accordingly in the various vehicles. We had started the day at 5 a.m. and although it was only eleven o'clock we were already tired. I was anxious to have a rehearsal to work out the kinks, but Minnelli said we weren't ready for a rehearsal. I was on the walkie-talkies to all my assistants. Minnelli was fiddling around with some minor detail. I said, "Vincente that doesn't matter in this shot. We are far away." Minnelli said to me once again, "Small details make great motion pictures." I said, "Please, let's have a rehearsal. Better yet, let's shoot the rehearsal. It's only film." Minnelli, in all his sarcasm, said, "So you know, when the Germans entered Paris, it was a beautiful sunny day." It was slightly overcast. I went to Kaplan and asked him to go to Minnelli. Maybe he would have more influence on him than I. Kaplan tried and failed. We had to call lunch for one hour. Remember, the French extras get a bottle of wine with lunch. Remember they hate wearing German uniforms, and remember a one-hour lunch usually takes two.

Meanwhile, the Parisians were upset with us. We had disrupted the traffic on all the streets leading into the Champs-Elysées, and we stationed German soldiers all over. It was after 2 p.m. when we reconnoitered. The extras were all disheveled; it seemed to take longer than before to get them into position. My assistants were worried that the citizens were getting extremely upset. They didn't know how much longer they could hold them back. I asked Kaplan to see if the gendarmes could help. They weren't very happy either. The weather was getting worse. It was now almost 4 p.m. I said to Minnelli, who was now on the scaffold looking through his viewfinder, "Vincente, we are ready. Let's get the shot. Let's get something on film."

"No, you are not ready," he yelled down at me.

"What's wrong now?"

Minnelli says, "So you know, during the war, Paris did not have yellow buses. I see a yellow bus."

"Where do you see a yellow bus?"

"Down the street, near the American Embassy."

I couldn't see anything from where I was standing. I said, "Fuck you. Roll the cameras…ACTION."

The vehicles started to roll. We got the shot—one take. It was getting too dark to do another. I told Kaplan I was leaving and that I never wanted to work with Minnelli again. I guess all the years of being frustrated with Minnelli eventually got to me. Besides, it happened to be the last day of the second unit.

By the way, that shot of the Germans entering Paris was never in the final print. As a matter of fact, very little of what we shot was used.

I never saw Minnelli again until many years later. I was standing inside of a crowded elevator at the Plaza Hotel in New York going down to the main floor when I suddenly heard someone humming the musical scales. This was a habit of Minnelli's. He was always humming. I stepped out of the elevator and stood to one side. Sure enough, it was Vincente Minnelli. I didn't speak to him. He more than likely would have had a very vague recollection of me.

During my stay at the Plaza Hotel, I had another "New York Experience." It was almost six in the morning. I was in a deep sleep when a woman with a strong German accent, screaming directly above my bedroom,

Frustrations with Minnelli.

"Ludwig, Ludwig, put that knife down," suddenly awakened me. "Ludwig...Don't!" was followed by a blood-curdling shriek. I wasn't sure if it was a dream but the woman screamed again. I immediately telephoned the hotel operator. I said, "This is Mr. Moonjean in Room 616. There is a woman directly above me in Room 716 who is about to be murdered." The operator said, "I can't be bothered. I am giving out the six o'clock wake-up calls." She slammed the receiver down on my ear. Welcome to New York.

Later on, as I was leaving the hotel, I went up to the front desk. I said, "I'm in Room 616. If there is a dead woman in Room 716, Ludwig did it." The manager looked puzzled and then said, "Oh, that must be Mrs. Kravitz. She's a bit crazy but she is harmless. We can't get rid of her. She comes down every day and pays her bill."

I returned home to MGM. Luckily for me, *Sweet Bird of Youth* was scheduled to be filmed. It was to be produced by Pandro Berman and written and directed by Richard Brooks. Pandro asked me to be the assistant director on the project. Brooks' contract stipulated that Tennessee Williams would have absolutely nothing to do with the script. Williams' only request was that a young actor by the name of Mike Stein was to have a small speaking part in the film. Paul Newman and Geraldine Page had created the roles on Broadway. Berman signed Newman to star in the film. The leading female role of the Princess was yet to be cast. Newman hoped that Geraldine Page would be in the film, but Pandro wanted to test her first.

Arrangements were made to have Page flown out from New York to the studio. A test was made with an MGM stock actor. It wasn't a good test—not so much the acting, but the way Geraldine Page looked. Geraldine was a very plain woman—certainly no beauty. Pandro said the Princess was supposed to be a great fading Hollywood beauty. He said he couldn't believe Geraldine Page was ever a great beauty. Geraldine was turned down for the role. Pandro then approached Ava Gardner to play the Princess. Ava said she would love to play the Princess—in Mexico. Pandro said, "Fuck her!" It was going to be difficult finding the right actress. Ava would have been perfect in the role. Paul Newman asked Pandro to reconsider Page. Paul said that he would come out to Culver City and he would test with her. Pandro said it wasn't her acting ability; it was the way she looked.

Now the Hollywood dream factory stepped in. Sydney Guilaroff was asked to make a special wig for Page. Guilaroff ordered hair from Italy. It seems that Italy has the best hair in the world for wigs. Orry-

Kelly, the very famous dress designer, was hired to create a gorgeous gown for Page. William Tuttle, the head of MGM's makeup department, a terrific and talented man, began experimenting with Page's makeup. The preparations took almost a month. Meanwhile, sets were being built for the production. Before the Page screen test was shot, Brooks, the Art Director and I flew to New Orleans to look for locations for the opening sequences of a convertible driving along the Gulf Coast. These scenes were subsequently shot in California—just above Laguna Beach. On our return, Brooks directed the Newman-Page test. Page's appearance was like a fairytale transformation. She looked perfect! Pandro set Geraldine Page for the lead.

One afternoon on my way to the Iron Lung to view the test I bumped into Gerry. (By now, Page was Gerry.) She asked me where I was going and I said to see her test. She asked if she could join me. She hadn't seen the test. I hesitated. It wasn't for me to show it to her. She pleaded with me. I said, "If anything is said, I'll deny I had anything to do with it." So, the two of us went to the projection room. Gerry was sitting next to me. I started running the test. I could hear Gerry whispering, "She's beautiful, she's beautiful," as she slid down in her chair, hardly believing her eyes, unable to refer to the glamorous creature onscreen as "I."

Meanwhile, Brooks was trying to talk Randolph Scott into playing Boss Finley. Brooks has a talent for casting against type. He had cast Shirley Jones in *Elmer Gantry* and Jack Carson and Burl Ives in *Cat on a Hot Tin Roof*, amongst others. Randolph Scott turned down the role. Brooks signed Ed Begley Sr. for the role of Boss Finley. Begley won the Oscar for Best Supporting Actor for his performance. Also cast were Shirley Knight as Heavenly, Mildred Dunnock as Aunt Nonnie, and my "friend" from *Cat on a Hot Tin Roof*, Madeleine Sherwood, as Boss Finley's mistress. Mike Stein, Tennessee Williams' friend, played the trooper watching over Heavenly. Rip Torn, who played Boss Finley's son, was Geraldine Page's lover in real life and later her husband.

In the meantime, Brooks was having trouble with the studio. Brooks, being a stickler for authenticity, insisted that he be allowed to use Smirnoff's vodka in the film. The vodka bottle was an important prop. The studio wanted a phony label. Remember, this was the era of "payola," and no one had yet figured out about getting paid for product placement in films. Brooks said he wouldn't do the film unless he could use the real vodka label. It wasn't an idle threat. The studio gave in to Brooks.

Filming began on schedule. Our biggest set, an entire beach-type hotel, was built on Stage 15 (the stage of the peacocks). Most of the filming was to be shot there. One regular problem I had with the policeman at the main gate who would call me on the stage and say, "There is a woman here who says she's on your film. Shall I let her in?" I would say, "Does she look like she hasn't combed her hair in a year?" He'd say yes. And I would say, "She's mine, let her in." It was Page, naturally.

In one flashback scene, Geraldine Page is having her hair touched up in her dressing room. I suggested to Brooks—why not Guilaroff? Brooks liked the idea. Guilaroff did it. Gladly.

Gerry had a very high-pitched voice. Before takes, she asked me not to roll the camera until she gave me a signal. I was to let her know when I was ready. When I said that we were ready to start filming, Gerry would start saying softly, "Help." She would repeat "Help" a dozen times—each time getting her voice lower and lower, deeper and deeper. She'd signal me to roll. I would and Brooks would yell "ACTION." Geraldine would do a great scene with a deep, resonant voice. Brooks would say, "CUT," and Gerry, now back to her high voice, would say, "How was I?" Geraldine Page was a real pro.

One day, Rip Torn hadn't showed up to work. My assistant called everywhere and couldn't find him. I said, "Call Gerry. He's probably with her." He wasn't. When Gerry came to the set that afternoon, she really told me off. "How dare you assume that Rip Torn was with *me*!" But, but…She had already forgotten about the incident the next day. Everyone knew they were lovers. Rip was in the stage play with her, as was Paul Newman and Madeleine Sherwood. Gerry and Rip eventually married. Early one morning, script changes arrived on the set, changes to do with what we were about to shoot that morning. In the original play, the two Hollywood gossip columnists referred to were Louella Parsons and a fictitious one. When Brooks wrote the script, he made the second woman Hedda Hopper, an actual Hollywood columnist. Remember, Brooks wanted authenticity. After reading the new changes, I saw that the second columnist had been changed back to the fictitious one—not Hedda Hopper. I went to Brooks and asked him why the change. Brooks, always ready to smolder, said, "If you must know, Hedda Hopper said she wanted $10,000 dollars and Pandro refused to give her any money."

"There are other columnists," I said. "You're such a stickler for fact. What's wrong with Jimmy Fidler or Walter Winchell?"

Brooks said, "That's a fucking awful idea. Come with me."
We walked to the stage telephone. He called Pandro in his office. "Pandro, I have an idea. Why don't we use Walter Winchell?" Pandro said it was a great idea, and to go ahead. Pandro knew Winchell and he knew Winchell would allow us to use his name without compensation. Brooks winked at me and walked to his chair and began smoking his pipe. It's moments like this that make you feel good for having made a creative contribution to a film. The scene in question called for the Princess to be talking on the telephone to the "phony female gossip columnist." With Walter Winchell, the Princess is now speaking to a man, though you never hear his voice. Suddenly, it became a more powerful scene. The Princess is virtually making love to the telephone. Brooks told me later that it was that scene that guaranteed Geraldine Page an Oscar nomination for Best Actress.

Mike Stein, who was the actor that Tennessee Williams wanted in the film, told me how Williams got the idea for *Sweet Bird of Youth*. Several years before, Williams was driving along the gulf coast in his convertible. Williams spotted Stein, a male hustler, hitchhiking and picked him up. They checked into a plush seafront hotel for several days. Tennessee Williams was the Princess and Stein was Chance Wayne. From this incident, *Sweet Bird of Youth* was born. A very successful play and a successful film. In addition to Begley and Page, Shirley Knight was also nominated for an Oscar as Best Supporting Actress.

Both of Richard Brooks' films, *Cat on a Hot Tin Roof* and *Sweet Bird of Youth*, suffered from the censors. In *Cat*, Paul Newman's character was a closeted homosexual. The word, or a suggestion, or any "gay" gestures were forbidden. If you had seen the play, you knew what the "problem" was. In the movie, it was very much hidden. However, it's pretty obvious that if a husband refuses to touch his wife and his wife is *Elizabeth Taylor*, he has a problem. In *Sweet Bird of Youth*, the play was more graphic and much more brutal. In the play, the Paul Newman character is castrated. In the film, his face is severely beaten up. The love scenes between Heavenly and Chance were tame.

One of Richard Brooks' eccentricities was that a complete script was not to be given to anyone, even to the actors. One script would be issued to the art department and one to the production department. Of course, all the executives had a script, but other than that absolutely no one else saw one. This was just paranoia on Brooks' part. It was part of his "act."

Admiring the brilliant Geraldine Page.

He threatened to fire anyone who defied his edict. This made it difficult for the casting and other departments. You can be sure that Paul Newman and Geraldine Page had scripts.

During shooting, Ed Begley came up to me pleading to see a script. He said, "I'm an actor. I must know what scenes are coming up. I must know where I'm going with the character. Please let me see your script."

I said, "There is a script in my desk over there in the corner. I'll be back in ten minutes." Begley was forever grateful for me defying Brooks' orders. Ed Begley was a true gentleman. He'd been in Hollywood for years. Boss Finley was his greatest role.

In the film, Madeleine Sherwood played his mistress. Her attitude had not changed since *Cat on a Hot Tin Roof*: everyone—including Begley, disliked her just as Jack Carson did on *Cat*. During one dramatic scene, Begley was about to present Sherwood with a large Easter egg, similar to a Faberge egg. In the egg is a diamond ring that Begley has no intention of giving Sherwood. Brooks had selected the egg weeks before. Since the egg had a sharp edge, I ordered a Styrofoam replica of it. Begley, as he presents the egg to Sherwood, is supposed to slam the egg on her fingers as she reaches for the ring. We rehearsed several times. When we got to the close angle of the presentation, I asked the prop man to bring in the dummy egg. Sherwood said, "What dummy egg?" I explained the reason for it. She said she was an actress and she could handle the "real" egg. I said, "Be my guest," with glee. The entire crew gathered around the set. This had to be seen. The camera turned and Brooks yelled "ACTION." After a few lines of dialogue, Begley slammed the egg on Sherwood's fingers as hard as he could. You could hear her screams all over the studio. Absolutely no one went to her aid. After all, she is an actress.

We shot an alternate ending in Long Beach, California. It involved Page and Sherwood fleeing the pandemonium at the hotel. The scene was scrapped after filming all night. *Sweet Bird of Youth* was a fairly successful film. Geraldine never looked so attractive. She was nominated for an Oscar that year.

Chapter 9
Cleopatra – Again

Cleopatra was ready to resume in Rome. I was ready to produce films with Eddie Fisher starring Elizabeth Taylor. We all left for Rome. Rex Harrison replaced Peter Finch and Richard Burton replaced Stephen Boyd. Joseph Mankiewicz replaced Rouben Mamoulian and Rome replaced London. Now, the fun began. Elizabeth and Eddie had rented a huge villa on the Appian Way. Elizabeth's three children, Michael, Christopher and Liza, were there as well as Richard Hanley, Elizabeth's right-hand man.

Elizabeth and Eddie wanted to have a child. Elizabeth could never have children after Liza's birth. On a trip to Germany, Elizabeth and Eddie visited an orphanage. They spotted a young girl who had major problems with her hips. Naturally, Elizabeth had to have that child. There were hundreds of orphans ready for adoption. Elizabeth, always for the underdog, wanted only that child. They tried every means to adopt the little girl. The German courts refused. It seemed that the German judge felt that Elizabeth and Eddie were doing it for publicity, which was so far from the truth. Finally, Elizabeth contacted Maria Schell, the famous German actress and a friend, to intervene. Maria Schell told the German judge that it wasn't a hoax or a publicity stunt—that Elizabeth and Eddie genuinely wanted the child. The judge relented, thanks to Maria Schell's intervention, and gave the approval for the tentative adoption with the understanding that for three months, there couldn't be any publicity about the baby. Otherwise, the child would be returned to the orphanage. In all the communications between Munich and Rome, the child was referred to as "the book." "When will the book be ready?" "When can the book be picked up?"

The ever-present paparazzi were camped daily outside the villa. They didn't know who I was. Elizabeth asked me to buy whatever a young baby required. I shopped for everything and brought it all to my apartment. Gradually, I would take the baby's things to the villa, in small quantities, so I wouldn't be observed. Try hiding a bassinet in a taxi.

Elizabeth asked me to go to Munich to pick up the "book" and bring the child to Rome. I flew to Munich, met a nurse at the airport holding a baby and we exchanged passports. We immediately returned to Rome. We took a taxi to the Hassler Hotel, which has two entrances. The two of us, and the baby got out of the taxi and we walked through the hotel and exited at the other end. We got into a second taxi. I may have seen too many spy films. As we approached the villa, I asked the nurse to get on the floor with the baby. We entered the villa undetected. The secret of the "book" was kept for several months. Elizabeth named the child Maria, after Maria Schell. For a short while, she was Maria Fisher. Elizabeth spent a small fortune on Maria's hips. It was not too long before Maria was running around the villa with her siblings. She eventually became Maria Burton.

On a trip to Geneva, Elizabeth and Eddie and I were walking along a boulevard and we came across an art gallery. We didn't go in but were looking at some paintings in the gallery's windows. Eddie zeroed in on a Modigliani painting of a long-faced lady. The painting was one and a half feet by three feet—a typical Modigliani. Eddie admired it greatly.

When we returned to Rome, Elizabeth asked me to go back to Geneva and buy the painting for Eddie. She wanted to give it to him as a Christmas gift. Christmas was around the corner. I flew to Geneva and bought the painting for $80,000. There was a great deal of red tape involved to get a famous artist's painting out of the country. But I managed to get it to Rome after much paper work.

The group that had access to the villa was called the "family." The "family" consisted of Richard Hanley, John Lee (Hanley's companion), Eddie's piano player, and Bob Abrams, a friend of Eddie's, and myself. We all chipped in $200 to buy Elizabeth and Eddie a Christmas present. What do you buy Elizabeth Taylor? We decided on an expensive tablecloth, and John Lee announced that the best tablecloths come from Florence. So Lee took the train to Florence.

Christmas was upon us; Elizabeth had mentioned in a recent Italian newspaper interview that she loved candlesticks. As a result, fans were sending her candlesticks from all over Europe. Elizabeth was loved worldwide. There were hundreds. Finally, Elizabeth told Hanley to "get rid of the fucking things."

The living room in the villa was huge. In one corner of the room stood a large Christmas tree. Gifts arrived for the Fishers by the carload. On Christmas Eve, the "family" was invited to dinner and gift opening. As I entered the living room, I could not believe the amount of gifts—all colorfully wrapped. There must have been several hundred presents. There was no room to get around. Gifts virtually covered the entire floor. In that maze, somewhere lay Eddie's Modigliani and our tablecloth. Elizabeth asked Eddie to play Santa Claus. The children gathered around. We squeezed around the room. Eddie would pick up the first gift and it was for Elizabeth. He would pick up another. That, too, was for Elizabeth. Elizabeth would open twelve packages and Liza would get one. Elizabeth would receive another dozen gifts. Eddie would get one. This went on all evening. She finally opened the box with the tablecloth. How sweet! And she put it aside. Along the way, Eddie got his Modigliani. He was thrilled and gave Elizabeth a kiss. He left the painting on the floor. I was worried about the painting. Children and dogs were all over the piles of tissue paper and wrappings. I thought for sure someone is going to step on the Modigliani. I felt around all the tissue papers and finally found it and I placed it on the mantelpiece. The mantel was full of ancient relics that the children dug up from the garden—arms, heads and other pieces of marble. The marble pieces would have been a home decorator's dream. Years later, I asked Elizabeth what happened to the Modigliani. She said she had no idea. I'm sure it is in some Italian household.

The next morning, we went to the villa for Christmas Day lunch. As I walked into the dining room, I saw Liza having breakfast on "our" tablecloth. It had egg and crumbs all over it. Liza, as I remember, was a poor eater. Often, she would be sitting over her meal defiant as Elizabeth said she couldn't leave the table until she had eaten her food. Liza would win out. She had those Taylor eyes that would melt your heart. Elizabeth entered the dining room in a flowing muu-muu. I said, "Elizabeth, that's an expensive tablecloth that should be used for special occasions." She said, "That's right, this is a special occasion." Touché.

One Sunday, Elizabeth, Eddie and I flew to Geneva. We were met at the airport by a limousine and taken to the jewelers, Baume and Mercier. The jewelers opened the store just for Elizabeth. We were ushered in. The entire staff was there. All the cases were full of jewels. Trays of diamonds and emeralds were brought in on black velvet trays. Elizabeth kept picking out various pieces. The scene reminded me of Lauren Bacall in *How to Marry a Millionaire* picking out jewels. "I'll take that and I'll take that and that one." Elizabeth kept telling Eddie to buy a watch. Eddie must have had a hundred watches. Elizabeth asked me to buy something. I said I didn't need anything, thank you. Elizabeth's generosity is unending. Elizabeth kept choosing more jewels. In the shadow box on the wall, there was a magnificent necklace of emeralds and diamonds. I admired it. Elizabeth bought that as well. "Hank, please take something." I needed a watchstrap. I don't remember how much Elizabeth spent. I'm sure it was over two million dollars. They threw in the watchstrap.

While in Rome, we heard that there was a new sensational French actor named Alain Délon. We made arrangements to see the Délon film entitled *Purple Noon* in the studio's projection room. As soon as Délon appeared on the screen, Elizabeth got up and said, "I can't work with him, he's prettier than I am." We left the screening room. But I do remember Elizabeth telling me she thought that the most beautiful actress in the world was Vivien Leigh. Many years later, when I got to know Vivien, I told her what Elizabeth had said about her. Vivien said, "She never told me that."

Whenever it was my birthday and I happened to be with Elizabeth, she would give me a small birthday party. She would always dress the way I found her most beautiful: in a muu-muu, her hair parted in the middle and large gypsy gold earrings. And no makeup. This birthday party was in Rome, and, unbeknownst to me, Elizabeth had invited Audrey Hepburn. Elizabeth was a bit drunk when Audrey arrived, looking like she just stepped out of an Yves Saint-Laurent showroom. Elizabeth said, "You remember our birthday boy, Hank Moonjean?" Audrey looked at me and said, "I don't think so." Elizabeth became upset and asked Audrey to leave. I was extremely embarrassed. Audrey, who appeared to be more embarrassed than me, just turned around and left. I was sorry the entire incident happened. I never saw Audrey Hepburn again. I said to Elizabeth there was no reason why she should remember me; *Green Mansions* was a long time ago.

During all the time *Cleopatra* was shooting, I only visited the set twice. The first time was to observe Cleopatra's spectacular entrance into Rome. Hermes Pan, the legendary choreographer, staged that scene. It was probably one of the most exciting scenes I've ever witnessed. It went on for weeks. If I had anything to do with it, I would have started shooting with Elizabeth first instead of last, even though she was to be at the end of the procession. Get Elizabeth first while you can. The second time I was on the set was when Cleopatra was to be presented to Caesar, hidden in an Oriental rug. I didn't want to go but Elizabeth insisted. I knew she had something mischievous planned. I could tell from her demeanor. The scene in question had been rehearsed many times with a double. It was very important that when Cleopatra was rolled out of the rug at the feet of Caesar, that she ended up facing him, and resting on her elbow. Finally, after all the logistics had been worked out, Elizabeth stepped in. Two Nubian slaves were to carry the rug with Elizabeth in it, to the designated spot and roll out the rug. The camera turned. Action! The unfurling was perfect and Elizabeth ended in the exact position—a perfect take. As she rested on her elbow, face in hand, she looked up at Caesar, who was perched on his throne, and said, "Fuck you." Rex Harrison was taken aback. He pinched the bridge of his nose and said, "That wasn't quite dignified."

One evening while playing Hearts, Elizabeth turned to me and said, "Someone told me that if you own a house in Switzerland, you can get a tax break." I said that's what I understood. She asked me to go Switzerland and buy her "one"—like buying a new sweater. I said, "Where in Switzerland?" Elizabeth said, "Where does Audrey Hepburn live?" I said either in Vevey or Gstaad. (Contrary to what Eddie Fisher said in his autobiography, *Been There, Done That*, it was I who found and bought the house in Gstaad—not Eddie.) Elizabeth gave me a signed blank check.

I flew to Geneva, drove to Gstaad and checked into an inn in the center of town. I went to my room, cleaned up and went downstairs to the bar. The bartender spoke perfect English. After a drink or two, I asked him if he knew of a house for sale in the immediate area. He said, to my surprise, that he knew of one. He said a wealthy Texan built a chalet just up the road from the inn and before he moved in, he had a fight with the architect and refused to take possession. The bartender gave me the name of the real estate agent. I called him and made an appointment to see him the next morning.

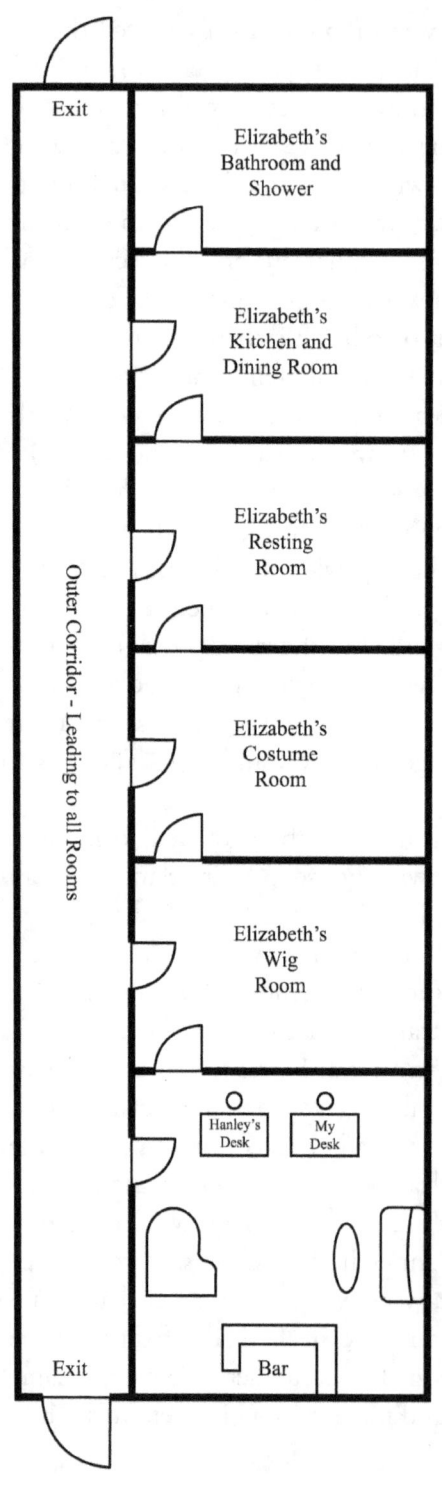

We met at the inn and we walked up a gravel road, and we immediately came upon this fabulous chalet. Although the building was brand new, it looked old. It's the custom to get wood from old buildings and use on the new facades to make the chalet look old and rustic. We entered from ground level into a huge lower basement with a small room for furs, a small room with a built-in safe, an air-raid shelter (Swiss law requires all new buildings have an air-raid shelter), and several other small rooms. I was thinking of space for the four children. We went upstairs. The view from the master bedroom was majestic, looking right up a mountain. There were the usual rooms—kitchen, dining room, etc. I was not sure if the chalet was big enough. I told the agent that the house was not for me; that I was looking at houses for a friend. (I never mentioned Elizabeth.) Would he arrange for a photographer to photograph the entire structure so I could show it to my friend? By the way, how much? He said, "$400,000." I went back to the inn. There was a message to call Elizabeth. (She had a code name.) I telephoned her and she said, "Where the fuck are you?" and I said, "I am in fucking Switzerland looking for a fucking house for you." She said, "Did you find one?" I said, "Well, I found a chalet. I am not sure it is big enough, I am having pictures taken tomorrow." She said, "How much?" I said, "$400,000." She said, "Buy it." I said, "But you must see it first." She said, "Buy it." I said, "I would like to bargain for the price, maybe I can get it for $390,000." Elizabeth said, "It's my money, buy it and come back to Rome so we can play Hearts." I went across the way to the real estate agent's office. I said I would buy the property. He was stunned and he was more stunned when he saw me fill in a blank check for $400,000 that was signed by Elizabeth Taylor Fisher. I flew back to Rome in time to play cards. Elizabeth not once asked me about the house. I was anxious to tell her about it. She was playing games with me.

I never saw the chalet again. However, it has been Elizabeth's home for years now, especially for the holiday visits with her children and grandchildren. I don't know if changes were made, but my guess is that they must have changed the chalet considerably to accommodate everyone.

As to Eddie Fisher's book, I found many inaccuracies from the time I first met Eddie until the time I last saw him in Italy. But a couple of things about his book that I agree with wholeheartedly were his remarks about Richard Burton and Roddy McDowall. About Burton he wrote, "I thought he was an arrogant slob. I know he was a coward and a user." And about McDowall: "Roddy McDowall, there's a phony. A hanger on." Incidentally, Roddy never liked me either. I never saw or heard from Eddie again. I was never mentioned in his book. Maybe it was just as well.

Richard Burton could charm anyone and everyone. And somewhere along the way while making *Cleopatra* Elizabeth fell out of love with Eddie, and fell in love with Richard Burton. Who's to say exactly when? Richard had the reputation of always bedding down his leading ladies and when the film ended, so ended the affair. I thought this time it was not going to happen that way. You cannot just hump and dump Elizabeth Taylor.

In the beginning, Elizabeth would ask me to have lunch with Burton and herself in her private dining area. (See Plan of Cinecitta bunker.) She was either afraid of him or of herself. I remember the glass top of a small dining table—Elizabeth on one end and Burton on the other and me in the middle. It was like attending a tennis match. I could see Burton (still in costume) maneuvering his foot beneath the table, flirting with Elizabeth—both oblivious to my presence.

My rare visit to the *Cleopatra* set with Elizabeth, Eddie, Paddy Chayevsky, and Joseph Mankiewicz.

I honestly believe that Elizabeth was frightened of Burton at first. She was frightened about being involved in another affair. She was frightened about being in another scandal. But it was not easy to escape the Burton charm. The affair was getting deeper and deeper. We all knew what was going on. Eddie was devastated. Strangely, the press did not pick up on it for several months. Many of the executives knew. Mankiewicz knew. Eddie was hoping it would pass. I felt bad for Eddie. I felt bad for Elizabeth. Two friends, so unhappy.

During rational moments, and there were many, the three of us discussed future projects. Actors are most anxious to know what film they are going to do next even while in the middle of filming. Elizabeth, Eddie and I decided that *Anna Karenina* would be a perfect follow-up film for Elizabeth after *Cleopatra*. I suggested that Charles Chaplin would be the perfect director. Elizabeth seemed excited about the possibilities. I contacted Chaplin's agent in London and was told after several days that Chaplin might be interested. He wanted to have a meeting in Switzerland.

Meanwhile, things got very hot and heavy on the *Cleopatra* set. I was anxious to begin working. I thought I was never going to produce *Anna Karenina* or anything else. Eddie and I had two subsequent meetings in Vevey, Switzerland, with Charles Chaplin, before the shit hit the fan. Oona Chaplin would sit on the sofa, coiled up like a cat and looking at Chaplin as though she were mesmerized. Chaplin himself was amusing and brilliant at the same time, a vibrant and fascinating man. He told us very proudly that one of his sons was working in a drugstore in the village and he was in love with one of the waitresses. I asked Chaplin whom he considered the best American comic in films today. Without hesitation, he said Jerry Lewis. I asked him what he thought of Gloria Swanson miming him in *Sunset Blvd*. He said that it was an embarrassment. I gathered he did not like her. At least I got to meet Chaplin, even though we would never work together. *Anna Karenina* ended before it began.

Meanwhile, back to Rome and reality. Eddie set up a meeting with Sybil Burton, Richard's wife, to discuss the situation. She told Eddie, "He always comes back to me. Don't make an issue of it." One day, Burton burst into our office and screamed at Eddie, "You leave my fucking women alone. They are both mine. Leave them alone." Burton stormed out. Eddie was suicidal. He was defending what he thought was his. Things began getting more complicated. There was more drama behind the camera than in front of the camera.

Inevitably, the world soon discovered that Elizabeth Taylor was in love with Richard Burton. Somehow the press found out. Surprise? I was driving to the studio one sunny morning. When I got to the studio, the main gate was crawling with reporters and television cameras, all trying to get into the studio. I inched my way into the studio and parked my car next to the bunker. I went into our office. Our office was at one end of the bunker. (Cinecitta was built before World War 2 by Mussolini and looked like army bunker.)

Hanley had a desk. I had a desk. There was Eddie's piano *and* the bar. What I witnessed would make a great scene in a movie. Picture this: Eddie pacing the floor ashen-faced. Eddie's pianist plunking away on the keyboard. The telephones ringing off their hooks. John Lee, Richard Hanley's companion, fluttering around, enjoying the drama. John was relegated to making Bloody Marys for Elizabeth. Richard Hanley was exasperated with all the phones ringing. When Eddie saw me, he said, "They've found out! They've found out! Elizabeth is in the back and she doesn't want to see anyone—not even you." I shrugged my shoulders and went to my desk. Hanley asked me if I would help him with the telephones. Hanley typed something on a piece of paper and handed it to me. It read, "Mr. and Mrs. Eddie Fisher have no comment to make at this time." Every time the phone rang, I would read off the message. It didn't matter who was on the other end of the line. During all this drama, John Lee, who was the only one allowed to see Her Ladyship, kept making Bloody Marys for Elizabeth. I thought this is it. I'm going home to resume my life and my career. What am I doing in Rome?

Suddenly, John Lee entered our office for the umpteenth time, and walked up to Eddie. Almost on cue, all the telephones stopped ringing. Everything was still. "Eddie?" We were all on pins and needles. News from the rear. "Eddie," John Lee proclaimed, "If Elizabeth keeps this up, *you* are going to have to get more tomato juice." I started to laugh. I thought that Lee was going to say that if Elizabeth keeps this up, she's going to be dead drunk. I couldn't stop laughing. Eddie saw no humor in it. I was laughing uncontrollably. Here we are in the middle of a multi-million project, two families are about to be destroyed, careers are at stake, and we are out of tomato juice. I walked out of the office and walked around the bunker trying to stop laughing. But every time I thought about it, I began to laugh, again. Finally, I settled down.

Years later, I told this story to Elizabeth. She said, "I never told Eddie you couldn't see me." She missed the entire point of the story. Perhaps she didn't think it was funny.

I stayed in Rome a little longer. For a time, it looked like Elizabeth and Eddie had worked things out. No such luck. Elizabeth, looking toward the future, had told me her next film was going to be the most important film of her career. She wanted to make sure that I was on it. She said she couldn't divulge the title. I had already guessed it was *Who's Afraid of Virginia Woolf?* She wanted to have me written into her contract as the first assistant director. I asked Elizabeth not to. I said I had enough credentials by now to try and get the position on my own. Besides, the director should be able to select his own assistant. These discussions were going on the same time that *Cleopatra* was filming and the Taylor-Fisher-Burton saga was at its height.

Irvin Kershner, a director, just had a success with his film *The Luck of Ginger Coffey*. I didn't know if Kershner was set as the director of *Virginia Woolf* or was being considered for the job. In any case, he wanted Elizabeth and Burton to see his film. The delivery of the print was delayed, probably by the Italian customs. After many transatlantic calls, a print arrived. Elizabeth kept insisting that it wasn't necessary to see the film. Kershner said that Elizabeth and Burton must see his masterpiece. Elizabeth, Burton and I went to a projection room at Cinecitta and viewed *Ginger Coffey*. After less than ten minutes, Burton stood up and said, "The film is shit." That was the end of the screening and that was the end of Kershner. Imagine what changes would have been made in motion picture lore if Kershner had not insisted on showing his "Masterpiece." We'll never know.

During all this drama, I decided to go to Istanbul, Turkey on the Orient Express. The travel agency said that I would have to get a special visa from the American Embassy in Rome as the train went through Bulgaria. Americans were not allowed to go to Bulgaria. I went to the Embassy and applied. Within a week I received a telegram stating: CITIZEN MOONJEAN'S REQUEST TO TRAVEL TO ISTANBUL TURKEY ON THE ORIENT EXPRESS DENIED. (signed) JOHN FOSTER DULLES. I thought with all the problems in the world, it was a little odd for Mr. Dulles to be worrying about Citizen Moonjean.

The drama at the Appian Way Villa was getting more and more intense. I was ready to leave Rome. Eddie begged me to stay. I said I had

had it. I was making arrangements to fly out of Rome. Eddie asked me to go to Florence with him just to get away. I could always fly home from Florence. When Elizabeth heard I was leaving, she phoned me and said, "I hear you're fucking off with my husband." I said, "Something like that. I love you, Elizabeth, but you do not need me here. I'll see you back home." She was crying.

Eddie, Bob Abrams and I drove to Florence. Eddie sped all the way. Elizabeth had given Eddie a brand-new green Rolls-Royce. Several times I thought we were goners. We checked into a swank hotel in Florence. That night, I think Eddie attempted suicide. Something was going on. Bob Abrams was running from bedroom to bathroom to bedroom extremely nervous and concerned. I didn't want to know. I had seen too much of my friends hurting one another. Nothing was said and next morning, I flew back to Los Angeles.

I believe that the studio made Elizabeth the "heavy" for all its problems on *Cleopatra*. Certainly, she added to it. But I think the culprit was Joseph Mankiewicz. He did not care if the film took five years to make. He was living like a king and enjoying every minute of it. Seldom did the actors get the script. He would not tell anyone what he had in mind. Expensive sets were built and never used.

I was one of the first people to return from Rome to Los Angeles who were indirectly or directly involved with *Cleopatra*. I was approached by a magazine and offered $50,000, in those days a huge sum, to tell everything I knew about the Taylor-Fisher-Burton story. I turned it down flat. It's the last thing I would do to my friends. Years later, I told Elizabeth of my grand gesture. At least, I thought it was a gallant gesture. Elizabeth said, "You fool, you should have taken the money."

I had been home less than a week. The television was reporting a giant Bel-Air fire out of control. I got an urgent call from Elizabeth in Rome asking me to go to her mother's home, which was in a direct line of the fire. Richard Hanley gave me Sara Taylor's address and I managed to get through the fire blockade. I was amazed that Elizabeth knew of the fire in Rome just as it was burning in Bel-Air. Bad news travels fast. Sara Taylor lived on a plateau and on both sides of her house were deep canyons. Houses were burning all around us. I ran into Sara's beautiful home. I'm sure Sara was in shock. She hardly reacted to me. She had been watching the fire coming up toward her from the lower canyon. She was standing in front of sliding glass doors. Although she hadn't touched the hot glass windows, her hands were burned. The heat coming through the glass was very hot. I was afraid the house might implode. Marshall Thompson, an actor who knew Elizabeth and lived nearby, also came to Sara's aid. Amazingly, the flames leaped right over Sara's house, burning the house behind her to the ground. Marshall took Sara into his car and drove away. I locked up whatever I could and ran out. Sara's all-white rooms were now a dirty gray. Sara's house survived. It was a miracle it didn't burn down. Many actors lost their homes in that fire. Joan Fontaine's beautiful home burned to the ground. Luckily, she had sold it a few months earlier.

Richard Harris on the deck of the *Bounty*. Note the "unhappy actor" standing next to the mast.

Chapter 10
Back To MGM and *Mutiny*

I was very happy to be back in the States after being away for so long. I immediately went to MGM, my "home" studio. Walter Strohm was glad to see me. MGM had just started shooting *Mutiny on the Bounty* in Papeete, Tahiti, and they were already in trouble. He said they had been shooting for only four days. He wanted to send me to Tahiti as a troubleshooter. I let out a moan. I still hadn't unpacked. Walter said it was imperative for me to go. There was no one else available at the studio. Besides, I owed it to the studio that gave me my first break. In any case, it was for only three weeks. In Hollywood, time means nothing. "It'll take five minutes" or "We can shoot that in two hours" is a fantasy.

Reluctantly, I agreed. Walter said I could take the next plane to Tahiti, arrive early on Saturday morning, rest on Sunday and begin work on Monday. I was armed with several versions of the script, contracts and all the documentation that I had to be privy to. The film starred Marlon Brando, Trevor Howard, Richard Harris and Hugh Griffith (the Arab Chieftain from *Ben-Hur*). Most of the remaining cast was from Britain. Other than Marlon, I did not know any of the other cast members. Sir Carol Reed, a successful British director, was set to direct. The cameraman was Robert Surtees. The producer was Aaron Rosenberg. The unit manager was (Mr.) Ruby Rosenberg. Luckily for me, I knew most of the crew having worked with them on previous MGM films. The first assistant director was Reggie Callow, a man who taught me a great deal in the early days. I was told to take the minimum of clothing; just shorts, bathing suits and sneakers. And only cotton fabrics, as wool rots in the tropics. I unpacked and repacked and was off to Tahiti—a brand-new experience. I read all the documents on the plane.

"I'll share screen credit with you over my dead body." Those were the first words I heard from Reggie Callow as I disembarked the plane. Nice greeting. I said, "Reggie, I have no intention of asking for screen credit."

When *Bounty* began, Tahiti had no jet airstrip and no fancy hotels. It was just a beautiful dot in the Pacific. By the time the film was finished they had built the airstrip and several new hotels. I was taken to my little shack near the sea. The walls did not touch the ceiling, therefore allowing ventilation as well as a passageway for the rats. There was no air-conditioning. Most of the key crew had similar accommodations along the sea front. We all lived within walking distance from one another. I unpacked my things and was anxious to get to the set to see some of my friends and to check out what was happening. There were giggling native girls all over. I was allocated a small Renault car. After showering, I went to the location where they were shooting.

I walked around to the nearby set. The scene that they had been shooting was of Captain Bligh (Trevor Howard) and his crew being welcomed by the native chief. Reggie introduced me to Sir Carol—a tall man with a red face and big red nose who wore a large floppy hat. Brando came by and welcomed me. He said he was having a party that night and he wanted to make sure I would be there. I was getting tired so I went

Celebrating my birthday in Moorea.

back to my shack. I took off my clothes and climbed in bed with only a sheet over my naked body. I was just about to fall asleep when a huge "something" fell on the left side of my neck and began crawling across my chin. I didn't move. I was terrified as I felt it crawl. I slowly pulled my arm up and swatted the thing off my face. It was the largest spider I have ever seen, big as a dinner plate. I quickly killed it. A native girl who heard me holler said I should not have killed the spider. It wasn't poisonous. Apparently, there is nothing in Tahiti that is poisonous—at least not on land. The only way you can get killed on land is if a coconut should fall on your head. The spiders eat all the insects. I told her I was not accustomed to having spiders crawling all over me and I would continue to kill them. Sorry.

That night I went to Marlon's party. All sorts of Tahitian delicacies were laid out on huge green fronds on the ground. A pig was being roasted. Everybody sat on their haunches eating with their fingers. The drums were drumming. The dancers were dancing. The singers were singing. It was very romantic. A beautiful South Sea Island moment. Any minute, I expected Dorothy Lamour in her sarong to come out and do the hula. At the party, I became reacquainted with two of Marlon's closest friends—Phil and Marie Rhodes. They knew Marlon during his New York City days. On *Bounty* Marie was Marlon's stand-in, and Phil was Marlon's makeup man. The crew called Phil "Horizontal." Often, Marlon would lean over the prone Phil while Phil applied makeup. Phil was too tired from the night before to stand up to apply Marlon's makeup.

Tahitians are very kind and hospitable. They are a simple people. They make no demands of others and they accept themselves as they are. The pure Tahitian is very plain looking with short stocky frames; the women as well as the men are built like football players. The beautiful women are usually of mixed blood. The German/Tahitian girl is extremely gorgeous. Many have Chinese or French blood. I'm sure by the time *Bounty* was completed; there were many children with American blood. Marlon's party was a great success, but I was getting tired. For me, it had been a very long day. I thanked Marlon and went home to my shack. I looked around for more spiders. I went to bed and immediately fell asleep. I awakened from a deep sleep. I heard what seemed like a girl in high heels walking across a marble floor. I switched on the light and saw a dozen or so land crabs tapping sideways across the linoleum. What next? Eventually, I fell asleep again. I knew that crabs couldn't climb up a bed. The next morning, Sunday, I put on my bathing suit and walked a few yards to the sea. Lying near on a beach chair was Bobby Webb. Bobby was in charge of the local casting. We knew each other from the studio. He welcomed me to paradise. As I was about to step in the water, I asked Bobby if he knew whether or not there were octopi in these waters. Don't ask me why I selected octopi. I could have said sharks or anything else. I must have had a premonition. Bobby said he didn't know. I stepped in about two feet of water and all of a sudden a three-foot octopus clung to my ankle. I stepped back on land with the octopus still clinging to my ankle. I didn't panic. I shook it off as it slithered back into the water. I watched its colors change as it moved away. I decided I didn't want to swim.

I got into my Renault and drove into "town" to look around. Papeete looked like a movie set. The island of Tahiti is shaped like the number 8. The main road went along the entire island between the sea and the land. I discovered a large white house on the outskirts of Papeete. It was a house of lepers. On most of the ensuing Sundays, I would go to the outdoor market and buy a large quantity of fruit to take to the lepers. I would get orange-colored watermelons, mangoes, pamplemousse (grapefruit) and all sorts of exotic fruit. I would deliver them in large wooden crates and carry them part way up the walk to the house and leave them. Slowly, the lepers would come out, wave to me, and take the fruit inside. Leprosy was fortunately on the wane. These unfortunates were the last of the community.

Marlon Brando's contract was quite detailed. Brando had script approval, director approval, leading lady approval and approval of the actor who was to play Captain Bligh. Also, the exteriors of the film must be shot in Tahiti in the actual locations of the book. Brando was a big box-office draw. The studio was anxious to cast Brando as Fletcher Christian, which would insure the success of the film. Consequently, all Brando's demands were accepted.

The first thing MGM did was to send a crew to Baja California to build the Tahitian village there, spending hundreds of thousands of dollars. When Brando got wind of this he notified the studio to read his contract. Somebody at the studio forgot this minor point. Already Brando was being made the heavy, as happened with Elizabeth Taylor on *Cleopatra*. Someone has to take the blame. Also, the studio neglected to check the weather conditions in Tahiti during the scheduled start date. Another minor point. Now, most importantly, the script was not ready. The script was never ever ready. It was being written and rewritten daily. The screenwriter was Charles Lederer. Sir Carol fell into the trap that many directors have, agreeing to a start date knowing full well that the script was in no shape to begin filming. When I eventually viewed the film that had already been shot, all I saw were entrances and exits. Reed never shot the "guts" of the scene.

On the first Monday, I was given an interpreter named Philippe. We went to the set. They were continuing the scene from the previous Saturday, Captain Bligh and his crew being welcomed by the chief, Hitihiti.

With Tarita. The future "Mrs. Marlon Brando."

The part of the leading lady, Maimiti, was yet to be cast. I went to Marlon and asked him if had found the girl for Maimiti. He said he hadn't, and, "By the way, I think I have a dose." That's all we needed. I said I would get a doctor to examine him. I asked him to give me the name of the girl—just in case his suspicions proved accurate. At the end of the day, he gave me a list of twenty-three native girls.

The shooting continued. Trevor Howard was feeling no pain. He was drunk most of the time but it never affected his performance. I preferred him drunk. He was a bastard when he was sober. It was getting close to lunch. They decided to break for lunch early as the scene immediately after lunch was going to be difficult. Reggie called lunch. The natives were asked to remain. The real chief stood up and spoke to all the natives in Tahitian. The Americans were already in the chow line. I asked Philippe what the chief was saying. It seems that a crew member had his wallet stolen. According to Philippe, the chief was upset with the theft. It was not the way of his people. The Americans were guests. He wanted the wallet left on a stone slab that he had pointed to. He said when they returned from lunch he expected to see the wallet onthe slab. The natives went to lunch. When we came back, the wallet was there intact.

The scene after lunch was memorable. Hundreds of young men and women came out from under the palm trees dancing the "tamure," a Tahitian dance. This scene was rehearsed the week before. They made sure that the natives in the foreground were authentic looking. All the women wore long black wigs. Short hair was the current style in Tahiti but not in the days of the *Bounty*. The scene was magnificent. The tamure is very hard on the dancers' knees and legs—especially dancing uphill for quite a distance. I think this particular scene was one of the highlights of all the location shooting.

Amongst the dancers was an unusually beautiful girl. Her name was Tarita. She was one-fourth Chinese, one-fourth French and half-Tahitian. Marlon had already spotted her. He went to her and he pulled her aside, speaking in fluent French. In about fifteen minutes Marlon came to me and said he had found Maimiti. Marlon introduced me to Tarita who spoke no English. I called Philippe over to translate for me. I told Tarita that I had to prepare a contract for her. I told her she would eventually be required to work at the Culver City studio for interior shooting. And I had to discuss her salary. She said in French, "All I want is a motorbike for me, and one for my brother and one for my boyfriend."

Soon to be Mr. and Mrs. Marlon Brando

I said I would arrange for the necessary papers. A proper contract was prepared and gave Tarita a fair salary. Marlon subsequently fell in love with Tarita and eventually married her. She bore him two children. But in the beginning, Marlon's competition was a short-order Dutch cook in some flea-bitten hotel. The cook gave Marlon a run for his money. Tarita could not choose between a local cook and one of the most famous actors in the world.

Bounty was the most unorganized production that I ever had been on. On a good day, we would get two shots. Everybody was on a paid vacation. There was nothing I could do. There was nothing anyone could do. My father used to tell me that if the fish smelled it was always from the head. In this case, it was the producer.

When we were at sea, Charles Lederer, the screenwriter, would be typing the scene that we were about to film. I would pull out the paper from his typewriter when he was finished and race it to where the camera was set up. I would hand the new script pages to Marlon. Marlon, without even looking at them, would toss the pages overboard. Marlon would say to me, "Hank, I told you that I will do any scene you ask me to do but I must have the scene at least two days before it's scheduled to be shot."

I was getting involved in the production, deeper and deeper. Reggie must have resented my intrusion and rightfully so. If he did, he never let on. You can't have two chiefs running the set. Eventually, a few months too late, the legendary director Lewis Milestone replaced Sir Carol Reed. The veteran director was called "Millie." Two directors with women's names—Carol and Millie. Millie was arthritic, very old and not very well. *Bounty* was a very physical production. Milestone had to be hoisted in a boson's chair whenever he had to get aboard ship.

Very early one morning, while the entire crew and cast were aboard, ready to sail out of the Papeete harbor, we noticed that Hugh Griffith, our token drunken actor, wasn't accounted for. Someone tried to reach him by phone. No luck. Finally, we could see his little Renault careening around the coast road. "Here he comes." The small car arrived at the dock and a native girl stepped out and then another native girl and then, two other native girls stepped out. It was like the circus act where all the midgets pile out of a small car. Hugh Griffith was the last one out. He was drunk and completely naked. I wasn't at all surprised. I never saw him sober in the entire time I was on the film. Of course, by now my original three weeks were long past. Griffith was a pathetic sight. He, too, was hoisted onto the deck. And we eventually sailed.

The sea was calm. The Bounty sailed toward the outer reefs. I felt great. I felt adventuresome. I went to the ship's bowsprit and straddled and shimmied up the long thick mast, nearly to its end. The crew were watching and waving and laughing, (Why were they laughing?) They foresaw pending disaster. I didn't. We eventually passed the outer reefs. Suddenly, the Bounty lurched and heaved. First, it lurched only 3 feet, then, 6 feet, then, 10 feet and I'm sure 12 feet. I was scared, nervous and felt less adventuresome. I held on the mast for dear life. Each time I came up from the depths, I was gagging from the salt water. The mast was wet and very slippery. Gratefully, we arrived at our destination and anchored the ship. To hell, with Errol Flynn movies.

One beautiful cloudless day, Philippe said it was going to rain tomorrow. I said he was crazy. How could he predict the weather? I said that it couldn't rain; we have too much to do. Philippe said it would be a "passing" rain. I said, "What is a passing rain?" He said, "Seven days." It rained the next day and it rained non-stop for seven straight days! It rained so hard that the only way you could see the roads was to follow the telephone poles. Raging brown waters cascaded down from the hills and

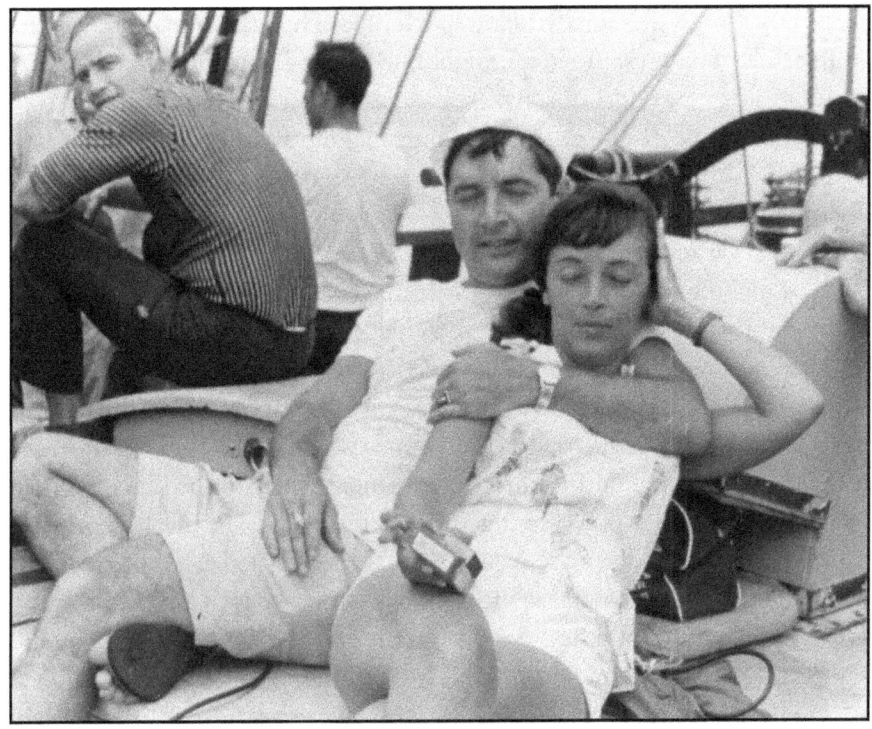

A tough day at the "office" in Tahiti. Brando observing.

into the sea. You couldn't tell where the sea began and the land ended. And when it rained all the telephones went out.

This particular day, while the company was shut down, Reggie and I made the rounds to all the actors to let them know what was happening. The last visit was to Richard Harris' house. We stayed and had a few drinks with Richard. It was still pouring. I said to Reggie that we'd better go before it gets dark. Reggie walked down the stairs to the yard where we had our car parked. I was right behind him. He stepped off the last step and sunk into the wet ground up to his navel. It looked like quicksand. Richard and I couldn't stop laughing. Reggie, always the good sport, was laughing the hardest. At the end of the seventh day, the rain stopped as Philippe had predicted. The hot sun came out and the ground looked like it hadn't rained in years. Everything was positively dry.

Production picked up considerably after Milestone took over. Plans were being made to return to the studio to begin interior sets. However, one major scene had to be shot before we returned to MGM. It was a scene where the natives show Bligh's crew how to catch fish Tahitian style. This scene was shot in the nearby island of Moorea. The fishing method is quite simple. The women stand in a straight line holding a gigantic rope net. The men are in canoes and boats with paddles and sticks. The men face the women at a good distance. The men start making as much noise as possible by beating the waters as hard as they can. The women begin to slowly form a semi-circle, gradually beginning to form a full circle. The frightened fish swim toward the net and get trapped. Once the circle is formed, the women close in making the circle smaller and smaller.

Our cast was with the native men helping out with the noise making. It was wisely decided to film this scene in shallow waters and have all the women on their knees. From the camera angle, it appeared that the women were standing in deeper water. This scene took three days to complete. I was in the water the entire time. The women never stopped giggling and talking. They didn't like wearing those awful wigs. They all thought we movie people were crazy. We would be near ready when the camera operator would tell me he could see the nipples on the fifteenth girl on the right. I'd walk to her and pull her hair over her breast. Then the operator would say he could see the nipples on the third girl on the left.

There were sea urchins in the water called sea cucumbers that looked like a penis. The girls would pick them up and squeeze them and liquid would shoot out. These girls were having a good time. We'd get closer to shooting and another nipple cropped up. On one of these days, one of the girls pulled down my shorts. I was wearing no underwear. They all laughed and pointed to my shrunken privates. You spend three days in warm salt water and see what happens! Finally, we were ready. The girls kept giggling or talking. It was difficult to hear anything. The camera began to roll. All the natives put their heart into what they were doing, still laughing and talking. All of a sudden there was complete silence. It was an eerie moment; one of the native men whispered, "Shark," and the women slowly fanned open the circle that they had formed—ever so gently. As they straightened out the nets, we saw thousands of fish swimming out to the open sea. We also saw the fin of a shark in the net. It was amazing how the natives knew there was danger. We never saw the fin or the shark during the scene. Like Philippe and his seven-day rain, they have a special instinct. We didn't see the shark again that afternoon.

A week later, when we were out to sea filming, it was so hot that at lunchtime I decided to climb down the permanent ladder alongside the ship to cool off in the water. I only lowered my body into the water to

Lining up the girls for the famous fishing sequence in Moorea.
NOTE: The *Bounty* in the background.

my waist. Suddenly, the ship's captain let out a yell telling me to get out of the water *now*. Foolishly, I did not realize that my white skin in the shimmering water would draw the attention of the sharks.

One day as Philippe and I were returning from location in my car, I said, "I'd give anything to go swimming in a lake or a cold stream." The ocean water is almost too hot and certainly not refreshing. Philippe asked me if I knew how to swim underwater. I said yes but exactly what did he have in mind? He said, "I'll show you." We drove several miles along the coastline. Philippe said, "Turn right here." I drove into the deep jungle as far as I could before stopping. We got out of the car and walked several hundred yards to a huge cavern set in the side of a mountain. Within the cavern, the shimmering water looked like a miniature lake. The blue-gray rainwater glistened like crystals. The cavern was beautiful. The cave's ceiling had trees and plants and exotic flowers growing upside down. The seashells and mollusks in the water threw reflections throughout the cave. Philippe and I removed our clothes and dove in. What relief. What joy. We swam for a while. Swimming naked is a different experience than with a bathing suit. Philippe said, "Are you sure you can swim underwater?" I said, "Yes." Philippe got out of the water and told me to follow him and do exactly what he did. I got out of the water. Philippe made a deep dive and I followed him. Something was above my head and back. We swam about twelve yards and Philippe suddenly went up. I followed. We were in the inside of a dead volcano. The volcano was fully lit by the sun. Above us, looking about the size of a silver dollar was the mouth of the volcano. The light from the sun streamed in. The base of the volcano was twice the size of the cavern that we just swam from. There were very few plants and nowhere to sit. I was getting tired as we were treading water. I said to Philippe that I was tired and we should go back. We dove under to return to the outer cavern. I followed. I scraped my back slightly. We came up into the outer cave. That experience was one I shall never forget; it certainly is my best memory of Tahiti and the *Bounty*.

The film took its toll on human life. The second unit lost five native men whose canoe tipped over a coral reef, immediately killing them. Falling on a coral reef is like falling onto a million razor blades. An elderly character actor from Australia died during a scene on top deck. Ruby Rosenberg, our unit manager, had a heart attack on top of a native girl.

On departure day, the airport was filled with all the Tahitians saying goodbye. They were all crying. There was much to drink. Flower leis were put around our necks. Leis of seashells were put around our necks. We were scheduled to fly out on a chartered prop plane to Los Angeles. The plane was late in taking off. More tears, more kissing, more crying and more booze. Finally, we began to board. All the flower leis had to be removed. Most everyone was feeling no pain. Trevor Howard and Hugh Griffith had to be carried onto the plane. Several of us were sober, including me. Finally, we became airborne. I was sitting near the front of the plane. The crew was giving the two stewardesses a bad time by grabbing them or throwing shells at them. About an hour out of Papeete, I looked out of the left side of the plane and saw flames shooting out of one of the engines. I called the stewardess. She looked out the window and said, "Oh, my God." She ran into the pilot's compartment.

The plane turned around and headed back to Papeete. The pilot notified Papeete that we were returning. The natives were also notified. As we reached Papeete, the entire village was there to greet us. While the mechanics checked out the problem, the initial departure scene was repeated. More flower leis and more shell leis. Soon, the plane was ready. The drunks were drunker. The flower leis were removed and Trevor Howard and Hugh Griffith were carried aboard the airplane again.

In flight, Hugh woke up in a drunken stupor. He went to the bathroom and locked himself in. He was in there for over an hour. I asked the stewardess to check the bathroom. She opened the door to see that Hugh had scrawled graffiti all over the walls with a red marking pen. Not an inch of wall space was spared. He also decided to decorate the ceilings in the cabin. We eventually reached Los Angeles. Most of the booze had worn off after such a long flight. But now nearly everyone was sick. The upshot of all this vandalism was that MGM was sued by the airline for $15,000 and Hugh Griffith was fired from the film. Should you see *Mutiny on the Bounty* some evening on television you will notice that Griffith's role is in and out and his character makes little sense.

Meanwhile, back at the studio, I was now in full charge of the unit, I ran set the set. Because Millie could barely walk, I directed all the storm scenes on Stage 28. Again, I was waterlogged. This time I was wet for three weeks. Whenever Millie couldn't handle a scene because of his condition, I would direct—with his approval. My three weeks became four months. After shooting in the studio for some time, arrangements were made to return to Tahiti and finish whatever wasn't accomplished the first go-round. I told Walter Strohm that I would not return to Tahiti.

At the studio on Lot 3, Lewis Milestone at the top of the gangplank.

Trevor Howard and the ailing "Millie" Milestone.

He understood. But no one else did. Millie, who said I was the best assistant director he ever worked with, begged me to go back.

Most of the MGM executives offered me bonuses, screen credit, whatever I wanted. I still refused. There were several reasons why I wouldn't return to Tahiti. The most important one was Reggie Callow. Reggie taught me a great deal when I started out as an assistant director. In his heyday, he was considered one of the greatest. By the time *Bounty* began, he was losing his zip and vigor and the booze was taking its toll. But the *Bounty* film credit was very important to him and this was my way of thanking him for everything he had done for me. I don't know if he ever realized it, but I hope he did in the end. The studio executives asked Marlon to intervene. I told Marlon I had my reasons for getting off the film. He dropped it. Reggie came to me and thanked me. Nothing else was ever said.

I stayed with the *Bounty* until they all returned to Tahiti—everyone except Hugh Griffith and me. Brando was blamed for all the overages and excessive cost to the production. While I was on the production, he was cooperative. Marlon never gave me a bad time. Marlon just didn't like authority. He didn't particularly like directors or producers or studio executives. He is happy with being with the crew. The film was badly planned. The first director wasn't prepared, the second director was too ill, and the producer was ineffective and the script was never acceptable. The film drew mixed reviews. However, all the people who went to Tahiti had experiences they will never forget and a great vacation, courtesy of MGM.

Chapter 11
The Prize

The timing was perfect. Pandro Berman was about to produce *The Prize* based on a script written by Ernest Lehman. This time the director was going to be Mark Robson. I never met Robson but he had a great track record. I was looking forward to working with him. The cast that Pandro had selected included Paul Newman, Edward G. Robinson, Diane Baker and German actress Elke Sommer. The film had to do with the Nobel Prize and the story takes place entirely in Sweden. Except for a small second unit, the entire film was to be shot in the studio. I took a small unit to Sweden and filmed several exterior shots, establishing shots and many background plates. I was in Stockholm for two weeks. For some reason, Robson had not begun working on the

Miss Elke Sommer
EUROPE'S MOST GLAMOROUS NEW YOUNG ACTRESS

Is arriving to begin preparations for her co-starring role with Paul Newman and Edward G. Robinson in MGM's "The Prize". It is her first visit to Hollywood.

Producer Pandro S. Berman and Director Mark Robson cordially invite you to meet her and discover for yourself why she has become the most talked about and written about young star in Continental Europe.

Cocktails	Wednesday Evening
Sans Souci Room	April 17
Beverly Wilshire Hotel	5:00 - 7:00 p.m.

R. S. V. P. 870-3311, Ext. 1605

film. I think he was just finishing up his latest film. And Pandro was anxious to get started because of the time constraints of various contracts.

One of the major scenes in the script was of thugs chasing Paul Newman. He runs into a building where a nudist group is listening to a lecture. This was a censor's nightmare at the time. I had an idea. I went to our cameraman, William Daniels—the brilliant cameraman that photographed Greta Garbo. I said, "Bill, I have an idea about the nudist colony scene. Often, when you are getting a tan under strong hot lights, you are required to wear protective eyeglasses. Supposing all the nudists are wearing these glasses. When Paul Newman runs into the outer lecture hall, he is made to undress. Instead of a towel, he is given a pair of these glasses. With these tinted glasses, when he has them full on, everything is washed out blurring the detail. When he raises them, he sees everything clearly avoiding any censorable body parts." Daniels thought it was a great idea and he would have fun experimenting with different colors and techniques. Fortified with Daniels' enthusiasm, I went to Pandro. Pandro loved the idea. He said this would probably avoid censor problems. Remember, the year was 1963. Today, this would have been a moot point.

Mark Robson finally reported to the studio. I was introduced to him. Immediately we got into a conversation about all that had transpired in his absence and what was yet to be accomplished. I liked him immediately. He had a great smile and a twinkle in his eye. The first meeting was with the art department.

The art director, Pandro, Mark and I began to discuss the sets from beginning to end. Mind you, I had just met Robson only three days ago. I was sitting next to Pandro. When we got to the nudist colony scene, Pandro kicked my crossed leg and said, "Tell Mark how you would shoot it." I was flabbergasted. Pandro, not known for tact or diplomacy, put me in a very delicate situation. An assistant director does not tell the director how he should shoot a scene. It's just not done. I fumbled through trying to explain my idea, which began to sound confusing. Mark just looked at me and said, "Interesting." Needless to say, we didn't do it my way. However, Mark never held it against me.

When we shot the nudist colony sequence, the MGM publicity department asked me to pose for a picture attempting to stop the non-existing press from entering the soundstage. That photograph of me was printed in newspapers all over the world. My nephew Richard, who was stationed in Japan, saw the photo in a Japanese newspaper.

This was the photograph that was in all of the newspapers throughout the world.

One Friday during production, I went up to San Francisco for a long weekend. I think it was a holiday. I was with Brad Bennett and some friends and we were carousing around the North Beach section of San Francisco. The four of us went into a girly magazine shop. The place was full of people thumbing through all the sex and porno magazines. After about five minutes one of my friends held up a magazine and said, "Look. There's a picture of Hank in this magazine." Everyone in the magazine shop turned and looked at me. Everyone gathered around to see what I was doing. It was the posed photograph of me stopping the non-existent press from entering the soundstage—the same one that appeared all over the world. For a quick moment, I felt like a celebrity. Not everyone can find his or her photograph in some girly magazine in a porno magazine stand.

Paul Newman said to me that he wanted to do his own stunts on the film. I said he had a great stunt double. Why take chances? Paul insisted. I told Pandro. Pandro said, "Let him do it." After I prepared the shooting schedule, I put all of Paul's stunts on the last day of filming. Weeks later I gave Paul my schedule. He immediately began to look for when he was scheduled to do his stunts. He found it on the last page. Paul said, "How come you have my stunts on the last day?" I said, "Paul, if you break your neck, we can still release the film." It was the only time in all thirteen

Arguing with Richard Brooks.

films that I worked on with Paul that he was openly upset with me. It passed quickly. Paul realized I was concerned with his well-being.

The only time Paul asked me to be sure we had a "closed set" was the day we were scheduled to shoot the Nobel Prize presentations. I had studio police posted at the stage entrances. This was going to be shot on Stage 5, the theater stage.

During the afternoon, as we were filming, Paul looked at me and said, "I thought I asked you to have a closed set." A closed set means that no visitors are allowed whatsoever. I said I made all the necessary arrangements. I turned around and saw Emily Torchia ushering in Hedda Hopper, the gossip columnist. I ran up to them before they reached Paul. I said, "Hedda, this is a closed set. I'm going to ask you to leave." She said, "You don't know me well enough to call me Hedda." I said, "I've met you a dozen times. Please leave." Sweet Emily was mortified. She didn't speak to me for weeks.

Elke Sommer was a good sport and good fun. I used to tease her about pursing her lower lip. Elke use to call her Mother "Mommie." We all loved Mommie. She wasn't a stage mother. I think she used to visit the set because she was lonely and missed her home in Germany.

Of the cast, Edward G. Robinson was one of my most favorite actors. He had a brilliant, keen mind. Of course, when I met him on *The*

Prize he was an old man. People told me that in his heyday at Warner Bros., he was hell on wheels. But with me, he was a pussycat. He would come to me around 5 p.m. daily and would say, "Boss, I'm an old man. Can I go home?" I would mimic him. He loved it. As a matter of fact, Eddie (as we all called him) offered to send me to RADA in London, the Cadillac of drama schools, to study acting. He said he would pay all expenses. Eddie thought I would make a good actor. I think he saw himself in me. Eddie never had any children. He had an adopted son who didn't amount to much. His first wife took the cream of his very valuable art collection in a divorce settlement. I said to Eddie that I wanted to work behind the camera, not in front of the camera. He tried many times to convince me otherwise. He was very professional and was loved by the entire crew. We kept in touch until his death.

Pandro credited me with saving a great deal of money on the film. For the filming of the Nobel Prize presentations, we required five hundred male extras. When you deal with that many extras, you can hire a certain percentage of non-union extras at a much lower salary. All you have to do is provide them with a box lunch. You can also ask them to wear one item of clothing. I asked the casting department to inform

With my friend Eddie Robinson.

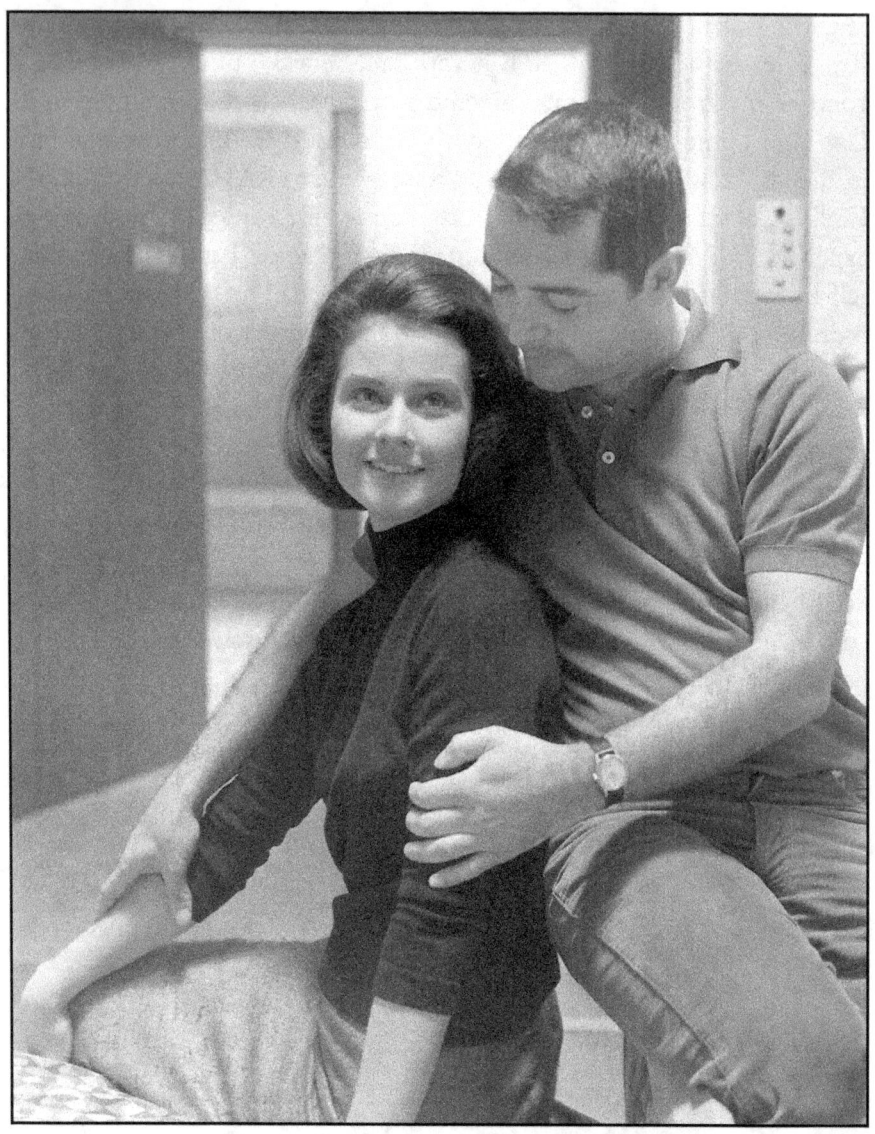

With Diane Baker on the set of *The Prize*.

them to wear a white dress shirt. I had the grip department bring out rolls of black grip cloth. Several hundred ponchos were made and hung over the heads of the non-union extras. From a distance, they all looked like they were wearing tuxedos. The union extras closest to the camera wore proper tuxedos.

Our script supervisor was a man named Stanley Scheuer. The script supervisor has one of the most important and difficult jobs on a film.

With Mark Robson.

They have to be sure that the dialogue is followed, and also to be sure that all the actors/movements are the same in each take. Additionally, the script supervisor must take the editor's notes. Stanley was one of the funniest men I ever knew. Incidentally, he was the script supervisor on *Cleopatra*, and when 20th Century-Fox had a trial investigating the mismanagement of *Cleopatra*, the studio asked Stanley to testify. Stanley said he would go to the trial only if his mother was invited.

Mark Robson had requested Stanley. Stanley was Mark's whipping boy. Often, if a director is upset with a star, rather than risking a confrontation, the director will take it out on someone else. In this case, Mark would turn on Stanley. Stanley didn't care, he was used to it. Once during a scene, Paul Newman asked Stanley whether the key was in his left hand or his right hand. Stanley said, "Yes." Stanley, who was in his late 60s, would always dye his hair with henna on the weekend. On Monday morning, the henna would be on his forehead. Bill Daniels began calling him "Red." Stanley would say, "Better men than you have insulted me." Stanley always ended up on top. In one particular scene, we were filming Paul inside a bedroom. The camera was outside the room at the doorjamb looking into the bedroom. Stanley was sitting along the wall. No way could he see the action in the bedroom. After several takes, Mark was frustrated with Paul about something. Mark turned to Stanley and sarcastically said, "Wouldn't you like to sit somewhere where you can see what's going on?" Stanley said without hesitation, "I thought I would sit here for the first ten takes and then go on the other side for the next ten takes."

After work one Friday, the key crew went to the San Pedro shipyards to look at a derelict ship that we were to film the following Mon-

On Sacramento location after passing my kidney stone.

With British actress Anna Lee.

day for three consecutive days. It was a filthy rat-infested ship. I said, "I don't think I'll be working in this hell hole. I'm planning to be sick for three days."

That Sunday I had a kidney stone attack and Brad rushed me to the hospital. The pain was excruciating. God was punishing me for being so smug. For the next three days while I was in the hospital, I drank beer and more beer, the theory being the more liquid I drank, the chance of passing the stone was surer. I thought I would leave the hospital a dipsomaniac but cured of my kidney stone. It seems the large kidney stone

E.G.R.

August 20, 1963

Dear Hank Moonjean:

No, I don't think it "corny" for you to have written me as you did. I've always had a warm feeling for you and have never been associated with a finer assistant director than yourself. In fact, I'm looking forward to the time when you will have attained the high potential which I recognize in you, and you will be my director in a picture rather than assistant director. I predict that you will be a great one.

Actually, I wasn't in a serious mood the time I called to your attention that you hadn't greeted me, -- it was just an impulsive comment, soon forgotten. However, whether or not we are objectively conscious of it, the primary purpose of practically everything we do is to make ourselves and others happy, and so human relationships are important, both on and off "the job", I feel. *You possess this quality in a great measure —*
Now that THE PRIZE is completed, I hope there will be other occasions for our working together, and please know that you have my best wishes for your continued and expanding success.

                                          Sincerely,

                                          Edward G. Robinson

EGR: BC

Mr. Hank Moonjean
2132 Laurel Canyon Blvd.
Los Angeles 46.

was at the lip of my bladder and all it needed was a little shove. Of course, I was also getting sedation. Edward G. Robinson visited me at the hospital. He said he wanted to make sure that I wasn't faking it. I went home on the third day and the three days of shooting in San Pedro went very well without my involvement. Everyone is expendable.

The next morning we all flew to Sacramento, California to film a night scene with Paul Newman on a bridge. We all checked into the local

Standing in for Paul Newman with Elke Sommer.

motel. The plane flight from Los Angeles must have jiggled the stone loose. I passed it. The stone was as big as a lemon seed. Those three days were the only times I missed work due to illness in my entire career. *The Prize* was a big hit at the box office. I had many more films to do with Paul Newman.

I followed *The Prize* with a small MGM film entitled *Drums of Africa* starring Frankie Avalon and Mariette Hartley. The best thing about the film was the footage taken from *King Solomon's Mines*. "Africa" was the Fox Ranch at Malibu, California. If you should ever have the misfortune of seeing this "dog" on television, look for the arrows sticking into the "rocks." Also, you might see the same extras, first as slave traders shooting at Arabs when actually the Arabs were the slave traders. We had a very small budget—small budget, small picture.

I discovered camels were the mode of transportation in the deep jungles as well as on the desert. The animal wrangler warned us about getting close to the camels. It seems that a camel can spit, with deadly accuracy, 12 feet into someone's eye, causing serious infection.

Not withstanding, there were laughs every minute. The funniest was a scene in which Mariette Hartley, one of the stars and a new MGM contract player, was playing the daughter of missionaries. The particular scene that I will never forget is that Mariette, Frankie and Lloyd Bochner (Another cast member) were enroute to the mission through the jungle. They come upon the smoldering mission that has been set afire by the nasty natives. Mariette is between Frankie and Lloyd. Bare in mind, that Mariette is a tall, sturdy woman. (And a method actress.} ACTION. The

With Mariette Hartley.

With Frankie Avalon.

men attempt to hold Mariette back. But she drags the 2 men across the rough barren ground about 30 feet before the director calls, "cut." This was the best shot in the movie, as far as I was concerned. The 2 men survived their ordeal. Unfortunately you will never see it. It remains in my memory.

Around this time, I worked on *How the West Was Won*. Everybody at MGM worked on this film—one way or another. It was a very long shooting schedule. There were three different directors on three different units—John Ford, Henry Hathaway, and George Marshall. Debbie Reynolds was the only participant who stayed through the entire film. I directed the sequences that separated the three sections of the film. I also directed Raymond Massey playing Abraham Lincoln. It was during this film that I realized I made the right decision to become a producer rather than a director.

Incidentally, two scenes in the film were taken out of *Raintree County*, which I worked on a decade earlier—the Cotton Blossom going down the Mississippi and the Civil War battle scenes.

Often I would play poker at Stuart Rosenberg's house. Other than Stuart's wife Margot, the other players were Jack Lemmon, his wife Felicia, Peter Falk and his wife, and occasionally the Milton Berle's. Milton's wife, during this period, was a retired WAC. She may have been an officer, but acted like a top sergeant. Berle was very funny and always "on". One of Milton's main claims to fame was that he was *extremely* well-endowed. Everyone in Hollywood knew it, and if they didn't, he made sure they did.

One poker evening, I brought a friend to the game. After introductions were made, Milton, suddenly with great relish, said to my friend, "Would you like to see it?" The WAC said, "For Christ's sake, would you put that fuckin' thing away." So much for decorum and new acquaintances.

Chapter 12
Molly Brown and Me

The Unsinkable Molly Brown was the first musical that I worked on from beginning to end as first assistant director. Again, I was with Debbie Reynolds—the hardest working actress in the film business. The MGM film also starred Harve Presnell, Ed Begley (my friend from *Sweet Bird of Youth*), Hermione Baddeley and Martita Hunt, the great British character actress whose face was her fortune, and what a face! The director was Charles "Chuck" Walters. Chuck was a difficult man. He didn't particularly like Debbie. He made no secret about wanting Shirley MacLaine to play Molly Brown. The studio told Chuck if he wanted to direct the film, he had to accept Debbie or they would get another director.

The producer was the veteran Lawrence Weingarten. The associate producer was Roger Edens, the brilliant composer and musical guru from the Freed Unit. There was an elaborate dance unit that was under the direction of choreographer Peter Gennaro. Peter was a small, vital man who had a speech impediment. When he spoke, he sounded like the cartoon character Sylvester the Cat. "A-five-and-a-shix-and-a-sheven-and-a..." Peter wore a hearing aid. Peter brought his assistant from New York City as well as two key dancers—Mary Ann Niles and Maria Karnilova. Both dance rehearsal halls were jumping. The very rare thing about *Molly Brown* was that virtually the entire cast either danced or sang or did both. Usually in most musicals, the two leads do the dancing and singing. Debbie was involved in every number. Peter would lay out the dance with a skeleton dance crew and with Margie Duncan, Debbie's dance-in. After Peter had worked out the dance routine to his satisfaction, he would show it to Debbie and Chuck. If it were approved, Debbie would start learning the routine. Unfortunately, Debbie didn't have much time to rehearse. She was needed with the first unit most of the time. At the same time, Roger Edens would be working on the songs, and the cast who had to sing would work with Roger on another unit until he was ready to record them.

Musicals are far more complicated than a straight film. Prior to the start of principal photography, there were extensive wardrobe and makeup tests done on Debbie. One afternoon en route to the projection room to view the tests, Peter Gennaro asked if he could join me. We entered the projection room and began watching the test. Most tests are shot without sound. As we are viewing the test, I see Peter banging on his chest and monkeying around with his hearing aid. He said, "I can't hear anything. I can't hear." I started to laugh. I said there was no sound. But he said that Debbie's mouth was moving. I said that Debbie's mouth never stops moving. Peter was relieved. Before the start of principal photography, all the songs are prerecorded. In the case of Martita Hunt, she was still in London. Her two lines for one song would be recorded when she arrived at the studio. When various cast members were not filming, they were either recording or with Gennaro rehearsing.

Morton Haack was the costume designer. Except for Martita Hunt, all the other cast members lived in Hollywood. Morton was able to measure, design and fit all the clothes at the studio. As for Martita, her measurements were sent to the studio from London. Haack had already designed and made her costumes. When Martita arrived at the studio, I met her at the main gate. She was a tall woman and wore a huge floppy hat much like Captain Bligh's. Martita must have been in her 70s. I thought she was the ugliest actress I had ever met. But her ugliness had a strange appeal. I escorted her to Helen Rose's salon, where Haack was temporarily headquartered. Haack had all of his costumes for Martita on dressmaker forms. I made the introductions. Haack asked Martita to go into the changing room and take off her clothes so that he could commence with the fittings. Within five minutes, Martita stepped out wearing only her hat and shoes. I thought that Haack was about to faint. Martita's breasts looked like deflated inner tubes. Her nipples were almost to her waist. Haack, turning his head away in dismay, asked her to put on her slip. Martita said, "I never wear undergarments." One of the seamstresses brought her a slip and the fittings began. Martita was cast as the Grand Duchess Elise Lupavinova. She headed the list of European royalty. The

The British Contingent, Hermione Baddeley on the left, Martita Hunt on the right.

other royal was a Greek actor named Vassili Lambrinos (we called him "Vaseline"). He played Prince Louis de Laniere.

Moyna MacGill, who was Angela Lansbury's mother, was part of the European royalty that Molly brought from Europe. During a very strenuous dance, Moyna fell and broke her arm. I called Peter Shaw's office. Shaw, an MGM executive and Moyna's son-in-law, immediately came to the set and took Moyna to the hospital. Several days later, Angela Lansbury came to the set with Moyna's costume. She said her mother wouldn't be returning but had enjoyed working on the film.

Martita, who liked a drink or four, was either feeling no pain or just drunk. Before appearing before the camera, she prerecorded a few lines for the "He's My Friend" number. In the scene in which Molly introduces the European royalty to Denver society, Martita was three sheets to the wind. Her entrance was to be made from the top of the staircase, down six or seven steps to a landing and down the last six stairs. I was worried that Martita might fall. I went to Walters. He said, "What do you want me to do about it?" I guess it was my problem. I got one of the special effects men to get me a metal waistband that stuntmen use. I took Martita aside and cut a two-inch slit in her dress at the waistline. "Dear boy, what the fuck are you doing?" I said, "Just relax." I started to insert the metal waistband under her dress and twisted it around like a belt. An eyelet, which was part of the metal belt, was at the base of Martita's spine.

The special effects man hooked a heavy wire through the eyelet and his assistant stretched the wire up to the scaffolding. This procedure took a half hour. I was holding up the company. Finally, we were ready to shoot, the camera turned. Action. Martita, who was the last of the "royalty" coming down the staircase, started her descent. The special effects man was guiding her along from the scaffolding almost like a puppet. At one point, Martita was actually off her feet. (If you should ever see *Molly Brown* you'll see a slight twisting motion.) As she was about to walk down the last set of stairs, Harve Presnell ran up to her and escorted her to Debbie. This action was not in the script. Harve thought she might fall. The major domo announces, "Her Royal Highness the Grand Duchess Elise Lupavinova." Martita actually made it without breaking her neck.

What followed was the largest song-and-dance number in the film. The entire cast was involved. Not only did we have the European royalty and the Denver social set, but also we had the Leadville crowd, stuntmen, scores of extras and musicians. The number began with the entire cast doing the "He's My Friend" number. Each actor did his turn—Ed Begley, Hermione, some of the Royals, Debbie and Harve and at one point Martita. This was all done to playback as all the actors had prerecorded the song earlier. The playback started with clicks. When Martita started her little dance, she ignored the clicks and heard herself singing on tape. She stopped dead in her tracks. "Who is that *dreadful* woman? Who is that dreadful woman imitating me?" Naturally, we stopped filming. I went up to her and said that was her voice. She had recorded it two weeks ago. "It is not." We began take two and the same thing happened. Martita refused to lip-synch to the song. Finally, Walters said to forget the playback. She did it her way. When she finished, she asked me if she could go home. "Dear boy, can I go home? I've done my fucking bit." I said she couldn't. When we reverse the camera, we would see her. She said, "Then, will you tell the fucking walk-ons to shut up." In England, the extras are called walk-ons. After several days, the sequence was completed. It remains the high point of the movie. Debbie's dancing has never been better.

One afternoon, Martita asked me to collect her living allowance check at the cashier. I said I couldn't do that. She had to pick it up herself. She said, "It's not dignified." Martita Hunt was a hoot.

The unqualified star of *The Unsinkable Molly Brown* was Debbie Reynolds. Debbie was the glue that kept the production together. As I mentioned earlier, no one works harder. She was more than generous with Harve Presnell. She helped him considerably, knowing it was his first time in a movie. Harve had created the role of Johnny Brown in the Broadway stage version but film was a new experience for him. Harve had a powerful voice. Debbie, knowing that Walters didn't want her (he made no secret of it), was determined to prove her capacity as an actress. And she did it. Debbie was nominated for an Oscar as Best Actress

We were shooting a big scene on Stage 30, when Debbie received a phone call, on her private line, from her assistant and arranger, Rudy Render. Rudy told Debbie that President Kennedy had been shot in Dallas. Everything came to a standstill. At that moment, we didn't know whether or not he was dead or alive. Someone brought out a radio and we all sat around trying to get the latest news. Some of the crew was crying. I called off the shooting for the rest of the day. Martita was pacing back and forth saying, "Dreadful Country. Dreadful Country." I told her to shut up. She said, "I need to go to a pub." I said there were no pubs nearby. She said there was one next door. She knew of the "Retake Room." We all eventually went home and the studio shut down for that terrible weekend of the funeral.

Hermione Baddeley played Buttercup Grogan, the mother of Denver's number one socialite. Amazingly, for an Englishwoman, she didn't drink, at least not during working hours. I met Hermione long before *Molly Brown*. It was at a party that Laurence Harvey gave. Harvey asked Hermione if she had ever met me. Hermione said, "No, but we've been exchanging glances." At the same party I met that great character actress Elsa Lanchester, Frankenstein's bride. What a fascinating face. The subject of garage sales came up. Elsa said, "I love garage sales. My entire house is a garage sale." Hermione was charming, witty, talented and well loved by everybody. We became lifelong friends. She reached fame by appearing in amusing London stage revues. She was called "the other Hermione." Hermione Gingold was her nemesis. They competed for every role. In *Molly Brown*, Hermione was Ed Begley's love interest. They both did a marvelous Irish jig in the movie. Ed had a ball on this film. He was a happy camper. Martita Hunt finally finished her role and was ready to return to London. She came by the soundstage to say her goodbyes. We were still filming. She said to me, "Dear boy, you've been a brick. It's been a great experience. It's been memorable." Movie star bullshit. I said, "Martita, I'm going to be in England right after we finish shooting." She

Rowe Wallerstein, my assistant and me carrying Debbie to the set.

said, "Dear boy, you must come up to my flat and have tea and watercress sandwiches." I said, "But I don't have your phone number." She said, "I'm listed."

I did eventually get to London. I had offices at Borehamwood, MGM's British Studio. One day I was sitting in Irene Howard's office and said I had a standing invitation to have tea and watercress sandwiches with Martita Hunt. Irene was head of casting and was also the sister of Leslie Howard. She looked like Leslie Howard. Irene said to be sure not to call Martita before 1 p.m. because she'll be hung over. I found her listed in the London phone directory—Hunt, M. 5 Primrose Hill. I waited until after one before I telephoned her. You couldn't mistake that high-pitched voice. "Hellooo."

I said, "Martita, this is Hank Moonjean."

"Whooo?"

I said, "Hank Moonjean."

Martita said, "I don't know any Hank Mooo."

I said, "I was the assistant director on *Molly Brown*."

She said, "Well, what do you want?"

I said, "You invited me for tea and watercress sandwiches when you were back in Hollywood."

She said, "There's no one here to make them," and then slammed the phone down. So much for being a "brick."

Molly Brown was a great experience for me. Debbie Reynolds and I became closer than ever. I did not enjoy working with Chuck Walters. He had a long mean streak. But I did get to visit scenic Colorado. And I enjoyed knowing Peter Gennaro, Mary Ann Niles and Maria Karnilova. Unfortunately, they have all passed on. But I shall always remember them.

Chapter 13
Peach and Beyond

At MGM, my next film was *A Patch of Blue* starring Sidney Poitier, Shelley Winters, Wallace Ford and newcomer Elizabeth Hartman. The producer was Pandro Berman and the director was Guy Green. I was both the unit manager and first assistant director. *Patch* was a "studio" film—only one week on location at the Westlake Park area of Los Angeles.

The story was about a poor blind girl who falls in love with a man who befriends her, not knowing he's black. Shelley Winters played the bigoted mother of the blind girl. Veteran actor Wallace Ford played the blind girl's grandfather. The most unusual aspect of this film was that it was the first time a white girl and a black man kiss in a film produced by a major studio. 1965 was still in the dark ages. When we shot this simple scene, studio police were posted at the stage entrances. No photographs were allowed. The set was partitioned off and all the nonessential crew was asked to leave the set just before we rolled the cameras. I think the entire episode was blown out of proportion. And I know it wasn't done for any publicity reasons.

Shelley Winters was a pain in the ass. But she was a "fun" pain in the ass. She would start drinking straight vodka during the day. She would insist on playing opera on her record player in her dressing room so loudly the crew was unable to hear instructions. She would often tell Green that no one told her what scenes she was to learn. Seldom did she know her lines. Green was getting on my back. I told my assistant that I would take care of Shelley in the future. At the end of each day, I would give her a written account of what time she was due in makeup, what time she was due on the set, and what scenes she was required to learn. She still wouldn't cooperate. Green consistently kept blaming me. Of all the Berman films that I worked on this was the first time I went to Pandro's office during a shooting day with a complaint. I asked my assistant to take over until I got back.

Pandro was the kind of producer who automatically assumed that whatever job you had on his films, you were the best at what you did. Pandro was very fond of me. I considered him my "Godfather." Pandro was never conscious of other people's importance; he didn't pander to stars or directors if they were in the wrong. Right was right and he would never pussyfoot around. I went to Pandro's office in the Iron Lung. His secretary Eleanor said that Pandro was waiting for me. Pandro always wore bedroom slippers in his office. He would throw one leg over the arm of the chair he was sitting on. "What's wrong kid?"

I said I was sorry to bother him but I needed his help. Shelley was the first star I could not handle. I told Pandro of her drinking, her lack of cooperation, her high-decibel opera playing, and everything else I could think of. Pandro buzzed Eleanor and said, "Call the set and have Shelley Winters come to my office immediately, even if we have to stop shooting."

I stood up and said, "I'll see you later," and started to leave. Pandro said, "Sit." What a situation to be put into. I still had six weeks more to work with Shelley. This was going to be embarrassing.

Pandro said, "I'll show you how to handle this situation." He buzzed Eleanor again and said. "Ellie, when Miss Winters gets here, have her wait. Just buzz me when she arrives." Pandro sat back and said, "And how have you been? The rushes look good. I think we have a winner." Pandro was making idle conversation. Within minutes, Eleanor buzzed to say that Miss Winters had arrived. Pandro said, "Keep her there for a few minutes and then have her come in." Pandro took the receiver off his private phone and placed it on his desk. Pandro winked at me.

The door opened and in walked Shelley. She looked straight at me. She knew exactly what was up. Whatever Shelley is, she is definitely not stupid. Pandro said, "Sit down."

Shelley, with great charm, cooed, "Pandro, darling, I..."

"Sit down. Hank tells me you've been drinking, always late, never prepared." (The list went on and on.)

Pandro pointed to the telephone. "I have Eileen Heckart on the phone in New York. She has always wanted to play your role. Now if you don't behave yourself, I will fire you and sue you for every penny you have."

With Guy Green in Westlake Park in Los Angeles.

"Pandro, darling, I promise to be good. Honest."

I got up and Pandro asked me to sit down again. Pandro said to Shelley, "Go down to the set and behave yourself. I don't want to hear any more complaints about you." Shelley left. Pandro placed the receiver back on the hook. "You won't have any more problems with her," he said. Pandro was right. Shelley was a pro for the remainder of the film. *And* she never held any animosity toward me for squealing on her.

Sidney Poitier, always the professional, was great to work with. This was my third movie with him. He was dating Diahann Carroll at the time. One night in Cohn Park on Lot 2, we were doing a rain sequence with Elizabeth Hartman and Sidney. Elizabeth had been left alone in the park. Her drunken grandfather had forgotten to pick her up. Sidney comes upon her. She is shaken and frightened. As we were filming in the "rain," I noticed the back of Sidney's hairline. It looked like he had a haircut. An actor cannot get a haircut during a production. His makeup man does the necessary trimming. Some films have a storyline that covers two days but it may take eight weeks to shoot. The hair has to be consistent. I asked Sidney if he had gotten a haircut. He said he hadn't. We continued to shoot in the rain. I kept looking at Sidney's hair. I would have sworn it had been cut. I said, "Sidney, are you sure you haven't had a haircut?" Sidney pulled me aside and put his arm on my shoulder. "Hank," he said. "You see, I'm a black man. When a black man gets his hair wet, the hair tightens up. I can't believe you are that observant." I was slightly embarrassed at my stupidity.

Elizabeth Hartman was from Youngstown, Ohio. *A Patch of Blue* was Elizabeth's first film and she received an Oscar nomination as Best Actress for her performance. She only made a few pictures after that. Not too many years later, she committed suicide. She was a strange and shy person. But she was sweet and everybody liked her.

Shelley Winters was a real character. After her meeting with Pandro, she became the epitome of a professional. She had a wicked sense of humor. She loved dirty jokes. For her performance in *Patch*, she won the

Elizabeth Hartman's first film – *Patch of Blue*.

With the great Sidney Poitier.

Best Supporting Actress Oscar.

I hadn't seen Shelley for many years. One day as I was waiting outside of Mike Nichols' apartment on Central Park West, standing by my limousine, Shelley ran up to me and said, "Are you my driver?" How quickly they forget. I worked on the two pictures she won Oscars for and she didn't know who I was. There won't be a third time. *A Patch of Blue* was a very successful film.

Shelley Winters trying to grab my privates.

Spinout is the only Elvis Presley film I received screen credit on. It was early in 1967. I was the Associate Producer. Although I worked on nearly all of Elvis' MGM films I wasn't given any credit because I only worked on them for a short time. On one occasion on the set, one of Elvis' cronies called me "Hank." Elvis blew up. He said, "Don't you ever call him by his first name again. You refer to him as Mr. Moonjean. He has an important job." I said to Elvis that I didn't mind, that everyone calls me Hank, but Elvis had an almost old-fashioned Southern propriety.

Once I went to Colonel Parker's office in the studio. I said, "Why is Elvis doing all these lousy pictures? The scripts are lousy. He has a director who is blind in one eye and can hardly see out of the other. Elvis is entitled to better scripts and better directors."

The Colonel said to me quite emphatically, "Stay out of it. You just make sure he sings eight songs. That's your only concern." Eight songs make an album. Elvis would make more money off the album than his movie salary.

Elvis and I often talked about doing an "important" movie in which he wouldn't have to sing. He had so much more acting talent than he was allowed to express in these movies.

After I left MGM and many years later, I read a short novella called *Being There*. I happened to be in New York at the time and I had recently met the author, Jerzy Kosinski. I made an appointment to see Jerzy at his apartment. The next day, I went to Jerzy and told him I had a great idea. What did he think about Elvis Presley playing the lead role of Chauncey Gardener? Jerzy thought for a minute and said he liked the idea. Jerzy gave me a year's option without any money being exchanged.

When I returned to Hollywood, I set up a meeting with George Cukor. Cukor once told me that he thought Elvis had the potential to be an important actor. Cukor said he would be interested in directing the film. I then went to Joe Esposito. Joe was the best of Elvis' "rat pack." Joe cared for Elvis and always had Elvis' interests at heart. I discussed *Being There* with Joe. He wasn't necessarily overcome with excitement. Joe knew that Elvis wasn't in any shape to discuss a film project. I hadn't a clue as to Elvis' condition. Shortly thereafter, Elvis was dead.

In all the years I knew Elvis, I never saw him take a drink, smoke a cigarette or even smoke a joint. I never heard Elvis say an unkind word about anybody. He was always the Southern gentleman. The film world lost a giant who never had the opportunity to fulfill his dreams. *Being There* was eventually made with Peter Sellers. The movie was excellent. It won many awards and accolades. The Sellers movie was not the story that Jerzy wrote. The lead character was a young handsome American stud—nothing like Peter Sellers. It would have been perfect for Elvis.

There were rumblings about *Who's Afraid of Virginia Woolf?* Several years had passed since the Cinecitta studio screening room where Elizabeth and Burton had rejected Irvin Kershner. Mike Nichols was set to direct this very important movie. My friend, Ernest Lehman, was to produce and write the script for Warner Bros. Elizabeth called me from New York City and asked me to meet with Nichols. Easter Sunday Nichols and I met at the Beverly Hills Hotel. Mike was charming and friendly but all the time weighing and analyzing me. You could tell he had a brilliant mind. How do you interview an assistant director? It's usually what you have heard about the individual from others. This time I had the star and the producer on my side. I did say to Mike that my long association with Elizabeth should not be a deterring factor. My allegiance would be to him and Elizabeth would acknowledge that. We spoke of a start date. He said the question of salary would be left up to Lehman. We shook hands and I left with the anticipation of being on a great film.

Later that evening, I received a phone call from someone who would not identify himself. He said for me not to count on doing *Virginia*

Woolf, that I would definitely not be on it. He hung up the phone. I was dumbfounded. I could hardly wait for the morning to find out exactly what happened. I knew it couldn't have been a crank-call because the man who called was privy to my conversation with Nichols. The next morning I called Nichols' office. I wanted an explanation. I never was able to speak to him. He was busy. I never told Elizabeth. I didn't want her involved. I assumed Nichols was worried about my closeness to Eliza-

With Glenn Ford.

beth and he had second thoughts about hiring me. I still would have appreciated an explanation. It was my first career disappointment. More disappointments would come.

My next film was *The Money Trap* for MGM. It was to star Glenn Ford, Elke Sommer, Ricardo Montalban, Joseph Cotten and Rita Hayworth. This was the first time I worked with Rita Hayworth. The director was Burt Kennedy—a charming and bright man. This was another "studio" film with the exception of one week of location work in the Hancock Park area of Los Angeles.

When you work with Glenn Ford, it's usually the same routine. The Saturday before the Monday start of his next film, he has a "party" at his multi-million-dollar estate in Beverly Hills with the principal actors and the key crew. Ford is known to be frugal. The word frugal is meant to be kind. You arrive at a designated time and have one drink. The one drink is measured with great accuracy. The bar lights start blinking before you can have another drink. The blinking light means the bar is closed and "dinner" is ready. We are ushered into a grand dining room. If there are twelve guests, you will find twelve hot dogs, twelve hot dog rolls, a bowl of potato chips, a jar of mustard and twelve paper napkins. No way could you get a second hot dog. After "dinner," we are led into his private projection room and have the privilege of seeing his last film. When the lights go on, you are expected to start saying your goodbyes.

One morning, I received a phone call from Howard Strickling's office telling me that Katharine Hepburn wanted to visit our set the next afternoon and to please keep a lookout for her. She would ask for me.

Many years before, in George Cukor's office, I had met Miss Hepburn. She was fascinated with my last name. She suggested that I change Moomjian to Moonjean. She said it would look better on the screen. At the time, I thought it was a good idea. But in retrospect, I'm not sure it was the right thing to do. I never denied my heritage. But the decision was already made.

I asked Virgil Apger, our set photographer, to take a picture of Miss Hepburn and me when she visited the set. The next day, sometime in the afternoon, the policeman at the entrance said there was a Miss Hepburn asking for me. I went to the door and greeted her. I'm not too sure she really remembered me but she was charming. She introduced me to her young nephew. I said, "We have been expecting you. Welcome." As we entered the stage, Miss Hepburn spotted Virgil creeping around ready to

With Agnes Moorehead and guest at a party.

shoot a photograph of us. "Virgil, you haven't changed and neither have I—*no* pictures." Hepburn acknowledged some of the crew by their first names. It was very similar to *Sunset Blvd.* when Gloria Swanson visited the soundstage after years of being away. I introduced Hepburn to Rita Hayworth and Burt Kennedy. It always surprised me when two famous actors such as Hepburn and Hayworth had never met. Hepburn said to excuse her intrusion and please go on with whatever we were doing. She stood next to me and her nephew, whispering. "That is called a boom and the sound goes through that pole. You know, I think we did *The*

Philadelphia Story on this stage…Fabulous Business. Fabulous Business." (At one time, I considered calling this book *Fabulous Business*.) After about 30 minutes, Hepburn left, thanking us, saying she hoped she hadn't been a nuisance.

Rita Hayworth, even in her later years, was still a beauty. I had never seen or met her before but we had many mutual friends. Despite having been a World War II pin-up girl, one of the biggest actresses in Hollywood, as well as a Princess, Rita was the shyest human being I had ever met. You felt uncomfortable being near her. More than likely this was the beginning of her Alzheimer's disease, which eventually killed her. I believe *The Money Trap* was one of her final films.

Rita presented the studio and the company with a major headache. She insisted that George Masters, a well-known hair stylist who was not a member of the hairdresser's union, was to do her hair and makeup. The union said it was absolutely impossible for Masters to work on the film. If he worked on the film, the union would strike. And it was not an idle threat. This issue became a serious problem. Rita said she would not do the film without Masters and that wasn't an idle threat either. The best thing about *Trap* was having Rita in the film. In her later years, Rita had become a formidable actress. I remembered the problems Elizabeth Taylor had with Guilaroff on *Cleopatra* during the London fiasco. That was resolved by Elizabeth having her hair done in a local inn very near the studio. Armed with this knowledge, I went to Bill Tuttle, the head of the MGM makeup department, with a proposal. Across the street from MGM, was the Aloha Motel. Many studio executives would hold "interviews" at the Aloha. I proposed that George Masters apply Rita's makeup and do her hair there. I told Tuttle that Rita's appearance in the film was imperative. Tuttle said he would discuss the situation with the union hierarchy. After several days, Tuttle called me into his office. The union had agreed to George Masters "doing Rita" at the Aloha but on these terms. Masters could not enter the studio for any reason; he could not view the rushes; he would not receive screen credit. Should he violate any of these rulings, the union would force the entire studio to go on strike. Masters agreed to do the film based on these terms.

I went to the Aloha and rented two adjacent rooms. I had a makeup table and full-length mirrors placed in the room. In the script, Rita is murdered by being thrown off the roof of a tenement building. That night scene was to be shot on Lot 2. We all knew that Rita had a drinking problem. She had been most professional during the entire film and had not once shown up drunk. However, we were going into the night schedule. I was apprehensive, and just in case of trouble I had a photo double for Rita standing by. The day began after lunch. We would shoot day scenes, break for dinner and resume with night shooting. Dinner would be served on Lot 2. Just before I called for the dinner break, I asked the two producers to take Rita to dinner or least bring Rita to Lot 2 and have dinner with the crew. They said they were too busy and couldn't be bothered. I was worried. I couldn't be in two places at the same time. I got things organized at the studio and had a driver take me to the Aloha—just five minutes away. I entered Rita's rooms.

In all my life, I never witnessed anything so bizarre. All the flowers that had been sent to Rita were strewn all over the room. Rita's hair was full of grease. It looked like axle grease; her caked hair was pointing in all directions. Her face was covered with red and black and orange grease paint. Masters and Rita were stoned out of their minds. Masters fluttered around the room like a crazed bird. Rita was intermittently laughing, yelling and crying. I said, "What in hell have you done with yourself? What are you made up for?" She said, falling over me, "No one told me how I should look when I'm thrown off the building." I said, "You look like you were thrown down the chimney." She started to laugh. I wanted to cry. To see such a beautiful creature in that condition. I told Masters to get the hell out of there and don't come back. I had no idea how he got home and I didn't care. I told my driver to go to the set and bring my assistant to the Aloha. I was careful not to let the driver know what was happening in the room. I was trying to protect Rita. Within minutes, my assistant arrived. I told him to stay with Rita and don't let her out of his sight. I went to Lot 2. They had completed dinner and were preparing the roof scene. I took Burt Kennedy, the director, aside and told him that Rita was in no condition to work. I was going to send her home. I went to Glenn Ford and told him what had transpired and asked him to help me get Rita home. After all, if it weren't for Rita Hayworth, Glenn Ford would be a nobody. Before *Gilda*, a very successful film with Rita, Glenn Ford only made mediocre films. Gilda placed Ford among the top stars of that period.

Ford said, "Fuck her. She's your problem, not mine." I lost whatever respect I had for him. I could have punched him in the mouth. With friends like that, who needs enemies?

I went back to the Aloha. Rita was incoherent. I sent my assistant back to the set and told him to send the car back for me. I called Hermes Pan, the famous choreographer, a very good friend of Rita's whom I knew well. I explained the situation. Hermes was there in twenty minutes, and he took Rita home. Fortunately, Rita's double worked out and shooting was not held up. A close-up of Rita lying in the gutter dying was required to complete the scene. I had the art department photograph the gutter and sidewalk so that it could be reproduced on the soundstage and we would be able to film Rita on the stage at a later date—during the day. The following week, we photographed Rita lying in the gutter on the soundstage. Rita made no mention of that night. Quite possibly she didn't remember it. I will never forget it.

Other than the Hayworth makeup incident the film was uneventful. Elke Sommer still pursed her lower lip. Ricardo Montalban and Joseph Cotten had lackluster parts. I was to work with Burt Kennedy again in the very near future. *The Money Trap* was not a blockbuster.

Before the film started, the production department tipped me off that Glenn Ford would come up to me every morning complaining that his wardrobe man had forgotten to lay out a jockstrap with the rest of his

With Rita Hayworth.

wardrobe. "Just ignore it. Tell him you'll look into it. Get him a jockstrap. Tell him it won't happen again." Ford must have 1,000 jockstraps at home. Ford had many idiosyncrasies. He refused to get on an airplane. He also suffered from "arithmophobia"—the fear of numbers. He would be afraid of doing a certain scene on a certain date. The numbers were "wrong." During the making of *It Started with a Kiss*, a film starring Debbie Reynolds and Ford, the studio went crazy trying to get Ford to

With the "swinging" nun.

With the "loving" nun.

Spain. Since he would not fly, arrangements were made for him to sail to Spain. But the cabin number didn't jive with the date or the level of the cabin. It went on and on until the studio made him fly.

Speaking of wardrobe men, Spencer Tracy had his own wardrobe man who strutted around the studio like he was a top executive. He was pampered and well paid. When the studio wanted Tracy for a film, they would submit the script to his wardrobe man. If the wardrobe man liked the script, Tracy would consider doing the film. Otherwise, Tracy would not be interested.

I was immediately assigned to another Debbie Reynolds picture—*The Singing Nun*. It was to be directed by the veteran Henry Koster. I loved Henry. Everybody loved Henry. The producer was someone named John Beck. The cast consisted of Greer Garson, Ricardo Montalban, Katharine Ross, Ed Sullivan, Chad Everett and the Fabulous Redhead, Agnes Moorehead. The story was about the Belgian nun, Soeur Sourire, who became a world-famous singing sensation.

The first thing we did was to take Debbie and a small unit to Brussels to do some second unit shooting for a couple of weeks. We then returned to the studio to resume shooting. From the beginning, the script needed a great deal of work. Henry Koster had a terrific sense of humor. He had a strong Hungarian accent. I would occasionally say, "Kill the juice," meaning turn off the electricity. Henry would say, "What do you have against the Jews?"

Henry often would come up to me and say, "Hank, can I go home? I am too rich and too old to be here."

"Henry, but you just got here," I would reply. Henry did not like the film and he wasn't overjoyed with Debbie. Debbie had her own ideas. But Henry, reluctantly, went along—bored and not really interested. He had lost his zest. This film became his swan song.

In the middle of the *Nun*, I got a call from back east. It was someone calling from the *Virginia Woolf* company. They were having trouble with the first assistant director that Mike Nichols hired and I was asked to take over. I said I wasn't available. The next evening I received another phone call. I said I was still not interested. The third morning I received a phone call from Elizabeth. "Hank, baby, we need you. I need you. Richard needs you."

"Elizabeth," I said, "I'm in the middle of a film. I can't leave."

She said she would call someone at MGM and get me off the film. "I really need you."

"I'm working with Debbie," I said.

Elizabeth said, "Fuck Debbie."

I said, "You fucked Debbie once but you can't fuck her a second time."

I heard Burton in the background say, "I don't know what all the fuss is about. It's like hiring the upstairs maid." That dumb son of a bitch

Carrie Fisher and Elisa Rich, Margie Duncan's daughter.

had no idea how important a good first assistant director is to a film. He should have guessed we were not just part of the scenery since they were prepared to fire the one they had.

In a recent interview, Ernie Lehman related this episode. Ernie was sorry. Elizabeth was sorry and I understood Mike Nichols was sorry as well. I would have never left Debbie. Never. Besides, my standing in the business would have suffered. You don't ditch one movie for the chance to

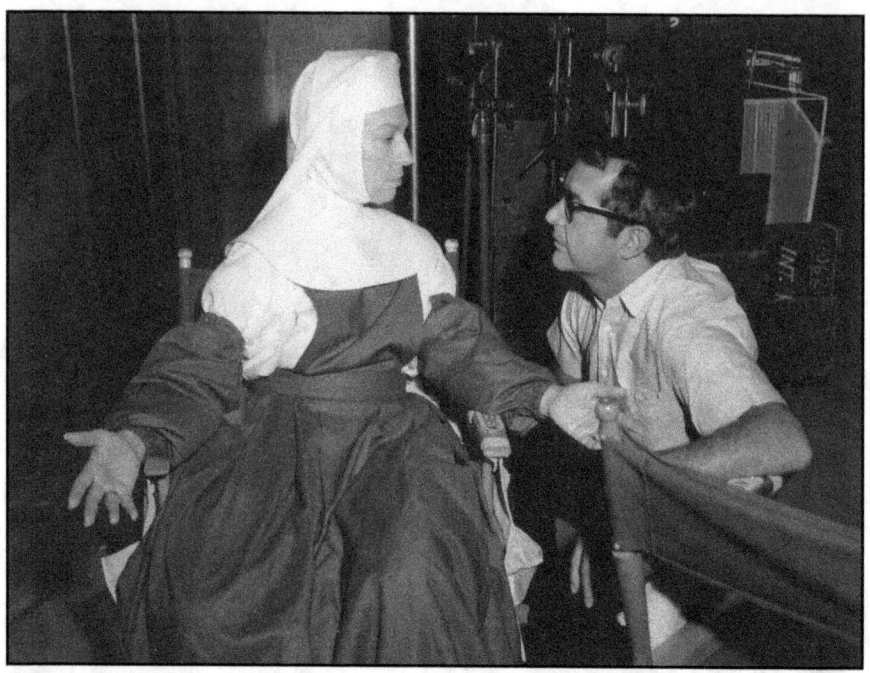

With Agnes Moorehead.

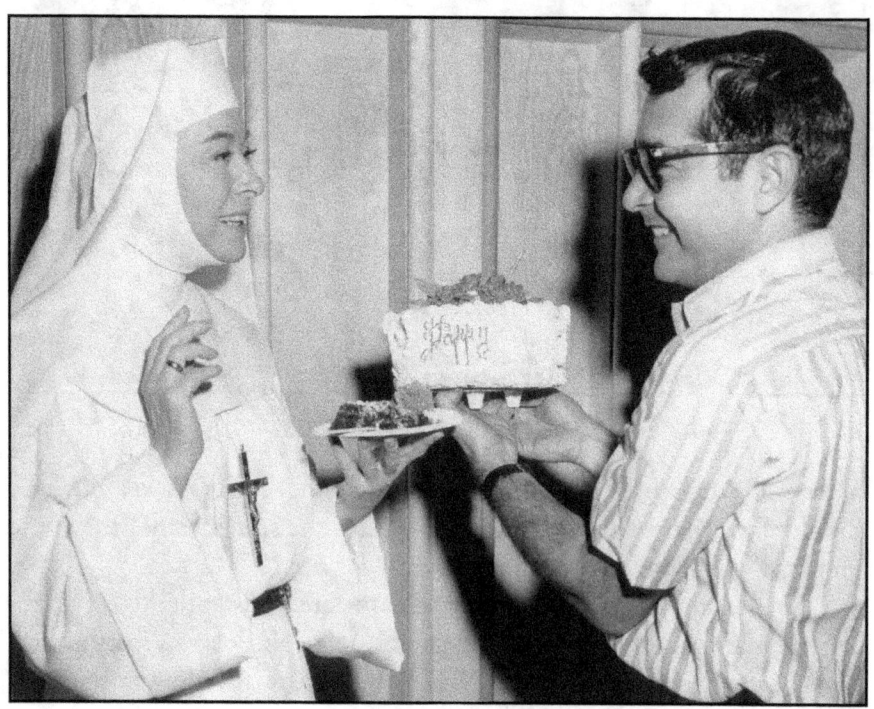

With Greer Garson.

work on a more appealing or important one—it's very unprofessional. Should you make such a movie, it would get around to the various studios.

Most professional actors know that the crew is responsible for making a film. Without them, there is no film. Most often, the crew roots for the success of the film, the success of the director and the performances of the actors, and one of the most important jobs on the film is the first assistant. He sets the tempo, the mood and the pace. He is a diplomat, a psychiatrist and an organizer.

The Singing Nun floundered along. Katharine Ross broke her arm horseback riding. Henry was becoming more and more remote. I was caught in the middle, and I just kept trying to keep the show moving.

Finally, Greer Garson reported to work. She was a welcome change, brightening all our moods. Her arrival was a red-letter day at MGM. The studio refurbished her *Mrs. Miniver* stage dressing room. I asked Henry what time he thought we would get to Miss Garson in the morning. Henry said 10 a.m. Her first day was on a small stage. We could not get her dressing room on the soundstage—only Debbie's. Miss Garson arrived at her dressing room, which looked like there had been a recent funeral, with flowers overflowing the room, pouring into the passageway. Most of the executives came to welcome her. After all, Miss Garson had been their biggest star during the war years. Unfortunately, 10 a.m. came and went. 11 a.m. came and went. I would go out to her dressing room and apologize for the delay. "Dear boy, I understand completely." While we were shooting with Debbie, I looked over my shoulder and saw Miss Garson sitting in her chair on the stage. I went up to her and said, "Miss Garson, we will be getting to you shortly."

"Thank you, dear boy."

I went back to the camera, which was in the opposite corner from where Miss Garson was sitting. Finally, Henry said we were ready for Miss Garson. I asked my assistant to get Miss Garson. From the far corner of the stage, he yelled, "HEY, GREER! YOU'RE WANTED ON THE SET!" Koster rolled his eyes. We had "Miss Garson-ed" her to death and now this. I told my assistant that I could have yelled just as well. I went to her quickly and said, "We are ready for you now, Miss Garson." She said, "That's better." (Of all my anecdotes, this one was Burt Reynolds' favorite.)

One of the nuns was to be played by a black actress. I tested Pearl Bailey, Cicely Tyson, Dorothy Dandridge, Juanita Moore and two or three other black actresses. All the nuns were on the stage at the same time—all in flowing white habits. Dorothy Dandridge was so drunk she barely was able to

The "singing" trio. Henry Koster, Debbie and me.

stand up. She was reeking with booze. It was sad to see someone so beautiful and so talented in that condition. Pearl Bailey, who was Debbie's choice, kept saying to me, "Give Dandridge the part. She needs it. She still thinks she's 'Bess' (from *Porgy and Bess*)." That test was probably the last time Dorothy Dandridge was in front of a camera. Although Pearl was Debbie's choice, the studio couldn't get insurance on her because of her heart condition. Pearl managed to live many more years. Juanita Moore was selected. She was the perfect choice. She was jolly and had a smile from here to there.

One morning on Lot 3, we were shooting a scene with Debbie. Quite often there would be other companies shooting on the lot at the same time. Lot 3 covered hundreds of acres.

I noticed my crew dwindling. "Where is everyone going?" Someone said there was a big fight going on near the Western Street. So we all rushed to see what was happening. It was probably more interesting than what we were doing. Debbie and I joined the crowd.

Sam Peckinpah, the mad director, was on top of someone, choking him. An assistant director standing nearby said, "Sam Peckinpah is strangling his script supervisor. But don't worry, they are best of friends. This happens regularly." It seemed so matter-of-fact. I guess the script supervisor mismatched something.

There was an executive at the studio that had a lesbian daughter. I won't reveal the executive's name. And I will call the daughter Phyllis, because she would want to be called "Phil" in any case. Phil was the butchest girl I had ever met. Before I began work on any MGM film, I would get a phone call from the executive asking me if there was a small role for Phyllis. It seems that Phyllis wanted to be an actress and wanted to become a member of SAG (the Screen Actors Guild). In order to receive a SAG card you must speak a line in a movie. This was not an easy request. I would take one look at Phil and know there wasn't a part, however small, that I could use her in. When I read *The Singing Nun*, I thought maybe I could use Phil as a nun. We needed twelve nuns for various one-liners. I went to Henry and asked him what he had thought of my idea. Henry liked and respected the executive as well. I went to see the executive who was extremely pleased that I was finally able to cast her. Phil was ecstatic. She went to wardrobe and was fitted in a nun's outfit. I said to my assistants that whenever Phil was in a scene, make sure she was seated. I didn't want her "thumping" through the set. The film went on and Phil was very professional—she hadn't done anything yet but sit. But we hadn't gotten to her one line as yet.

The day of reckoning. Phil's scene is upon us. The setting is in the office of Mother Prioress (Greer Garson). She is at her desk opening her mail. At this point, Sister Ann (Debbie Reynolds) is stationed in Africa. As the Mother Prioress opens a letter, she beams with excitement and walks to the convent room where the eleven nuns and Phil are wrapping bandages for the Sisters in Africa. She announces that she has received a letter from Sister Ann. One nun had to react verbally to the news. Phil was perfect for the one-liner. We had a rehearsal with Greer and the other nuns and we began lighting the shot. After about thirty minutes, we were ready to shoot. We got Greer and all the nuns in place. Action. The camera was on Mother Prioress and as she stood, she walked to the convent room, waving a letter. The camera panned with her as she reached the threshold of the room revealing the twelve nuns. "Sisters, Sisters, a letter from Sister Ann." Suddenly, from out of nowhere, we heard Phil's basso profundo "READ IT, MUDDER!" Henry was shaken by this mysterious unexpectedly masculine voice. I couldn't stop laughing. Another Moonjean discovery. Needless to say, we had to loop the line. But Phil got her SAG card and we made the executive happy.

During production, I was called to Benny Thau's office in the Iron Lung. I had never been in his office. Thau was a small man who had the second most important position at the studio. He dealt mainly with con-

Trying to talk Henry Koster into not quitting the picture.

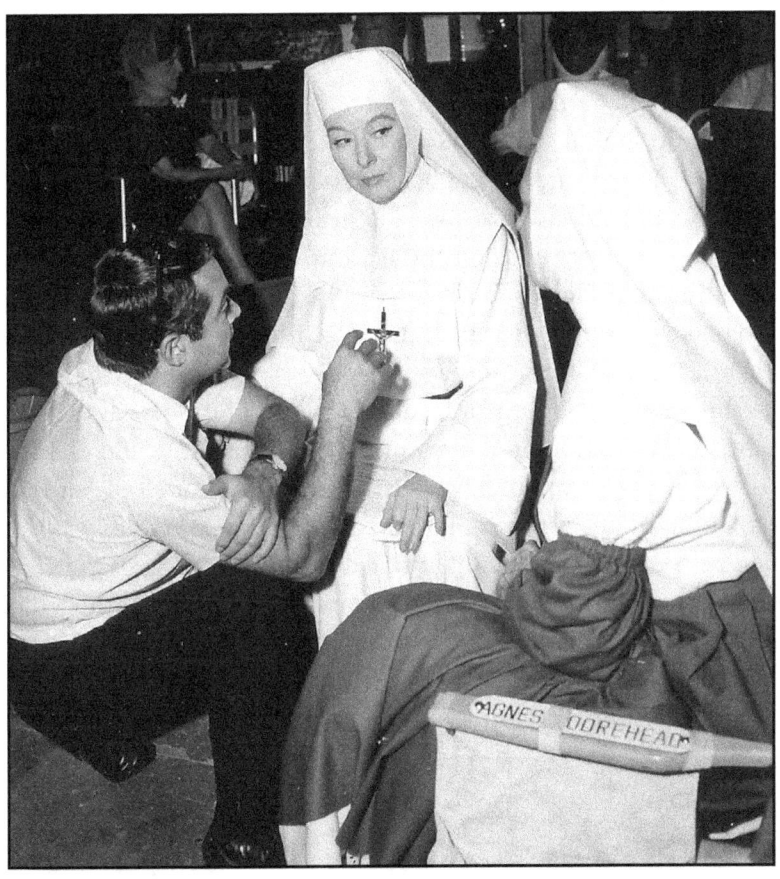

With Greer Garson.

tract actors. He had a large office and a huge desk with a glass top. I assumed he called me to ask me about *The Singing Nun*. Thau had a very, very low voice. I couldn't hear him. I was practically draped over his desk trying to hear what he was saying. To this day, I don't know what he was talking about. Every time I would say, "I can't hear you, Mr. Thau," his voice would get lower. I finally said, "I'll look into it," and left. I never knew exactly what he wanted.

The end of the *Nun* is set in Africa. Sister Ann has been assigned to a hospital in the jungle. I hired a black extra to be a nun in some of the scenes. These scenes were shot on Lot 3 near Tarzan's lagoon. When Margaret Booth, the wicked witch of Culver City who edited out African-American performances for the southern audiences, saw the rushes she became hysterical. She went to Ed Morey, the new head production manager, and wanted me fired. Morey called me into his office. He said Booth wanted to know why I put a black nun in those scenes. How stupid of me. I don't know what got into me. I never gave it a serious thought. Certainly, why should a nun in the heart of Africa be black? It makes no sense. I said, "Tell Booth to look up page 126 in her script." I walked out of Morey's office. Page 126 indicated that a black nun was helping Sister Ann.

The Singing Nun was a flop. The real nun, Soeur Sourire, made a fortune, gave up the sisterhood and became an "outed" lesbian and eventually committed suicide. You must give Debbie credit. She worked very hard to make the film a success. It just wasn't there. We all did our best to help her. It was not meant to be.

While at MGM, John Ford, considered one of the best directors of all time, began production on a film entitled *7 Women*. It would be his final film. I would have loved to have been on that film but all of Ford's films were a "family affair"—much like Alfred Hitchcock. The film was set in a Chinese Missionary Compound. It starred Patricia Neal, Margaret Leighton, Betty Field, Flora Robson, Mildred Dunnock (Elizabeth Taylor's mother in *BUtterfield 8*), Sue Lyon, Anna Lee and the only male, Eddie Albert. A week or so into production, Patricia Neal had a massive stroke, which was near fatal, and Anne Bancroft replaced her. The Ford set was a closed set—

Koster directing Debbie.

positively no visitors. One of the assistant directors was Rowe Wallerstein, a great guy who had assisted me on many films. I said to Rowe, "I know it's a closed set but if there is ever a chance to smuggle me in without you getting into trouble, I would be grateful." Rowe said, "I doubt it but I'll try." I wanted to see the master at work.

One morning about 8 a.m. my office phone rang. It was Rowe. He said to meet him by the schoolhouse. (MGM had its own little red schoolhouse where many of the child stars got their education.) Rowe said he could get me on the set. But he wanted to explain the situation. It seems that on the previous day, while Ford was staging a scene with the entire cast around the mission's dining room table, Betty Field, one of the missionaries, interrupted Ford with a question. Ford became irritated, got up and went home.

So, now it's the next day and they plan to pick up exactly where Ford left off. It was a beautiful sunny California day. Rowe took me onto the stage and hid me behind one of the dressing rooms. I could see everything. It was near 9 a.m. The entire cast assembled in the exact positions they were the previous day, like good soldiers. The set was already lighted. The camera was in position. John Ford's chair was next to the camera. Lew Borzage, an accordionist, worked on most of Ford's films. Borzage played mood music whenever Ford wanted to be inspired. Everything was ready. There were a few whispers but every actor and crewmember was in position. There was an old-timer assistant prop man who worked with Ford in his silent days. The prop man had a clubfoot. He was stationed at the stage entrance waiting for Ford's arrival.

On the dot of 9 a.m., the stage door opened and a stream of bright sunlight poured onto the stage entrance. Out of it stepped John Ford. Lew Borzage started to play "Red River Valley" on his accordion. The prop man with the clubfoot approached Ford. Ford was fumbling with his eye patch trying to put on a pair of glasses. Clubfoot extended his arm and Ford rested his arm upon Clubfoot's arm. Together, they limped, toward Ford's chair next to the camera. Ford reached the chair and the moment his butt touched the seat, the accordion music stopped—like clockwork. Ford said, "Good morning. Are we ready to work this morning?"

Suddenly, Betty Field, who was the cause of the problem the day before, spoke up. "Mr. Ford, about yesterday, I…"

Ford stood up and turned. "Red River Valley" started up again. Clubfoot limped over to Ford, extending his arm and they walked to the stage entrance limping. Ford was gone for the day. All the actors pounced on Betty Field. "Why did you speak up?" "You should have kept your mouth shut." "You know he's touchy."

Betty said in an angry voice, "I'm an actress. I'm entitled to speak my mind." This was my close encounter with John Ford. I didn't know whether or not to laugh or to cry. "Red River Valley" is a very sad song, but I decided to laugh. What I just witnessed would make a fabulous scene in a movie. Rowe told me that Betty Field was told that if she ever spoke up to John Ford again, she would be replaced.

Chapter 14
Cool Hand Luke

Cool Hand Luke is the film I'm asked about most often. It seems that it is everyone's favorite. It happens to be my favorite, too. The film starred Paul Newman, George Kennedy, Jo Van Fleet, Strother Martin and Dennis Hopper. The producer was Gordon Carroll. The director was Stuart Rosenberg. The cameraman was Conrad Hall. The production manager was Arthur Newman, Paul's older brother, and the script supervisor was Betty Crosby. The year was 1967. We shot most of the film in Stockton, California, even though the book is set in the Deep South. The interior of the prison barracks was built on a soundstage at Warner Bros., the studio that produced the film. The only other thing we shot at the studio was the opening scene of Luke cutting off the heads of parking meters. *Luke* was a difficult film. It was hot, dusty and quite physical. The entire cast and crew were housed in the same motel in Stockton. We worked on a six-day schedule. Each morning, everybody would board the busses to go to a nearby location. *Cool Hand Luke* was an assistant director's dream. Why? Because all the actors were chained together. And there was never any question as to who you were next to. I never got any flack from the actors such as, "That's Paul's scene and I'm not required."

"Yes, you are, because you are chained three bodies away from Paul, and we will miss seeing you."

The script was written by Frank R. Pierson and Donn Pearce, and was based on Pearce's book. The characters all had odd prison nicknames; Tramp, Alibi, Big Blondie, Society Red, Koko, Blind Dick, Gambler, Loudmouth, Sleepy, etc. The week before shooting started someone decided to arbitrarily switch the names of all the characters around. Alibi became Blind Dick, Koko became Loudmouth, Big Blondie became Sleepy, etc. Betty Crosby and I were getting mixed up. Rosenberg would say to me, "Get so and so." Betty and I would figure he means Blind Dick who used to be Alibi. I finally wore a card with all the names around my neck indicating who was who then and who was who now. Betty still didn't know if Big Blue was the dog or the dog's caretaker.

Many of the extras playing prisoners had no experience in making movies. A few of them were picked up on Los Angeles' skid row. They were not very cooperative. When we were ready to shoot, I'd call for all the actors to take their places. The responses were varied. "Fuck you." "Kiss my ass." "Get lost." "Don't fuck with me." This went on shot after shot. I was getting frustrated.

I went to Rosenberg and said, "You know, a word from you would make my life easier."

"Look, these people are animals," Rosenberg said. "I don't want them to feel regimented. I want them to act like animals."

"Okay," I said. "If you have the time, I have the patience."

Often, some of them would be smoking a joint. Some of them didn't even know where they were. We had one actor with the name of Tattoo. I had the makeup man draw a figure of a naked girl on his chest and fill it in with color. I, then, had the still man take a Polaroid of the tattoo so that each day the makeup man would match the original design. The makeup man never had to do it a second time. He just had to touch up the color because Tattoo never took a shower for the entire production.

Several times, we shot scenes of the prisoners coming back to the compound after the day's roadwork for head count. They were to count off numbers as they entered through the gate into the prison compound. "One, two, three, six, ten…" CUT. Rosenberg would back them up. ACTION. "One, two, buckle my shoe…three, four…open the door…" CUT. This would go on take after take. I must admit it was very funny.

Betty Crosby was the only female on the crew; except for the one day that Jo Van Fleet played Paul Newman's mother, and another day when Joy Harmon played the girl washing the car. Betty took all sorts of abuse from the actors. Every swear word was said fifty times a day. One night Betty came to my room in tears. She said she was going to quit the picture.

"I've heard all those words before," Betty said. "I even know what some of them mean. I grew up with two brothers so that's not the main problem." The straw that broke the camel's back was when Ralph Waite entered the "box." The box was like a narrow phone booth cage where prisoners were placed in for insubordination. "I was shocked!" Betty cried. "He wore no undershorts and was completely naked. I've seen naked men before, but I was married to them and I wasn't prepared to see a naked actor."

I felt terrible. I said I had too much respect for her to force her into doing something she didn't want to do.

"Why don't you sleep on it?"

Betty shook her head, "I'm leaving as soon as you get a replacement."

I told Rosenberg that Betty was quitting. Rosenberg liked Betty. The actors and crew liked Betty. I loved Betty. Rosenberg ordered flowers to be sent to Betty. We wrote a card. "Dear Betty, please don't go. We all love you. So some of us swear a little. So what the fuck!" When Betty received the flowers, a box of candy, and the note, she fell apart with laughter. Betty stayed on. I think the box of candy did the trick. I spread word among the actors to watch their mouth around Betty. They couldn't do enough for her. But the swearing stopped only for a day or two.

Every night, an alternating seven of us would play cards in the poker room either before or after dinner. It was great fun and lots of laughs. Paul Newman, after his nightly sauna, would come into the room wrapped in a towel with $200 folded over his waist. We fought to give Paul a seat. He would play for about twenty minutes and lose it all. He'd say, "I'll see you tomorrow night." Paul was not a good poker player. One night, one of the card-playing actors invited a stranger passing through Stockton to join us. The stranger said he had heard about the game. He would like to throw us a party. So that night six of us and the stranger played poker. The stranger had an attractive wife who was mixing drinks and making sandwiches for all of us. All was very friendly. The next day on the set, we were talking about last night's card game. Then and only then, did we realize we were taken. We figured between us, we lost over $3,000. The "kind" couple had checked out of the motel early that morning.

Everyone living together in one complex has its advantages and also disadvantages. Once, in the middle of the night, I would get a call from the night manager. "Do you have a fat actor working on your picture?"

"I have several fat actors," I said. "What's the problem? You know it's three o'clock in the morning?"

"Well, your fat actor just bit the ankle of one of our female guests."

"I am only responsible for the fat actors during working hours." I hung up the telephone.

A few nights later, around one in the morning, I received a call from one of my actors. This appeared to be more of a serious problem. "Come to the parking lot right away, 'Rabbitt' [Marc Cavell] just got his balls smashed in the door of his car." That must have hurt. I quickly put on my clothes and ran down the hallway. All the way to the parking lot, I was trying to figure out how one would get his balls caught in a car door. I could understand the other private part getting caught, but the balls? I got to the parking lot and "Rabbitt" was rolling on the ground in tremendous pain.

"Marc, how did it happen? No, seriously, *how* did you do it?" Marc wasn't in the mood for explanations. He screamed, "Take me to the hospital, please!" Some of the actors helped Marc get into my car and I drove to the Stockton hospital. On the way, I kept wondering how this could have happened. I got Marc to the emergency room. A doctor saw him immediately. He gave Marc a sedative and Marc finally passed out. I asked the doctor how he thought this could have happened. He said he hadn't a clue. Marc was in the hospital for a week. When he returned to the set, everyone wanted Marc to restage the incident, but he refused. It still remains a mystery.

Jo Van Fleet, who played Susan Hayward's mother in *I'll Cry Tomorrow*, came to Stockton to do one scene with Paul, as his mother. The scene took only one day to shoot. If she had more to do in the film, she would have gotten an Oscar nomination for sure. She was that good. In a subsequent scene, when Luke finds out that his mother has died, he walks into the barracks and climbs up on his upper bunk. All the prisoners in the barracks watch Luke as he reaches for his banjo. He softly starts to sing a spiritual as the camera slowly moves in on him, tears run down his cheeks. I think that shot was about the best piece of acting Paul Newman had ever done. I also believe that *Cool Hand Luke* was Paul's best film. By the way, he did that shot in one take.

George Kennedy, as Dragline, was brilliant in *Luke*. George was a real pro and a gentleman. He didn't horse around like the other actors. He just minded his own business. I imagine he realized he had a great

Holding Jo Van Fleet.

part and he was going to make the best of it. A role like Dragline comes along once in a lifetime. George won the Academy Award for Best Supporting Actor for his role. He deserved it. It couldn't have happened to a nicer guy.

During production of *Luke*, I lost a very close friend. Her name was Mary Barron Hilton Saxon. She was the first Mrs. Conrad Hilton and the mother of Nick, Barron and Eric, sons of Conrad. Mary was also

Tough day on the set. Wayne Rogers in the background.

Elizabeth Taylor's first mother-in law. Mary had a fantastic personality and a great wit. I only mention this now because when I left to go on location for *Luke*, she said she had a premonition that she would never see me again. Unfortunately, this proved to be true. I was a pallbearer at her funeral.

Everyone's first question to me about making *Cool Hand Luke* inevitably concerns the hard-boiled egg-eating contest. Paul Newman never swallowed one egg. He would bite an egg and chew on it, and after the cut, he would spit it out. We had buckets all around him. This went on egg after egg. Every student who hopes to be a film editor should study this egg-eating contest. The cutting was excellent. As for the "full stomach," Paul could contort his stomach so that he looked bloated. Paul had a routine. At the end of the day, Paul would drink a six-pack of beer and then take a long hot sauna. In all the years I knew Paul, his weight never varied.

Many evenings Paul would sit at the first banquette table in the motel's dining room, with oil and all sorts of herbs in front of him, trying to concoct a new salad dressing. I'd walk by and he would say, "Sit down and try my new salad dressing, Sport!" I once saw Paul using water in his concoction and I said, "You are not suppose to use water in an oil

Boring???

dressing. That's just not done." How wrong could I be? Paul has made a fortune with his salad dressings as well as other Newman products, and all profits are given to various charities. Paul, and his wife Joanne Woodward, are very caring people, none nicer.

The second most asked about scene in *Cool Hand Luke* was the one of "Lucille" washing her car. The actress' name was Joy Harmon. Rosenberg decided to shoot the scene in two sections. The first section was the chain gang spotting the girl—only we didn't have the girl at the location. They reacted to no one. Rosenberg was afraid the chain gang would go ballistic. They were all so horny. The only actor who actually worked with Joy was George Kennedy. George was the one calling out "Lucille" and salivating. Rosenberg did a brilliant job filming Joy.

It could be one of the most erotic scenes ever shot by a major studio. It was extremely sexy, extremely suggestive and at the same time in good taste. You thought any second the safety pin holding her blouse shut would snap open and her huge breasts would pop out. And all those soap suds. That sequence was one of the high points of the film.

"What we got here is a failure to communicate." That line from *Cool Hand Luke* is remembered by millions of movie fans all over the

"Showering" with Paul Newman.

world. Strother Martin uttered those words. Strother was a brilliant character actor with an unusual voice. He played small roles in scores of films and in his later years he was more widely appreciated, getting better roles. When Strother finished his work in *Luke*, he came to the set and kissed every man on the cheek, saying he was sorry to be leaving. He went to Betty Crosby and shook her hand. After realizing what he had done he said, "I think I'd better see my shrink. I need help."

Donn Pearce, who wrote the novel and screenplay, was an actual convict on a chain gang. He played one of the convicts in the movie. I think his acting role in the film was part of his author's contract. Even though *Cool Hand Luke* is supposed to be a novel, I'm certain that the book was autobiographical. Donn would strut around the set. He was proud of his background. Not everybody can be on a chain gang. Pearce took great pride in showing everybody how he could get his leg chains over his head. He would give demonstrations on request. He never got out of his convict's uniform on location. Pearce thought the entire company was "queer" and he had no use for "Hollywood trash." He thought we were ruining his book. No one paid any attention to him.

Morgan Woodward played Boss Godfrey—the guard with the mirrored sunglasses. It was Morgan's first film. The publicity at the time of *Luke's* release was that Morgan might be the first post-silent era actor to win an Academy Award nomination without ever uttering a word in the entire film.

Betty Crosby, who was loved by everybody, was given a plaque at the end of the film. It read:

>
> Presented To
> Betty Crosby
> For Gallantry
> At the Battle
> Of Stockton
> Love
> *Cool Hand Luke* Co.

I also was presented with a gift from the cast. Cliff James made a speech on behalf of all the actors. I opened a small box. There was a Derringer revolver in the box. The box had an inscription on a gold plaque. It read:

> To
> Henry Moonjean
> For Contribution Above And
> Beyond the Call of Duty
> *Cool Hand Luke* Cast

I was touched. As I said before, it was the film I enjoyed the most. Many of the actors went on to bigger and better things. Ralph Waite became Papa Walton and ran for Congress. Joe Don Baker became a leading man on several films. Wayne Rogers was a big hit on *M*A*S*H*. Harry Dean Stanton and James Gammon became respected character actors. Lou Antonio became a fine director. And I am still trying to figure out how "Rabbitt" got his balls caught in the car door.

Chapter 15
Three More Comedies

he Odd Couple was my first picture at Paramount. This successful film starred Jack Lemmon and Walter Matthau. The versatile Neil Simon wrote it. The producer was Howard W. Koch. The director was Gene Saks. Before the start of principal photography, we all sat around a table and read the script. Every so often, Neil Simon would laugh. It was a strange laugh—more like a short yelp. A very odd man.

Howard Koch sent me to New York City to film some establishing shots around the red light district on 42nd Street, and also along Riverside Drive. With the exception of shooting one week in New York, the entire movie was made on the Paramount lot. Once, when we were in New York, we were shooting with Matthau around Amsterdam Avenue, and Matthau spotted his mother on the street. He yelled out in the middle of a take, "Hey, Ma, I'm shooting around the corner. I'll see you later." We had to shoot the scene over. I thought Walter Matthau was a better comedian than Jack Lemmon. Matthau was more spontaneous.

After filming in New York, we began shooting in continuity at the studio. The first two days of filming had to be reshot because the apartment looked too neat. We added more newspapers, cigarette butts and beer cans. We discovered we had to exaggerate everything to get the effect we were trying to reach—a complete mess.

Our director Gene Saks, resided in New York City. I telephoned his apartment and asked to speak to Mr. Saks. The voice at the other end said, "He's not in." I said, "May I speak to Mrs. Saks?" The rough voice said that she was Mrs. Saks. I said, "No, you don't understand. I want to speak to MRS. Saks." The voice barked back. "OH, But I AM Mrs. Saks." I thought it was a man. It was Beatrice Arthur, Gene's wife. Talk about embarrassment. Nothing too noteworthy happened on the set of *The Odd Couple*. The "Pigeon Sisters" were amusing and the four poker players were all pros. Midway in the film, Matthau turns on the radio to listen to a ballgame in progress. You hear the announcer say, "And Hank Moonjean goes up to bat." To think that I am immortalized in a Neil Simon script and film.

The Secret Life of an American Wife was a 20th Century-Fox film. It was produced, written and directed by George Axelrod. I was the associate producer and assistant director. Our cameraman was the multiple-Oscar-winning Leon Shamroy. "Shammie" was a real character in the old Hollywood tradition. One day, an actress asked Shammie if the right side of her face was better than the left side. Shammie said, "Honey, what you need is a fucking plastic surgeon." When colleagues of mine heard that I would be doing a film with Leon Shamroy, they said he was death on assistant directors. That was so far from the truth. He turned out to be one of my favorites. The cast starred Walter Matthau, Anne Jackson, Patrick O'Neal and Edy Williams in her screen debut. Edy is the nut-case sex-bomb who often made a fool of herself at the Academy Awards ceremonies in the '60s.

George and I shared a bungalow on the Fox lot. A bathroom separated our offices. When the bathroom doors were open, we could see each other across the toilet. George would say, "It's always pleasant seeing you across the toilet every day." We had a secretary named Therma. Every time she started to laugh, she would wet herself. That's dangerous for someone who works for a comedy writer.

Anne Jackson's husband, Eli Wallach, would say, "Annie is rediscovered every five years by Hollywood." Anne was a delight to work with, "up" all the time. Walter Matthau was always letter-perfect, always helpful, and never a problem.

Edy Williams was a young teenager playing a young teenager. She was either 16 or 17 years old. Edy's scenes were with a very handsome young actor who was playing a delivery boy. She would mouth to him. "I'd like to fuck you," when the camera was on her back. "I would really like to fuck you." It would throw the poor guy. I'd say to her that's not in the script. She just would glare at me. This sweet thing's mother was five feet away, sitting next to the schoolteacher ever so proud of her daughter.

George Axelrod was great fun to work with. He had a brilliant mind. He was a very successful playwright. Unfortunately, the film was not a success.

During the making of *American Wife*, my Aunt Mary visited me from Boston. I asked her if she would like to visit the studio. She had been to MGM but never to 20th Century-Fox. She asked if it was possible to meet Frank Sinatra. He was her idol. Luckily, Frank was doing a Tony Rome film at Fox. I told my aunt I would try but that Frank was a very busy man. I didn't want to tell her he seldom saw visitors. I called Gloria, Frank's secretary, and asked her if it would be at all possible to have my aunt come by any day at Frank's convenience for a minute or so. Gloria called back within five minutes. Gloria said Frank remembered me from *Never So Few*. "Bring your aunt tomorrow at 2 p.m." The next day, I brought Aunt Mary to Frank's bungalow. He couldn't have been kinder or warmer to her. We were there for about forty minutes. And I know he did it for me. Seldom do you hear of Frank Sinatra's kindnesses. He made my aunt feel like a million dollars. So did I.

The April Fools, in 1969, was my second film with Stuart Rosenberg and my second with Jack Lemmon. Betty Crosby was again our script supervisor. Someone had to follow the dialogue and match the action. This was also Catherine Deneuve's first film shot in Hollywood. The film

The "happy" trio. Cameraman Leon Shamroy, Director George Axelrod, and me.

Rehearsing with Myrna and Catherine.

Jack Lemmon shooting his version.

also starred Myrna Loy, Charles Boyer and Peter Lawford. We had extensive shooting in New York City and the Connecticut countryside.

Working with Myrna was a thrill. I loved and admired her in all the films she did at MGM. She was still a great beauty with that amazing profile. Charles Boyer was equally a treat to work with. Loy and Boyer must have made over one hundred films between them, yet this was the first time they ever worked together. Before casting Boyer, we asked Myrna

With Catherine Deneuve.

if she thought William Powell would co-star with her in the film. She said that he was too ill and unable to work anymore. It would have been a great coup to have the Loy-Powell team back together again. They made many films together playing Nick and Nora Charles in *The Thin Man* series. Nevertheless, Charles Boyer held his own. I asked Boyer about the film he did with Marlene Dietrich. He said, "She was something else," with a special twinkle in his eyes and a big smile. I told Charles about being invited on the Paramount lot by Marlene when I was a teenager.

Myrna was a very left-leaning liberal, almost radical. One day while shooting on a soundstage in New York City, word came that Hubert Humphrey was going to visit the set. Myrna was upset. "I don't want to see him and I certainly don't want to have a picture taken with him," she said. Humphrey was a Democrat, and certainly his politics were to the left of center, but to Myrna he might as well have been Senator Joe McCarthy. When Humphrey, who was running for President, finally came to the set, Myrna ran out of the side door. She didn't return until he had left. Once Myrna said to me, "Why aren't some of those black extras carrying brief cases?" She resented the fact that in films in those days, the black extras never appear to be lawyers or professionals, only servants or the lower class. She would make that observation on all her films. She cared for the underdog.

Catherine Deneuve was as cold as ice—the beautiful stone face. She had that "French" attitude. It took me quite awhile to thaw her out. Again, we had hairdresser problems. Deneuve insisted on bringing her own French hairdresser. By this time, the studio system was slowly becoming a thing of the past, and the unions were losing some of their power. More and more, European cameramen, designers and art directors were being allowed to work in Hollywood. It was agreed that Deneuve could bring her hairdresser, who could work on her hair at home or in the makeup department—but not on the set. We had to have a standby hairdresser. I hired Agnes Flanagan, Elizabeth Taylor's hairdresser, as standby. Agnes was also Marilyn Monroe's hairdresser. I believe Agnes did all of Marilyn's films.

When Marilyn died tragically, Sydney Guilaroff was too distraught to arrange Marilyn's hair in the casket. The job fell into Agnes' hands, who jumped at the opportunity to make a few bucks. Although I never met Marilyn Monroe, for some unknown reason, Agnes asked me whom she should send the bill to for arranging Marilyn's hair. Agnes had made

With Peter Lawford on *The April Fools*.

tens of thousands of dollars working on Marilyn's hair and now Agnes was concerned as to how she was to be paid for the final hairdo. Unbelievable.

Catherine did not like Jack Lemmon. I think it was mutual. Catherine would say to me, "His breath is making me sick." Jack smoked cigars. Catherine could be obstinate. She called me "Honk." I wasn't "Henri" this time.

Catherine's agent had told us to never mention the recent death of her sister, the actress Françoise Dorléac. Françoise, Catherine's older sister, was killed in a car crash. Catherine responded to her sister's death by refusing to speak to anyone, including her parents, about the tragedy. In 1997, Catherine began speaking publicly for the first time about her overwhelming grief.

We filmed in New York City for about three weeks. One of our locations was the TWA terminal and lounge at JFK airport. The studio asked me to see if Catherine would agree to an interview with a respected journalist from the *New York Times*. Catherine had previously refused all interviews. I asked her if she would grant the one interview, and she reluctantly agreed. We would hold the interview at the airport during the dinner break. The journalist arrived and asked for me. I had arranged for a table for two in the area where we were all eating. I specifically told the journalist not to mention Catherine's recently deceased sister. I introduced the journalist to Catherine. As he was about to sit down, he said, "Why am I not allowed to speak of your sister?" Catherine looked at me, got up and left. That was the shortest interview this asshole ever had, and probably the longest he ever deserved.

I often used the word "asshole." One day, Catherine asked me what it meant. I explained it to her. She liked it and began using it herself with a distinctive charming French accent. Jack Lemmon would often come up to her and say, wiggling his fingers, "Pick a finger! Pick a finger!" No one knew what it meant. Catherine said to me, "I theenk that Jack ees an asshole."

The "Safari Club" was a scene with Lemmon and Deneuve in a rather erotic and exotic nightclub built on a soundstage. Seductive women were hanging from the ceiling. Seductive women were in animal cages and amongst these women were real caged animals—lions, tigers, orangutans and monkeys. The club was filled with extras. For some reason, as we were preparing this scene, the animals began going crazy. They were roaring and banging around in their cages. We were afraid that they would break loose. The head animal trainer came up to me and said, "Get all the women off the set." I said, "Why?" He said, "For Christ's sake, get them off the set." All the women left the stage. It seems that one or more of the women were having their period and the animals could smell the blood. I had to find out who was menstruating and send them home. Gradually things got back to normal and we were able to continue. Just another typical problem for an assistant director.

The April Fools broke no records. The problem may have been that Jack and Catherine never quite clicked. But I had a lot of fun, which sometimes beats being miserable on the set of a blockbuster.

After *The April Fools* I left for London. I was becoming a real Anglophile. I was enjoying working in Europe and already accumulated many colleagues and friends. One evening, I went to a party in Chelsea. Judy Garland was there, and we greeted each other with hugs and kisses.

The forever-beautiful Myrna Loy.

The equally beautiful, Betty Crosby, script supervisor, with Myrna Loy.

It was a spectacular evening. Judy had had a few drinks. She said, "Let's go for a walk." We walked along the embankment of the Thames River, Judy clutching my arm. We walked along, giggling and reminiscing. Suddenly, Judy stopped and with that unmistakable Garland pose, she pointed her arm to the full moon and said, "What a beautiful moon. Why the fuck do they want to fly to it?" It was the day after the first moon landing. And the last time I saw Judy Garland.

Chapter 16
Rosenberg – Three Times More

W*USA* must have been a very unusual film. As far as I know, there has never been a VHS video in existence. It is seldom listed in the volumes of film and movie books. Only occasionally is it listed in Paul Newman's film credits. The film was made at Paramount Studios and starred Joanne Woodward, Laurence Harvey and Anthony Perkins. The producers were Paul Newman and John Foreman and the director was Stuart Rosenberg. I was the associate producer and assistant director. Betty Crosby was our script supervisor. The film was based on a novel entitled *Hall Of Mirrors* written by Robert Stone, who also wrote the screenplay. The story takes place entirely in New Orleans. It is a complex script because there are four different stories being told at the same time. We had extensive shooting in New Orleans' French Quarter. We all stayed in the same hotel.

Anthony Perkins introduced me to pot. I had never indulged. It never interested me. I like to know what I am doing at all times. It seems that people who enjoy marijuana like to get others to indulge. Tony kept pushing me to try it. He would say, "This is great stuff. It's Columbian." I didn't know Columbian from Eskimo. We were on our way to dinner one night and I finally relented. He lit a cigarette and handed the joint to me. I've seen enough movies to know how to smoke marijuana. You just suck it in. I took a deep drag. I took a second deep drag. Suddenly, I didn't know where I was. New Orleans is the flattest city in the world. But I was walking along the streets holding the sides of the buildings as though I was on the hills of San Francisco. That was the last joint I ever smoked. Perkins couldn't stop laughing.

Joanne Woodward crocheting.

One day, while working in Potter's Field (a cemetery for vagrants) in the blistering heat, I noticed that the crew was dwindling. I saw them at the far end of Potter's Field cutting something. I went to see what was happening. Someone found marijuana plants flourishing. The crew was grabbing at the marijuana leaves like vultures. That night, every closet in almost every room in the hotel was filled with marijuana drying by a light bulb.

Another day, after returning from location, Perkins said to me, "You

"Legs" Woodward.

buy a *Time* magazine and I'll buy a *Newsweek* magazine and then we can exchange them." For some reason when John Foreman heard this, he went ballistic with laughter. I didn't know Tony was on the frugal side. And I felt bad because Foreman went around and told everyone. I didn't think it was so ridiculous.

New Orleans had many antique shops. Joanne Woodward and I would scour the shops for good buys. This was the first picture I ever worked on with Joanne, although I knew her for many years because of all the films I had done with Paul. She was a great sport.

After an extensive stay in New Orleans, we returned to Los Angeles to commence with the studio shooting. One afternoon, Paul and Joanne were working on a scene, and toward the end of the day, Paul had to leave on some important business. Paul was most apologetic to Joanne because he couldn't stay to feed her his lines on her close-up. Joanne said, "It'll be okay. Hank will read your lines." When we finished the shot, Joanne said to me, "If I lose the Oscar, it'll be your fault."

Cloris Leachman had a small part but she was great in the role. Laurence Harvey still bathed himself in witch hazel. He played a phony man of the cloth. We had to shoot a major scene in the Los Angeles Coliseum. It involved several hundred extras. We had dozens of stuntmen and stuntwomen. It was to be a political rally that goes awry. This was a major task. Fortunately, we had many assistant directors helping out. All went well. But it was a rough week. The picture was not successful. I think the title *WUSA* wasn't particularly inspirational. It was the fictitious call letters of the local radio station, and it just didn't scan well as a movie title.

The next Rosenberg epic was a real turkey. It was the strangest film that I ever worked on in my entire career. It was called *Move*. Pandro Berman's wife, Kathryn Hereford, brought the book to Rosenberg's attention. Pandro decided he wanted to produce it for 20th Century-Fox. The movie starred Elliot Gould, Paula Prentiss and a young British actress named Geneviève Waïte. We shot in New York City. One scene we had to do was Elliott Gould walking backwards in Times Square. Easier said than done. We also shot in Riverside Park.

One afternoon a young woman pushing a baby carriage came up to me and said, "Hello, I'm Barbra Streisand. Where can I find Elliot Gould?" I pointed to where Elliot was. I had met Barbra Streisand years before at a cocktail party at John Foreman's house. I remember standing next to her when someone came up to her and said, "Are you Barbra Streisand?" Barbra said, "Paul Newman I'm not!"

Meanwhile, back at the studio, the fun was about to start. We had to do a nude scene with Paula Prentiss. Rosenberg kept bugging me about that scene. He said he would fire anyone that made cracks or snide remarks about Paula's nudity. He wanted to make sure that there would be no visitors and wanted the set sealed off. Okay, I'll take care of it. Relax. In the meantime, we were going to do a nude scene with Genevieve Waite. Her turn came first. We started her scene on a Friday. She was completely nude but we had things strategically placed so that you couldn't see what you shouldn't see. As luck would have it, we were unable to finish the scene that day. We had to pick it up Monday morning.

Monday morning arrived and Rosenberg came up to me. He said, "*You* have a problem. Genevieve dyed her pussy red over the weekend. We've established it with her natural color. You'll have to get it back to the normal shade." All of a sudden Genevieve's pussy is my problem. I went to her and said, "I understand your pussy is currently red. Didn't you like the color God gave you?" She said, "I was so bored this weekend that I decided to dye it red." I said, "Go to the makeup department and wash it or whatever you have to do to get it back to its natural state." The things an assistant director has to do for a living. My biggest problem was trying to keep a relatively straight face and yet try to look professional.

Rosenberg was still pestering me about the Prentiss nude scene. "Don't you worry; I'll take care of it. When the time comes, you'll be astounded by what I've done." Lynn Reynolds was our makeup man. He had to be one of the funniest men I have ever met. He had a dour sense of humor. He said to me one morning in the makeup department that he was the only makeup man in Hollywood that had safety belt around his makeup chair, so that the actors wouldn't fall off.

The day finally arrived to shoot the "Prentiss nude scene." I can't tell you too much about the storyline of this movie. I worked on it for months and I still couldn't figure out what it was all about. The "Prentiss nude scene" was in some sort of office. Everything was white—the walls, the furniture, the rugs, the typewriters. Sitting at a desk was supposed to be a nude secretary. Rosenberg began rehearsals with Paula. After the rehearsals, the stand-in took over for the lighting. Rosenberg said, "I'll fire the first person who makes a crack." What a ball breaker. I said to Paula to go to her dressing room and get a full body makeup. When the cameraman finished lighting, I had "wild" walls rolled in to hide the set from the peeping Toms. No problems yet. After about fifteen minutes, the body makeup girl came to me and said Paula was ready. I told the crew that wasn't needed to go off the stage and have a cup of coffee. I said to my assistant to get Paula. Rosenberg said to me, "You go get her."

I walked across the long stage. Paula is a very tall lady. She had a high hairdo and always wore very high heels. She appeared to be seven feet tall. I knocked on her dressing room door. She swung open the door wearing her high-heel shoes and nothing else. She said looking around, "Where is everybody?" She stepped down out of her dressing room. I said, "Don't you have a robe or something?" She said, "Why?" She held my arm and we sauntered toward the set. On the way, Paula asked if she could suck my thumb. I obliged. This must have been a sight for Rosenberg who slightly gasped. His five-foot, seven-inch assistant walking with a seven-foot leading lady in the nude with his assistant's thumb in his leading lady's mouth. "Where is everybody? What is going on?" Paula kept asking. "Here she is," I said to Rosenberg. "She's all yours." The film was obviously a disaster. Pandro Berman retired after that film—never to produce another film. Pandro was the last great giant of Hollywood's golden era.

Pocket Money was my last film with Stuart Rosenberg and Paul Newman. This movie also starred Lee Marvin, Strother Martin and Wayne Rogers. It was a modern Western set in New Mexico. I wasn't the assistant director. I'm not exactly sure what my position was. I remember making a deal with the local Indian chief near Santa Fe. The company wanted to use some of their lands. The Indian "village" consisted of Cadillac cars resting on the ground without wheels, and little shacks scattered around. The entire area looked ramshackle. I was told that this particular tribe was supposed to be very wealthy. The chief wanted cash. I wonder where all the money went.

Candice Bergen visited the set in New Mexico toward the end of the schedule to take some publicity photos for the studio. She was a brilliant photographer. I had met Candy years ago through Carrie Fisher. Stuart Rosenberg, Paul Newman, Candy and I took the Warner Bros. Lear jet back to Burbank at the end of the shoot. Candy and I were playing gin rummy when all of a sudden the plane began spinning around in circles. What a weird feeling. I was about to discard a card from my hand but it wouldn't drop. Nothing moved. Candy was terrified. I was getting nauseated. This was one of daredevil Newman's pranks. He had asked the pilot to have some fun and games. No one else thought it was funny.

Shortly after, I received a call from Paramount Pictures asking me to come in to have an interview with Herbert Ross. He was going to direct a film called *T.R. Baskin*, to be made entirely in Chicago. I had never met Ross before but I knew he was a well-respected director. I went to the studio and met with Ross and the producer, Peter Hyams. This was to be Hyams first film. They offered me a small percentage of the movie and I was to be the Associate Producer. A good start. The three of us left for Chicago to check out the locations. The film wasn't scheduled to start shooting until the early spring. When that wind whipped up over Lake Michigan, the chill factor sent the temperature below twenty degrees. I have never been so cold.

Herbert Ross was well over six feet. He had a full-length fur coat down to his ankles and a fur Cossack hat. With his full moustache and his lanky frame, he looked like a Russian spy. In fact, he looked utterly ridiculous. The three of us scouted for several key locations. Hyams was from Chicago. He was the grandson of the great impresario Sol Hurok, and he had an ego larger than Lake Michigan. We'd look at some tall buildings along Lake Shore Drive and Hyams would say to me, "You're supposed to be so great, how many arcs would it take to light that twenty-story building?" I would just ignore him. That was no way to talk to someone who is supposed to be a partner. This went on day after day—snowstorm after snowstorm. Hyams would say the three of us would

make a great movie. Yet, the three of us often became two. Ross and Hyams would always stand away from me, out of earshot, and begin whispering. I really didn't care what they were talking about, but if it had to do with my work, I needed to know. I was getting more and more frustrated so I decided to leave the project.

I met with Ross in his hotel room to tell him that I had decided to quit the project. This was the first and only time I ever quit a film. Ross tried to talk me out of it. I said, "Herb, I know that I will never get along with Hyams and it wouldn't be fair to you. Besides, the start date is a long way off. It's not like I'm leaving two days before the film is to start." He had plenty of time to get a replacement. I went to Hyams to tell him of my decision. Hyams couldn't understand why I wanted to leave. He pleaded with me to stay. I was embarrassed by his sudden change of attitude toward me; it was odd, too, because after all, there are hundreds of capable people who can step in without causing a ripple to the plans. I finally understood what his real problem was when he said, "I hate to think that the first person I've hired in the movie business has quit on me." "Life is full of disappointments," I said. I met Peter on a set at Warner Bros. many years later. He was now a director and had been fairly successful. We spoke of Chicago. And I liked him. I don't think *T.R. Baskin* was much of a success.

A side note. Herbert Ross' wife, Nora Kaye, had been a successful prima ballerina. Friends had told me she had been a brilliant dancer. Now she was involved in her husband's film. When I met her I mentioned that I had friends who thought she was one of America's most accomplished ballet dancers. She said, "How nice."

Chapter 17
The David Merrick Saga

The beginning of 1971 was the start of a new phase of my career and it began with David Merrick.

David Merrick was considered the most powerful and successful Broadway producer of the '50s and '60s. He was a shrewd businessman. He was a lawyer who decided to be a Broadway producer. Everyone hated him. At any given time, he would have a dozen lawsuits pending. It gave him pleasure. *Child's Play* (not the Chucky film) was initially an unsuccessful Broadway play that Merrick had produced. Paramount wanted the rights to *The Great Gatsby*, which Merrick owned. Robert Evans, the then-head of Paramount Pictures, wanted the rights to *Gatsby* so that his then-wife Ali McGraw could play Daisy Buchanan. He concocted a clever scheme. Merrick would give Paramount the rights to *The Great Gatsby* if Paramount would first produce *Child's Play* and if David Merrick produced both films. This didn't sit too well with Robert Evans. Evans wanted to produce *Gatsby* himself. Merrick would not budge. There was a standoff but Merrick finally won.

Merrick had never made a movie. It was all new to him. Merrick made a separate deal with Paramount on *Child's Play*. I never knew the exact terms but it amounted to Merrick pocketing whatever money was left over from the original budget—a very sweet deal if you can keep the costs down. So, if the budget was $1,720,000 and the movie came in at $1,517,000, Merrick would get the difference—in this case, $203,000; this, along with his salary as producer. The only one who made money on *Child's Play* was David Merrick.

Merrick approached my friend Joshua Logan to direct *Child's Play*. Josh said he would direct if Hank Moonjean would be on the film. Merrick didn't know me from Adam, but he put in a call to me. He offered me Associate Producer credit and a fair salary. I said I would accept only under one condition—that I have a pay-or-play contract. A pay-or-play contract means I get my entire salary whether or not I make the film or if the film is never made. This is standard practice for independent producers. Logan was anxious to get me to New York so that we could get working. I refused to go until my contract was fully negotiated. Merrick's reputation had reached Hollywood. Eventually, I flew to New York. No sooner did I get there than Joshua Logan was taken off the picture. Some Paramount executive remembered that there was a big fiasco with *Paint Your Wagon* and didn't want anything to do with Logan, who had directed it. Now I'm in New York and Merrick is stuck with me. And this man is not about to pay me off for not having done any work.

Enter Sidney Lumet. Lumet was hired to replace Logan. Lumet, who always worked with his own team, inherited me. I'm sure he wasn't thrilled with the situation and I didn't blame him. But he was stuck with me and I was stuck with him. Lumet was reservedly pleasant.

The film had to do with strange happenings in a boys' Catholic high school. Marymount School, in the wealthy New York suburb of Tarrytown, was picked for the film even though it was an exclusive Catholic girls' school. James Mason was selected for one of the two leads. It was an all-male cast, most of whom were repeating their stage roles. Lumet wanted Marlon Brando for the other lead. Merrick was pleased with the idea. All of a sudden the film became important. Lumet spoke to Brando. Brando had some reservations about the script. No surprise there. Lumet agreed to all the script changes that Brando requested. However, Merrick wasn't privy to any of the suggested changes. Brando came to New York with every intention of making the film. In fact, I took Marlon to the insurance doctor to be examined for cast insurance. While in the doctor's office, I received a telephone call from Merrick. He wanted to see Brando immediately.

We went to Merrick's office in the St. James Theater's building. Merrick said to Brando that he would have to stick to the original script. Merrick also told Brando that his suggestions changed the entire storyline. It is my guess that Merrick got his nose out of joint because Lumet did not include Merrick in the initial story conference calls. Brando never said a word. He just listened to Merrick. I dropped Brando off at his hotel. I knew then and there that we had lost Brando, even though he didn't say a word. About 2 a.m., Brando called me to say he was leaving for Los Angeles. That was the end of Brando. When I told Merrick the next day, he got very upset.

"I'll sue the son of a bitch."

"For what?" I said. "Marlon asked for specific script changes and they were agreed upon by Lumet."

Merrick said, "Lumet had no right to make any promises without discussing them with me." Nevertheless, we lost Brando, which was a shame. There were no lawsuits. Within a few days, Robert Preston was set for the part. The third role went to Beau Bridges. Merrick wasn't getting along with Lumet, and Lumet was just putting up with Merrick. Lumet was very low key. I never saw him lose his cool but I did see him smoldering.

The first day of shooting at Marymount was disastrous. Merrick and his sidekick, Alan DeLynn, came to the set. They both looked like undertakers, dressed in somber suits and coats and wearing hats. I thought how nice it was of Merrick to come to wish us luck on our first day. We hadn't started shooting yet but the entire cast was assembled and ready to go. Merrick turned to Lumet and said, "Not only are you a fucking hack, you are a fucking phony," in front of the entire company. Merrick and DeLynn left. Lumet said nothing.

The first scene we were going to shoot before Merrick's interruption was Beau Bridges' most dramatic scene in the film. For some reason, Lumet chose to start with that scene. The scene in question is Bridges telling his superiors about a student getting killed in the school's gymnasium. Beau, in tears, is wearing sweats that are covered in blood. Priests surround him. As I watched the rehearsals, I noticed that one of the priests standing next to Beau was smiling. Beau was crying his heart out and here this priest was smiling.

I went to the smiling priest and asked him not to smile. He said, with a smile, "I am not smiling." I realized the poor man had some sort of facial distortion—probably from a stroke. Lumet continued rehearsing. Beau continued crying. And the priest, who said he wasn't smiling, continued smiling. Quietly, I suggested to Lumet to move the smiling priest away from Beau. The smiling priest was playing against the scene. There were several priests. It would have been easy—nothing had been shot. Lumet refused. He wasn't about to have the Associate Producer tell him how to direct—whether I was right or wrong. Lumet said to me, "Sweetheart. Brown Eyes. Angel. Don't worry about it. I'll take care of it." Lumet spoke like that to everybody. You could get diabetes listening to him. I thought this is only the first day. What would the next seven weeks be like? It didn't bode well.

We had taken over the entire Marymount School—the classrooms, the corridors, the gym and even the church. Most of the nuns wore ordinary clothes, while the older nuns still wore their habits. The Mother Superior and all the nuns were very helpful. When we needed boy students as extras, we would get them from the nearby Iona Prep School—a school for wealthy Catholic boys. Rich Catholic boys should marry rich Catholic girls.

At the end of the third day, we all went to the Deluxe Labs in Manhattan to view the first day's rushes. Lumet sat between his cameraman and script supervisor. Merrick and DeLynn sat by themselves. I sat alone. As the rushes started, I could hear Merrick say, "I can hear them but I can't see them." DeLynn would whisper, "You'll see them tomorrow in the reverse shots." Merrick was that unfamiliar with filming. Merrick didn't understand the editing procedure. These were probably the first rushes he ever witnessed. We watched about another ten minutes of film. The lights came on in the projection room. Merrick turned around and said to Lumet, "Why was that priest smiling?" Lumet looked directly at me and I looked up at the ceiling. Even with Merrick's lack of understanding when it comes to film, he immediately picked up on it. It was that obvious. I had been around long enough to know better than to get between the director and the producer. Lumet never said anything to me about it but I assure you that he naturally assumed I went directly to Merrick. I just let the incident die. Whatever I would have said would have made it worse.

Ruth Morley was our costume designer. She was just as successful on the Broadway stage as she was in film. Ruth was the one who created the *Annie Hall* look, which Diane Keaton still thinks is in fashion. Ruth was wickedly funny and great fun. One day she came to me and said, sotto voce, "I know it's none of my business, but you know that the girls here are from very wealthy families and I wouldn't want the company to get into any trouble."

"What are you getting at?"

"I'm afraid some of the girls are having hanky panky with some of the crew in the boiler room," Ruth said.

"With all the work I have, that's the least of my problems," I replied. Weeks passed and one afternoon I happened to pass the boiler room. I thought I would investigate. I did and, lo and behold, there was Ruth in the arms of the assistant cameraman. I decided never to check the boiler room ever again.

One day Merrick charged into my office. He threw the budget of the film at me. I threw it back at him. I said, "Don't you ever throw anything at me again." My secretary ran out of the office. Merrick screamed at me, "I will *not* sign it." I said, "I don't give a shit if you ever sign it." Producers are supposed to sign the final budget to indicate that it's all been approved. Merrick, being a lawyer first, refused to sign anything, especially as he had money coming from it. However, eventually, he had to sign it or there wouldn't be a final deal. I found myself stuck between a madman and a unhappy director..

Merrick was a very complicated man. He was not very attractive and he was balding. On a breezy day, his hairpiece would flop over. I also think he was ashamed of his heritage. Merrick was Jewish; his real name was Margulois. He never wanted to talk about his past. He would always skirt around it. He was on his third marriage. His first wife bore him a child who was mentally handicapped. He was currently married to a beautiful Scandinavian woman named Etan. We would call her Nate—Etan spelled backward. They had a beautiful daughter. Sometimes, I felt sorry for him, knowing he was probably the most hated man on Broadway.

One evening on the way back from Tarrytown headed for Manhattan, we passed a large billboard on the side of a building advertising Merrick's current musical, *Sugar*. It said "Coming to Broadway." It had been playing for months. Unfortunately, without thinking, I pointed this out to Merrick. The moment we arrived at his office, Merrick called his lawyers. He told his lawyer to sue the people responsible for that billboard.

My offices were also in the St. James Theater building, next-door to Sardi's, on 44th Street. One day before filming started I decided to go to the corner falafel stand on 8th Avenue for lunch. As I walked out of the theater toward 8th Avenue, I saw a man hit by a car. If that car didn't kill him, the second car that hit him must have. The ambulance was there in minutes. I crossed the street to the falafel stand and ordered my lunch. As I was watching all the police activity across the street, I felt a sharp tug on my jacket. I looked down and saw the ugliest black female dwarf smiling up at me. Her head was twice the normal size. She said to me, "You want to have a good time?" I said, "I'm sorry, honey, but I got to get to work. Some other time." I didn't want her to feel rejected. She grunted and went on her way. I finished my falafel and turned to cross the street. There was a sweet, old gray-headed lady who appeared to be at least 75

Sidney Lumet pondering the next set-up on the set of *Child's Play*. Robert Preston in background.

years old waiting for the signal to change. She looked like Norman Rockwell's grandmother. She was toting two heavy bags of groceries. I said to her, "Can I help you cross the street?" She said, "Keep your fucking hands to yourself." So much for my Boy Scout training. I crossed the street and just as I reached the other side, directly in front of me, a Latino man bounced off a wall, shot by police. His body fell about twenty feet in front of me. In one half hour, I had seen a man killed by a car, been propositioned by a dwarf, I been told to fuck off by a sweet grandmother, and seen a man shot to death. Welcome to New York City.

I didn't enjoy working with Lumet. He didn't like anyone to think. He directed by a master plan and everyone was his robot. Everything was measured and calculated. James Mason and Robert Preston did their best, as did Beau Bridges. The play had been a flop and so was the movie. The only one who made money was Merrick. He ended on top. But, in a way, so did I. Merrick asked me if I would like to work on his next film, assuming that the British director, Jack Clayton, approved of me. The film was *The Great Gatsby*.

Chapter 18
The Great Gatsby – Stateside

David Merrick told me that Jack Clayton was at the Plaza Hotel. Merrick's secretary made an appointment for me at 3 p.m. the next day. The next afternoon I went to Clayton's suite. The minute I saw Clayton, I had a good reaction. Clayton was a slim man, not very tall, with piercing blue eyes. He had long white hair but was bald at the top of his head, much like Benjamin Franklin. He was very English. He was wearing a blue cashmere sweater and Levis. (This would be his "costume" for the next two years.) Obviously, Merrick had spoken to Clayton on my behalf. Otherwise, I wouldn't be there being interviewed. We spoke about mundane things for about two hours. I felt he liked me. He finally asked me to call Merrick and tell him I was hired. I was pleased. Jack Clayton had never worked in the States before. He had directed only a handful of films in England. He started his career as an assistant director and worked his way to the top. He became a highly regarded director and was well respected by actors. *The Great Gatsby* was going to be his first American film.

The Great Gatsby, based on F. Scott Fitzgerald's novel, was produced twice as a film. There have also been several stage versions and recently there was an opera based on the book. The first film was a silent picture produced by Paramount in 1926, starring Warner Baxter, Lois Wilson, William Powell and Neil Hamilton. In 1949, Paramount again produced *Gatsby*, this time starring Alan Ladd, Betty Field, Macdonald Carey and Ruth Hussey. Neither film was successful. The only print of the 1926 version was in Moscow. We asked the State Department to see if we could borrow a print to study. The Russian government refused. It appears that the Russians have more respect for film than the Americans. They have prints of virtually all American films that have been lost or destroyed through neglect. But they weren't very generous with their treasures at the time.

F. Scott Fitzgerald's books have never made a successful transition to any other art form. They say there is a curse on his works. Truman Capote wrote the first script. It was discarded. Clayton was tight-lipped about Capote. He just didn't like Capote's approach to the book. Francis Ford Coppola was asked to write the script. He wrote it in five weeks. Other than writing the script, Coppola had nothing to do with the production.

Meanwhile, Jack Clayton was fully aware of what had transpired between Robert Evans and David Merrick as to who was going to produce the movie. Ali MacGraw had left Evans and went off with Steve McQueen. Needless to say, she would not be playing Daisy Buchanan. Now the search for Daisy began. It was similar to the search for Scarlett O'Hara. Clayton went on record stating that whoever wanted to play Daisy must go through an extensive screen test. He would be sorry later about his edict. Clayton tested every eligible actress in London, Hollywood and New York, the very cream of the crop of 1972. We tested Candice Bergen, Katharine Ross, Mia Farrow, Ann Turkel, Lois Chiles (who ended up playing Jordan Baker), Faye Dunaway and several others. Dunaway was a big pain in the neck. For someone hoping to get the most important role of the year, she certainly didn't ingratiate herself to Clayton or anyone else. She kept everyone waiting. Whatever chance she may have had, she blew it. Clayton and I met with Cybill Shepherd at the Polo Lounge in the Beverly Hills Hotel. We didn't know whether or not she was nervous, or uncomfortable, not really interested, or maybe not very bright. She replied to all of Clayton's questions with one word. That ended Shepherd.

Jack Clayton wanted to test Tuesday Weld. I knew secretly that she was Clayton's first and only choice. Clayton said that Tuesday looked most like Zelda Fitzgerald, F. Scott's wife, the character Daisy is based on. Tuesday Weld refused to test. And because Clayton made that edict, he had to stick to it. Weeks later all the Paramount executives, Merrick and Clayton viewed the screen tests. It was a unanimous decision to cast Mia Farrow. Her screen test was brilliant.

We had one great advantage that the other *Gatsby* productions didn't have. F. Scott's daughter, Scottie Smith, his only child, was an advisor. She was helpful to Coppola and to Clayton. We learned from her that Daisy was definitely based on her mother, Zelda. One of the most significant things Scottie told us was that her father intended Gatsby to be Jewish, even though that was never intentionally made clear in the novel. That would be a factor in casting Gatsby. Every major star in Hollywood wanted the part. Jack Nicholson's name came up. Warren Beatty's name came up. Almost every other big name came up. My choice was Robert De Niro. De Niro was dark and Semitic looking. The studio would never have considered it. De Niro had only made a couple of films. You could see he was a tremendous talent but he wasn't a major star yet. Finally, Robert Redford was chosen. Based on what Scottie Fitzgerald told us, Robert Redford was physically the wrong choice. Redford is the most waspish-looking actor in Hollywood. My objections weren't because of his ability. It was his physical appearance. But I was only the Associate Producer, so what did I know?

By this time, it was decided to start shooting the film the following year. I had been on the film almost 10 months at this point. I dealt mostly with Jack Clayton. David Merrick was involved with his Broadway plays. The next order of business was to secure the locations. The story of *Gatsby* is set on Long Island and Manhattan. I scouted locations all over Long Island. Because of the specific logistics, I could not find the right location for the Gatsby estate on Long Island. Either there were modern buildings in the area, or no room to build specific requirements and a myriad of other problems. Someone suggested Grosse Point, Michigan. Jack and I went there. Again, the perfect estates were near a marina or modern buildings. I then went to the New Jersey shore and, again, I had the same problems. I finally ended up in Newport, Rhode Island. There was the perfect location for all the exteriors and for some of the interiors. Somewhere along the way, it was decided to shoot the interiors at Pinewood Studios outside London. Although Clayton lived near London, this decision wasn't based on him being close to home. It was more financially practical. Meanwhile, more time had elapsed. I had been on *Gatsby* almost a year. We finally had a start date. We were to start the production in Newport, Rhode Island, on June 11, 1973 and shoot there for four weeks, move on to Manhattan for one week and then leave for London for seven weeks of additional shooting.

The key crew had to be selected. The film was now considered a British production. The key crew had to be British. John Box, the Academy Award-winning production designer, was set. Box won Oscars for *Lawrence of Arabia*, *Doctor Zhivago*, *Oliver!*, and *Nicholas and Alexandra*. And, eventually, Douglas Slocombe (Dougie) was to be Director of Photography.

Jack and I met with everybody who sewed a dress. We interviewed designers in Paris, London, New York and Hollywood. The look of the film was of the greatest importance. We were running out of dress designers. In New York, someone had recommended Theoni V. Aldredge, a tall slim Greek who was known in the theater world. Late one evening, we waited to interview Theoni in Jack's hotel room. In walked this elegant woman who immediately exuded class. Introductions were made and Jack asked to see some of her sketches. Theoni said, "I haven't asked to see any of your films, why should I show you my work?" In a normal situation, she would be on her way out. For some reason, Jack respected her comment. Later on he said to me, "Good for her." Theoni became part of the team.

Norman Cohen was our production manager on the American segment of *Gatsby*. Norman and I had worked together previously in New York City. I needed someone with his knowledge of the New York unions. They respected him. And I knew we would be having union disputes because of having a partial British crew. (Norman had union problems virtually every day—there was even a daily threat of a strike.) We had planned on bringing John Box, Douglas Slocombe, his camera operator and assistant cameraman, the assistant director, the film editor, the chief makeup man, the chief hairdresser and the script supervisor. All in all, twelve members of the crew came from England. Obviously, it is important to have the same look. You can't have two different cinematographers, two different makeup artists and two different hairdressers. Continuity of appearance was most important, especially on a film whose success is based so much on the visual. *Gatsby* is about wealth and opulence and the idle rich. It had to look right.

So, Norman had his hands full with the New York unions who claimed that Newport, Rhode Island was in their jurisdiction. As a matter of fact, on the very first day of shooting in Newport, Teamsters arrived from Boston, Providence *and* New York City all claiming Newport jurisdiction. I saw rifles in the cabs of the trucks. Norman and I approached them. I said that I could only hire one group of Teamsters. This was an internal problem amongst the Teamsters. Of course, New York City won out. The company had to hire a New York standby crew for all the British personnel. Additionally, we had to give the New York cameraman's' union $50,000 for their employees' fund. That didn't sit too well with David Merrick. He was furious with that decision, but had no choice.

Preparations were in progress in Newport. A major set had to be built at Rosecliff, the estate that was selected for the Gatsby Mansion. A small house abutting the Gatsby estate was built. This would be the house of Nick Carraway. (Sam Waterston was hired for that role. It was Sam's first major role.) When you analyze the novel, you realize the largest role, in film terms, was that of Nick. But you couldn't call the film *The Great Nick*. Norman made arrangements to shoot various scenes in several of the great estates of Newport—the kitchen in one, the hallways in another, the ballroom in another etc.

Hammersmith Farm was selected for the exteriors of the Buchanan estate. Hammersmith Farm was the home of Janet Auchincloss, Jacqueline Kennedy Onassis' mother. As a matter of fact, JFK and Jackie's honeymoon was spent on that estate. Jackie grew up there. I made arrangements with Mrs. Auchincloss to rent the fabulous lighthouse on her property for Jack Clayton and his wife, Haya Harareet. Also, I made arrangements for Robert Redford and his family to rent the oldest house in Rhode Island, which was also on the Auchincloss estate. When I rented the spacious rooms for myself above the garage, Mrs. Auchincloss apologized that there wasn't a room above the garage where flowers could be arranged. I said I would try to manage. Separate houses were arranged for the other cast members all over Newport. The other remaining actors were Bruce Dern playing Tom Buchanan, Scott Wilson playing Mr. Wilson, and Karen Black was cast as Myrtle. Scott and Karen would only work in England.

The personnel arrived from England. Norman had the New York crew and the standby New York crew also came to Newport. We were getting close to the start date. Merrick hardly spent any time in Newport. Two weeks before the start date, we had a meeting at the local restaurant mainly to introduce the two crews and go over all the loose ends. Douglas Slocombe was a very bad stutterer. A major stutterer. The chief electrician that Norman hired from New York was also a major stutterer. I did not know this at the time. At the meeting, introductions were made. Clayton was sitting next to me. The most important person on a movie for the head cameraman is the chief electrician, the gaffer. They are in constant discussion. When Slocombe was introduced to the electrician, he said, "I, I, I, am looking fffforward to wwworkking with yyyyou." The electrician said, "Sssssooo aaammm I." I said, "It sounds like this is going to be a very looooong picture." Jack Clayton started to laugh. He couldn't stop laughing. As a matter of fact, whenever I would see Jack through the years, he would still laugh at that luncheon in Newport.

The remaining cast was settling. The extras were hired locally. They were some of the richest people in the world. It was the start of the Newport social season, and everybody wanted to be in the movie. Much earlier, we had taken out newspaper ads in the *Boston Globe*, the *Christian Science Monitor* and the *Providence* newspaper asking for period cars to be hired as well as period boats and yachts. We would hire the cars and the owners of the cars would drive their vehicle in the film. I made a separate deal with the owner of the car that was to be Gatsbys'—a 1926 Rolls-Royce. The owner of the car was from Boston. I said that I wanted to contract the car for two years. (The publicity department wanted the car for promotional purposes after the film's release). It would be shipped to London; we would paint it yellow and then restore it to its original color. He said, "It's a deal," and he charged the company one dollar. After he signed the contract, I asked him why he only asked for one dollar. I would have given him considerably more. That car was as important to the film as the actors. Obviously, the man wasn't needy. He said to me that when we returned the car it would be far more valuable because it was used in the film.

The week before the photography started, Janet (Mrs. Auchincloss and I were now on a first name basis) said she would like to have a party for some of the people on the film. Janet said, "You decide who should come," and added, "I'll ask the children to come as well." The children were Jacqueline Kennedy Onassis and Princess Lee Radziwell. The party was planned for about 3 p.m. on the Saturday before the Monday we started shooting. I asked Jack and Haya, Mr. & Mrs. Redford, Lois Chiles, Douglas Slocombe, Bruce Dern, David and Etan Merrick and Mia Farrow. Mia asked me if it would be all right to bring her two sisters who were visiting. Andre Previn, Mia's husband, hadn't arrived yet. I said it would be okay.

The day of the party, we all drifted in. Janet introduced us to Jackie Kennedy, Princess Radziwell, Doris Duke and some of Janet's other neighbors, who were, of course, at the very top of the social and economic ladder. The house wasn't like the big estates in Newport—not like Marble House or the Duke estate or the Breakers. It was a large simple country home with a veranda around it with a spectacular view of the bay. Mrs. Auchincloss was most gracious as were Jackie and Lee. I took a big liking to Doris Duke—not because she was one of the richest women in the world and not because her Newport estate was considered the best in the entire state, but because she had a dour sense of humor. She was no beauty. She was at least six feet tall and very, very pale.

An early dinner buffet was served. There were servants all over. Everybody was having his own group conversations. Mia and her sisters were sitting on the floor in the middle of the room giggling like children—having a happy time. Jackie was sitting between her sister and Doris on a divan. Suddenly, from the center of the room where the Farrow sisters were sitting on the floor, one of them said, "I wonder who has the biggest cock in this room." The three ladies on the divan bolted up. Everything came to a standstill. Everyone heard it. Mia, the next day, denied that either she or her sisters said anything of the sort. The jury is still out. Anyway, everyone regained his or her composure and conversation resumed.

I was walking around the rooms looking at all the paintings and bric-a-brac. I sauntered into the dining room where the desserts were displayed on the table. There must have been thirty different desserts—everything imaginable. As I was deciding what I should take once dessert was announced, Jackie came in wearing her trademark smile. She, too, was admiring all the desserts. She looked at me and I said, "Your mother is pushing the apple pie." I don't think that's the cleverest line I ever said, but Jackie started laughing and continued laughing. Doris ran in thinking she must have missed something. Anyway, the afternoon and evening were memorable. Mrs. Auchincloss was the perfect hostess and all her guests and family were a delight. It's a day I will never forget.

The film started without any fanfare. Other than flowers, telegrams and "Good Lucks," it was a normal day of shooting. It took me over a year to get to this point. Norman had arranged all of our offices across from Rosecliff in another mansion. It made it very convenient, as it would take only a minute or two to get to the set. I had contracted with Cartier's in New York to use some of their jewels in the film. There was no charge for the use of these very valuable stones. They only asked to be given screen credit and that a Pinkerton detective be on hand whenever the jewels were out of the safe. Other than the prestige of using jewels from Cartier's, it is difficult to tell the real thing from the copies. However, the actors tell me that when they know they are wearing something around their neck that may cost a million dollars, it gives them an attitude, which helps their performance.

We had approximately two weeks of day shooting which went along smoothly. The remaining two weeks was allocated to night shooting. Mainly, these last two weeks were devoted to Gatsby's famous parties, which Fitzgerald described so vividly in his book. These weeks were probably the most difficult in the entire production. We had hundreds of extras in elaborate costumes and hairstyles, we had dancers, we had musicians and we had the fragile weather to contend with. In the meantime, Norman and I and all the office staff would be in the offices by 8 or 9 a.m. We would have long days. The shooting crew and actors didn't have to report to work until the late afternoon.

Late one evening, I heard a scratching noise on the window behind me. It was Doris Duke. I thought she was standing on something but she wasn't. I told you she was tall. I opened the window. She said, "Hank, would you take me across the street? I would like to see the filming. I don't want to go alone." I said, "Of course, I'll be right out." I hadn't been on the set that evening, so Doris and I walked over to Rosecliff. The movie party was in full swing. Clayton saw me and said, in front of the crew, "It's nice of you to come and see the working people," rather sarcastically. I said, rather sarcastically, "I was here before you ever got up this morning. Besides, Doris and I have been thinking of buying Paramount Studios and have you fired." Clayton broke up.

Next evening, a very distinguished gentleman came up to me on the set and said, "Mr. Moonjean, may I go home?" From his outfit I could see he was playing a butler. I asked him if there was anything wrong. He said, "I've been serving drinks for two nights. I have just served my own servants cocktails. I'm tired of standing." It seems that he was one of the wealthiest men in Newport, and with unusual irony, the casting department had made him a butler.

Clayton and I had an unusual relationship. He was extremely fond of me as I was of him. He had a vile temper. He also liked his brandy. A lot of brandy. Most nights he felt no pain. Remember, he was English. Very late one evening, near dawn, Clayton came into our offices fuming. Norman was there as well as Haya. He was crazy with rage at me. I had never seen anyone that angry. The secretaries fled in fear of their lives. I couldn't figure out why he was so mad. Hanging in my office was an antique mirror shaped like a toilet seat that I had bought at a local flea market. Clayton picked up a chair and was about to throw it in the direction of "my toilet seat." He immediately realized what he was aiming at and turned and threw the chair somewhere else. I knew then he wasn't that mad at me. Haya was near tears. She had put up with him for years. I still didn't know what was bothering him. I think it was a combination of exhaustion, frustration and brandy.

Clayton and Merrick had their twice-weekly arguments. At one point, Clayton wanted Merrick barred from the set. I never gave too much importance to their fights. I had a film to finish. I said to Merrick, "Why do you take this abuse from Clayton? Why don't you just stay in New York?" Merrick said, "I was told I must visit the set at least fifteen minutes each day." (This is not true. I've known of producers who play golf all day during production and get nominated for an Academy Award.) Merrick, as brilliant as he was, really did not understand how movies were made. In the theater, the boss is the producer. In films, not only does the producer have to answer to all the executives but you have a corporation on your back as well. Merrick did not like filmmaking at all.

Watergate was in full bloom at that time in 1973. Everyone was listening to the news on the radios. Clayton admired the American way of justice. He would say that Watergate could never have happened in England.

We wrapped up in Newport and headed to New York City. I thanked Mrs. Auchincloss for her generosity. I don't think Newport was ever the same. I understand they had *Gatsby* parties for years to see if they could spot themselves in some of the scenes.

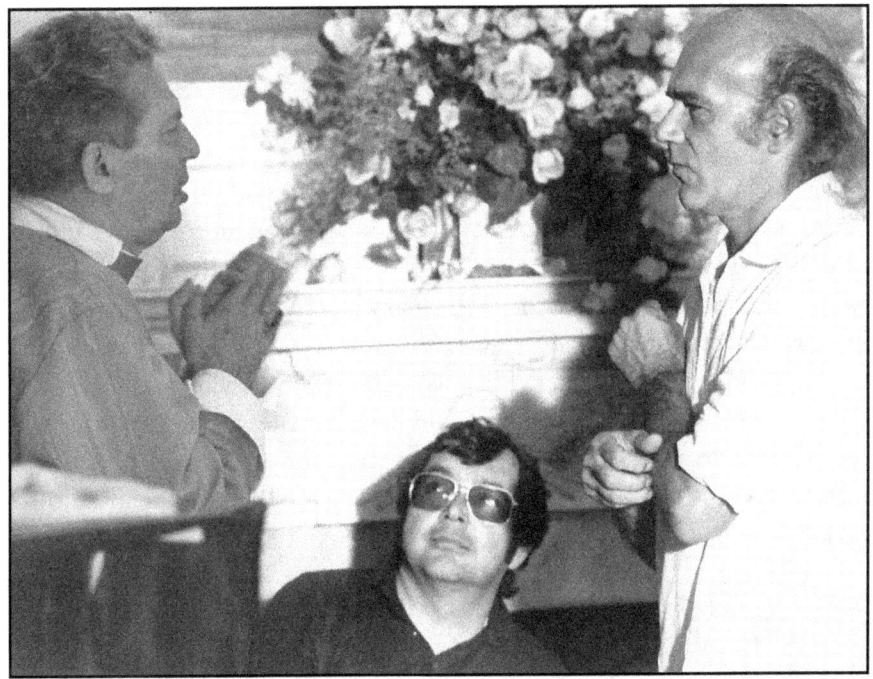

Peter Finch visiting the set of *The Great Gatsby* at Pinewood Studios.

Jack Clayton and I with Bob Evans.

New York City wasn't as hectic. First of all, we had no night shooting. We filmed on the Queensborough Bridge one Sunday morning. We filmed near Riverside Park, near Trinity Church in lower Manhattan, on Third Avenue and finally, the exterior of the Plaza Hotel. At the end of the shooting, we all left for England. I was sorry to leave Norman Cohen, my terrific production manager. He was a tremendous help to me and, as corny as it sounds, I don't think I could have done it without him. He was not allowed to work in London. Other than the actors and myself, the only other American allowed to work in England was Robert Redford's makeup man.

Chapter 19
The Great Gatsby – London

London. We arrived at Pinewood Studios to check the sets that John Box had built. We had two days of preparation before we started filming in the "Valley of the Ashes" set. That was the garbage dump between East Egg and West Egg—a key location. That was where Wilson's garage was and that was where we would resume shooting at Pinewood. Clayton, Slocombe, Box and other key members and I were studying camera angles from the plans. Alongside the garage was a billboard advertising Dr. T.J. Eckleburg, an oculist. The billboard was a huge pair of black- rimmed eyeglasses. This billboard was an important story point. As they were discussing the garage scene, I kept looking up at the billboard. Something bothered me. As Box and Clayton were on the ground studying the set plans, I said, "I think 'ocultist' is misspelled." Box, who didn't particularly like me, just ignored the remark. (Production designers do not like production people and vice versa. They like to spend a lot of money, and we like to save money.) I said, "I think 'ocultist' has one C, not two." Box looked up at me and said with great exasperation and authority, "I swear on my four Oscars that it is the correct spelling." Who am I to argue with a man who has four Oscars? We started filming in Pinewood Studios on July 20, 1973.

A few days later, while viewing the first day's rushes, I was still bothered by the spelling on the billboard. After the rushes, I went to my office and looked up the spelling. I was hoping there were two spellings for oculist. There wasn't. I had to go to Clayton and tell him. He went crazy. We had filmed the Eckleburg billboard for several days and it would have been too expensive to reshoot. Henceforth, whenever we would see the

With Jack Clayton and Robert Redford.

billboard in subsequent scenes, there would be a shadow over the word "oculist." I learned one important thing from that incident. I should always go with my instincts. What I should have done was go to my dictionary immediately when I spotted the error and not have listened to a four-time Oscar winner. Especially since they don't give Oscars for spelling.

While I was filming in London, Agnes Moorehead came to do a television movie. I had rented a large house in Chelsea and Agnes stayed with me. She was great company. Our cars would arrive at the same time. I would go to Pinewood and Agnes would go to Shepperton Studios. While there, Agnes was invited to the Royal Command Performance of *Lost Horizon*. She asked me to escort her. Queen Elizabeth would be there. I was excited, as I had never seen the Queen in person. On the night of the premiere, we got to the theater before 7:30 p.m. If you weren't there by that time you weren't allowed in. I was fascinated by the way everything was handled. Agnes and I sat in the balcony just off center.

Exactly at 7:30 p.m. sharp, the curtains in the cinema opened up and we could see the Royal cars arriving on the screen. They had cameras on the outside of the theater photographing the arrival. We could see her Highness step out of her limousine. She was presented with flowers and there were many curtsies. As she entered the theater to be presented to the cast and executives of the film, the cameras were turned off. She is never photographed while she is being presented. The curtains in the theater closed. There was about a ten-minute delay while the presentations were being made. (I had that experience years later when I was presented to Princess Diana.) Finally, ever so slowly, she entered the balcony from the opposite side where Agnes and I were sitting. Everybody stood up. I don't remember if they played "God Save the Queen." We couldn't see her that well. She walked very slowly down some stairs and sat in the middle of the first row. Almost everybody could see her from the main floor as well as the balcony. A small spotlight from the ceiling fell upon her tiara.

The movie began. It was a terrible film—nothing like the original. When the movie ended, the lights came on. Everyone rose when the Queen stood up. Now, she was exiting from the opposite side from where she entered. This time, again ever so slowly, she was walking right toward us. She got about three feet from us. Agnes made a slight curtsy; I swear

Celebrating Robert Redford's birthday on location at an English countryside.

she was looking at me. When I mentioned that to some of my British friends, they say she gives that illusion to everybody. Here, I thought she had recognized me.

Another adventure with Agnes in London was on a Saturday morning while we were window-shopping in Knightsbridge. Agnes spotted a beautiful red and pink gown in Harvey Nichols' window. Harvey Nichols is a chic department store. She said that she would like to go in and look at it. We entered this very elegant store and went to the gown department. Agnes asked the saleslady if she could see the red gown that was in the window. The saleslady, not recognizing Agnes said, "Madam, that is a very expensive gown." I said, "Madam did not ask the price. She asked to see it." Slightly embarrassed, the saleslady asked someone to get the gown from the window. Meanwhile, several patrons recognized Agnes. You couldn't miss that red hair. The red gown arrived and Agnes went into the dressing room to try it on. In minutes, she made an entrance, looking magnificent. Now, the actress in Agnes came out. She began swirling around the room. The dress looked like it was made for her. She was parading around for her small audience. She then went and looked at herself in all the many mirrors. She studied the cut and style and twirled around for a few minutes more. She said to the saleslady she wanted to take it off.

She came out of the dressing room. Agnes thanked the saleslady. I said, "Aren't you going to buy it? It looked perfect on you." Agnes said, "Darling, I can have that gown made in Los Angeles by my dressmaker for a third of what it would cost me here. I know exactly how it was made." Agnes and I made a dramatic exit.

We had many visitors on the set of *The Great Gatsby*. It was considered a very important film at the time. I met Maureen O'Sullivan, Mia's mother, who had played "Jane" in the *Tarzan* pictures. Ryan O'Neal, who co-starred with Mia in *Peyton Place*, would visit the set often. He was filming *Barry Lyndon* at the same studio. In the Pinewood commissary I saw my old "friend" from the *Bounty*, Trevor Howard. I went up to him and said, "Hello, Trevor." He turned and said, "For Christ's sake, can't fucking people leave me alone." I think he had been drinking. He was his usual charming self.

The making of *The Great Gatsby* was not easy. We were fraught with problems from the very beginning: studio executives at odds with Merrick, union problems, threats of strikes, constant feuds between Merrick and Clayton, Clayton's rage and drinking, the moving of the entire company to England and the final pressure of getting the film out before the end of the year in order to qualify for the Academy Awards.

Finally, the movie was ready to be released. The film world had been waiting two years for *The Great Gatsby*. There was a great deal of publicity about the movie long before it was released. The fan and fashion magazines were filled with the "Gatsby look" long before the movie had even begun. There were "Gatsby" pots and pans. I think by the time the movie was released the public was tired of it. The world premiere was held in New York City. I was proud to see my name in gigantic letters along the top of the buildings in Times Square.

The studio had asked me whom I would like to take to the premiere. Without hesitation, I said Paulette Goddard. I was in love with Paulette when I was a small boy. Of course, I would never have told her that. And I knew she lived in New York City. She had a permanent apartment in the Pierre Hotel on Park Avenue. All the arrangements were made.

With Mia Farrow, David Merrick and Maureen O'Sullivan (Mia's mother) at Pinewood Studios.

I arrived decked out in my tuxedo and asked the limousine driver to wait. I was announced and took the elevator to her apartment. Paulette opened the door and let me in. She looked pretty good for her age, which must have been around sixty-five or more at the time. She appeared slightly uncomfortable, as was I. After all, we had never met, although as old Hollywood hands we were both used to having to meet new people all the time. We also had a lot of goodwill toward each other that made the getting-acquainted stage easier. She was wearing a gorgeous gown and had another splendid gown hanging on the door. A huge necklace made of rubies, diamonds, and a gigantic emerald hung around her little neck. Paulette was well known for her fondness for jewels, and given her film goddess past, one could guess she had a serious collection of gems. She had been married to Charles Chaplin in the '30s, and her last husband was the author Erich Maria Remarque.

As I entered the living room, she asked if I would like some champagne. I sat on a sofa in front of a long coffee table. She popped the cork and sat next to me. She poured me a glass of champagne.

"Do you like my gown or do you prefer the one hanging on the door?" she asked.

"The one you have on looks great," I said. We were beginning to warm up. Suddenly, she bent down and reached under the coffee table and pulled out a can of Beluga caviar. I dislike caviar and champagne, I never appreciated this expensive combo. She then produced two small plates and a fork. She opened the tin and served me the caviar. She saw me fiddling around with the caviar.

"Don't you like caviar?"

"Only with egg and onion," I said and was immediately embarrassed by my honesty. Paulette smiled, reached under the table and presented me with a shelled hard-boiled egg and a small whole onion. As nice as the gesture was, neither she nor I was about to peel an onion. I resisted peeking under the magical coffee table.

Paulette rambled on about her expensive rugs at her estate in Switzerland. It seemed that recently there was a flood and she was concerned about their condition. I was getting fidgety and said we better leave for the theater. She went to get her wrap and when we stepped out of the apartment, she began locking the door. In typical New York fashion, she had several keys and several locks. It seemed to take forever. We got on the elevator. When the elevator reached the ground floor she said, "Oh my God, I forgot to lock my safe." We took the elevator back up; she unlocked all the locks, ran in, came out and locked all the locks again. Here I was anticipating an exciting, important moment in my life, shared with the magnificent Paulette Goddard, and we were screwing around with keys.

We arrived at the theater. It was like an old-fashioned premiere—Klieg lights, bleachers for the fans, television cameras. Army Archerd, the *Daily Variety* columnist, was interviewing the guests as they arrived on the platform. Army knew Paulette and me. He greeted us and asked Paulette what she thought of the film. Paulette said, "How would I know? I'm just about to see the movie." We were ushered into the loge section of the theater. The seats in the loge section moved forward and backward with ease. Every so often Paulette would fall forward. The weight of the necklace was pulling her body forward. By this time, I had seen the film at least fifty times. There were no surprises. After the screening, there was a fabulous party at the Waldorf-Astoria Hotel. I sat at Jack Clayton's table with Mike Nichols and Annabel Davis-Goff who soon would become Mrs. Nichols. Annabel was the script supervisor on the film.

At the New York premiere with Pauline Marion Goddard Levee aka Paulette Goddard James Chaplin Meredith Remarque. NOTE: The necklace.

The Great Gatsby ended production on September 24, 1973. It took a lot of sweat and tears to get *Gatsby* to the screen. It won two Academy Awards. One went to Theoni V. Aldredge for her magnificent costumes. Well-deserved. The other went to Nelson Riddle for his musical score. That, too, was a popular win.

David Merrick, who never ceased to surprise me, told many people in my presence that it was Hank who produced the movie. He gave me a new sports Mercedes in appreciation. The reviews were fair to bad. I firmly believe the problem was the casting of Robert Redford because of the reasons I mentioned earlier. I thought Mia was brilliant as a spoiled, selfish Daisy. The rest of the cast was also very good. Another problem was the script and that may have been because of Redford's celebrity. When you have a major star such as Redford, you expect to see him throughout the film. When you read the novel, you realize there are not many visual scenes involving Gatsby. The entire book is about Gatsby. Who is Gatsby? Where is Gatsby? I compared it to *Rebecca*. In *Rebecca*, the story is all about Rebecca. In that case, she was dead. By casting

Redford, scenes had to be created to give Redford more screen time. Fitzgerald did not write these scenes. They slowed the movie down as far as I was concerned. I think Clayton had fallen in love with the beauty of the scenes and his actors and the surroundings.

The only time I really tried to convince Clayton to do something my way was the scene in which Myrtle is hit and killed by Gatsby's car. I pleaded with him to let the audience see Myrtle get hit by the car. The story point is that we are not supposed to know who is driving the death car. I said there were several ways it could be staged where we wouldn't see who was driving Gatsby's car. We would naturally assume it was Gatsby at the wheel. Also, at this point in the film, it added a needed "zip." I begged him to shoot it. If it didn't work, we wouldn't use it. No amount of cajoling on my part worked. I certainly don't mean to insinuate that if we had seen Myrtle get killed, it would have made a better movie. Fitzgerald scholars for years to come will discuss the Fitzgerald movie "curse."

In 2001, there was a television version of *The Great Gatsby* that was terrible. The year before, Andre Previn wrote an opera based on *The Great Gatsby* that premiered in San Francisco. That was a flop too.

The final crowning *Gatsby* experience was that many months after the film's release, the doorbell of my home in Los Angeles rang. I opened the door. A well-dressed stranger was standing there. He said, "Is this the home of Hank Moonjean?" I said, "I am Hank Moonjean." He said, "I am so and so and I am from the FBI." He showed me his credentials. I started to laugh. As I showed him in, I said, "David Merrick sent you, didn't he?" He didn't say anything. I knew Merrick was still upset we had to pay the New York Cameraman's union the $50,000. He thought there was a payoff involving some sort of graft. At the time, there was nothing we could have done about it. The FBI agent recorded my "testimony" relating to the union problems. As far as I was concerned, nothing illegal had transpired. He left. I never heard from the FBI again.

Chapter 20
Another Disappointment

I returned back home to Los Angeles. Just about this time, I received a phone call from a Universal executive. He asked me to come to his office the next morning. I met with him and he said that Universal was going to produce a film entitled *Jaws*, to be directed by Steven Spielberg. Would I be interested in producing it? Would I? I was extremely impressed with a film that Steven Spielberg directed earlier called *Duel*. I would love to produce *Jaws*. The executive said to me that, to be perfectly honest, I was one of three producers that Spielberg was going to meet and consider. Fair enough. May the best man win.

The morning of my appointment with Spielberg came. I arrived at his office at Universal on time. I went into his office. Sharks were hanging from the ceiling. It appeared that Spielberg had been doing a considerable amount of research. I introduced myself. I was a little uptight. How do you interview a producer? It's usually by word-of-mouth or by past credits. The moment I started speaking, I knew he was just going through the motions of meeting someone the studio had recommended. He was bored to death. He had already made his decision. He couldn't wait for me to leave and I couldn't wait to go. My parting words were, "Mr. Spielberg, I wish you all the luck and should you select someone else, I would appreciate a phone call." I never heard from him.

Many years passed. *Jaws* was made, released and became a big moneymaker—thanks to Verna Fields. It was Verna, a film editor, who made *Jaws* the film it became. She had taken all the footage to her home. In her swimming pool, she would shoot close-ups of the "shark," a stuntman with a fin tied to his back, to intercut with the existing film.

Because of her contribution to *Jaws*, Verna was made vice-president of postproduction at Universal Studios. Unfortunately, she didn't live too much longer to enjoy her fame.

Years later, I was on the Paramount lot speaking to producer Larry Gordon when Steven Spielberg came up to Larry. He started talking to Larry, when Larry said, "You know Hank Moonjean." He looked at me. I saved him the embarrassment and said, "Oh, I'm the one who is still waiting to see if I can produce *Jaws*." Spielberg turned around and hoofed out.

With the fine actor, Ricardo Montalban.

Many years passed and I received a phone call from Spielberg's right arm, Frank Marshall. I knew Frank when we were both assistant directors. Frank said, "You are considered the best at what you do. Steven Spielberg and I want you to do a film called *Congo* in Australia for our company." I said, "Frank, I would love to do *Congo* in Australia. But before I accept, please ask Spielberg if I can produce *Jaws*."

When I was at Universal doing a film, someone asked me what I thought of *E.T.: The Extra-Terrestrial*. I said, "If that ugly son-of-bitch came into my house, I would have shot its head off." I have never had any respect for Spielberg, not just because of *Jaws*, but because of all the stories I hear about him on the set. The trick is not to see how much money you can spend. That's easy. It's to try to stay on budget and on schedule. And maybe to show some respect to those talented hard-working directors of the past who made tremendous films, made an effort to come in under budget and under schedule.

Chapter 21
Finally, Nichols

Mike Nichols and I finally connected. It was nearly ten years since the *Virginia Woolf* meeting, which was my first career disappointment. The movie Nichols asked me to do was called *The Fortune*. The producer was Don Devlin. I was made Executive Producer. This was the first time I received that credit. I can't remember if it was Devlin or Nichols who actually wanted me on the production. It was probably both men. I knew Devlin socially and I admired him. He was a true gentleman. He certainly was in the wrong business. He was too honest. And, I guess, Nichols really wanted to know how I ticked. The film starred Jack Nicholson and Warren Beatty. It was based on an original script written by Carol Eastman, a great friend of Nicholson's. I thought the script was brilliant. It's about an unattractive heiress whose fortune is derived from the manufacturing of female pads. What's the nice way to say Kotex? The men are down-and-out fortune hunters.

The part of the heiress had not yet been cast. The first name to come up was Bette Midler. I went with Nichols to the Beverly Hills Hotel where Bette was staying. Mike had asked me to join him. Our appointment was for 10 a.m. Bette kept Nichols waiting. She was having a massage. I thought to myself this is the end of Bette Midler. You don't keep someone like Mike Nichols waiting. Nichols eventually went up to see her alone. Goodbye, Bette. Jack Nicholson suggested Mama Cass. There is a scene in the script where our "heroes" stuff the heiress in a trunk and toss the trunk in the ocean. Mike said, "She'll never fit in the trunk." There was a sick joke going around shortly after her untimely death: "If Mama Cass [who choked on a sandwich] had given her sandwich to Karen Carpenter [who died of anorexia] they would both be alive today." Goodbye, Mama. Then, Stockard Channing's name came up. We met with her and she was everyone's choice and a good choice at that. Hello, Stockard.

Sets were built at the old Selznick Studios in Culver City on their back lot called "40 Acres." That's where *Gone With the Wind's* "Tara" once stood. Richard Sylbert was the talented production designer. Sylbert had worked on almost all of Nichols' films. Sylbert built an entire typical California bungalow courtyard. Additionally, he built a gas station, streets, garages and the facades of several apartment buildings. It had the perfect 1930s look. Over half of the film was shot at that location.

The cameraman was John Alonso. He was of Mexican descent. He asked me on the first day of shooting why there weren't more Mexicans on the film. I said, "The crew was chosen for their ability and experience—not by their ethnic background." Besides, Mike Nichols usually had the same crew. Alonso would invite his wife to view the rushes. Not only that, but she commented on what she saw—much to Mike's irritation. This is never done. I asked him not to have his wife come to the rushes. He said, "She always comments on my work." I'm sorry, but not on this film.

One day, I was walking by an open soundstage and I saw our painters, painting lines for a tennis court. I asked them what they were doing. They said that John Alonso requested that they set up a tennis court for him. It seems that Alonso is a tennis enthusiast. I told the painters to put everything back the way it was and come back to our stage. I went to Alonso. I was going to enjoy this. I said, "What's this about setting up a tennis court on Stage 6?" Alonso said, "There is so much time between takes, that I thought I'd play some tennis." I said, "I'm sure as hell glad you don't like polo!" Alonso was not one of my favorite cameramen. And he didn't play tennis on Stage 6.

We were shooting a complicated scene on the stage. It wasn't going well for Mike. He was getting frustrated about something. He looked up at the boom operator who was working off the scaffolding. The boom operator looked bored. (I didn't like him either. He acted as though he was doing us a favor.) Mike looked up at him and said, "I sure wish Clint Althouse [Mike's regular boom man who wasn't available for this film] was up there."

The boom operator looked down at Nichols and said, "I sure wish Peter Bogdanovich was down there."

Nichols insisted that I fire him. I said, "I can't fire him. You started it." Mike said, "Either he goes or I go." Goodbye, boom operator.

I had to appear before a Union board to explain the incident several weeks later. They knew all the facts. I lost the case. The boom operator was paid his regular salary for the run of the entire film. Mike was furious at that decision but there was nothing anyone could do.

One day, I was going over all the outstanding bills. I came across a bill for just under $10,000 for window shades. Window shades??? I took the bill to Richard Sylbert and asked him about the bill. He said he ordered hundreds of window shades for all the windows. I said, "We don't get near ninety-five percent of all the windows. What ever happened to tacking brown wrapping paper on the windows, suggesting shades?" Remember, production designers do not get along with production people. In this case, I liked Sylbert. I was doing my job and he was doing his. Sylbert resented my interference. I told him one of my jobs was to save money. The next day Mike said to me, "Get off Sylbert's back." I said to Mike, "I don't tell you how to direct. Don't you tell me how to produce." I've used that line before.

During production Mama Cass died. Nicholson was devastated. We closed down the production for the day. Nicholson said maybe if Mama Cass had been in the movie, she would have still been alive.

Shooting went on without further incident. There were many days of sheer laughter on the set. Don Devlin was a great friend with a tremendous sense of humor. He has given Hollywood a great legacy—his son Dean Devlin, who has become a top film producer. Dean produced *Independence Day*.

There wasn't a commissary at the Selznick Studios. Often, Nichols, Nicholson, Beatty and I would go to the local restaurants in Culver City for lunch. I don't ever remember Beatty ever picking up the check. He has the first penny he ever made.

Once on a street location in Culver City, Beatty came up to me and said he saw the girl who had been stalking him. I immediately called the police. From Beatty's motor home, we could see "the stalker" amongst the crowd who came to watch the shooting. She looked like a very ordinary young lady. She wore a trench coat. There could have been something under the coat. I even went and stood next to her. She didn't know who I was. We had several plainclothes policemen stationed around, but nothing happened.

Beatty's secretary called me early one morning and asked me if I would pick up Julie Christie, the Oscar-winning British actress, and take her to the location. We were shooting an airport scene in the desert, about two hours from the city. Christie was one of Beatty's current girlfriends. I picked her up at her friend's house. I had never met her and she appeared to be shy—why shouldn't she be? Taking a two-hour car ride with a total stranger? She was carrying a blouse on a hanger. We drove along—each of us making trivial conversation.

About half way to the location, I asked her if she was hungry. She said she was and I pulled over to a small desert diner. We ordered breakfast. She appeared less shy by now. We continued on our journey. She asked me to let her know when we got near the location. More chitchat. Finally, I said we should be at the location in about five minutes. I looked over at her and she was removing her blouse. She wore no bra but she had beautiful breasts. She changed her blouse and was ready to greet Beatty. And I had seen more of Julie Christie than I ever had on the silver screen.

There was a small one-day part for an actress to do a scene at the used car lot where Beatty played an automobile salesman. I asked Mike Nichols if he knew Jody Gilbert. I recommended her for the part and Mike said okay. Jody was a very large woman who appeared in over one hundred movies. I hadn't met Jody Gilbert. I was just a fan. I knew she would add something to the small role. Jody died a couple of years after *The Fortune* was completed. I saw in the obituary column in the *Daily Variety* that I was named an honorary pallbearer. I guess that was her way of thanking me.

There was a small juicy part of the manager of the courtyard. The actress that Mike wanted had already turned down the role. Mike asked me to meet with this middle-aged Oscar winner to see if I could talk her into it. Around 9 p.m. I went to her apartment. I could tell she had been drinking. She wore a pink negligee and sat directly across from me. In minutes, she pulled her legs up and her negligee fell open. No underwear. She began "flashing" me. She turned down the part and I turned down her advances.

The Fortune got mixed reviews. I think it was Mike Nichols' most unsuccessful film. I don't understand to this day why it was such a flop. Jack Nicholson was very funny. Warren Beatty was Warren Beatty. Stockard Channing stole the show. Maybe the problem was very simple;

Jack Nicholson was playing broad comedy, a la Laurel & Hardy, Stockard was playing sophisticated comedy a la Carole Lombard and Warren Beatty just wasn't funny. The three of them didn't mesh.

I admired Mike Nichols very much. He was probably one of the best directors I ever worked for. He had a natural instinct to get to the core of the problem. One word from him to an actor would suffice. Maybe it was because he was also an actor. However, I decided not to work with him again. He never seemed to be happy on the set—everything was a problem. Even when things were running smoothly, he complained about everything. He had no reason to be unhappy. I enjoy my work and I like to be around people who do as well. Of course, it wasn't perfect all the time—nothing ever is. But it would get depressing after awhile. After all, it's only a movie. As I said, I really couldn't understand him. He is probably the most successful director in theater as well as films. He has won every award possible. In any case, as we were winding down *The Fortune*, Mike asked me to produce his next film. I think it was called *Bogart Slept Here*. I turned him down. He said it was a comedy for Warner Bros. to star Robert De Niro. I asked him, "What makes you think De Niro can do comedy?" I wouldn't reconsider Mike's offer. Mike went on to make the De Niro film with Ray Stark. After one or two weeks into filming, the De Niro movie was canceled. I went on to bigger and better things. I will always admire Mike and will always consider him a friend.

Chapter 22
Beauty and the Beast – 1976

I will always be grateful to Norman Cohen, my *Gatsby* production manager, for recommending me to produce *Beauty and the Beast*. This famous literary piece has been made into a film numerous times. This version was a Palm Films-Hemdale Production. Thomas M.C. Johnston was the executive producer and Sherman Yellen wrote the script. The "Beast" was George C. Scott and the "Beauty" was Trish Van Devere, Scott's wife at the time. The other actors were Bernard Lee and Virginia McKenna. The director was Fielder Cook. The film was to be made for television for the US and Canadian markets and released as a feature film throughout the rest of the world. The entire film was to be made in London and Cheltenham, England. No studio shooting. This would be my first venture into the television business, not counting my few months at Desilu Studios. It was also the first time I received full screen credit as a producer. This was a red-letter day for me to finally reach my goal in my chosen career.

George C. Scott was a maniac. Talk about tempers and temperament. But I think he was one of the finest actors to ever come out of America. The "Beast" was depicted as a wild boar. Del Acevedo was Scott's makeup man. Every day, Acevedo would apply three sections of prostheses on Scott's face. First, the forehead, second the snout and finally the jaw. This process took over two hours. On one occasion, Scott broke out in a rash around his face. I called for a dermatologist to come to the set. I was in the makeup room with Scott when the doctor arrived. Del said, "The veterinarian…I mean the doctor is here."

When people visited the set, they would always ask me why George C. Scott was hired when you don't see him as Scott until the last three minutes of the film. He is the beast for almost all the film. They would say, "Anyone could have played the beast." And I would say, "Every student of acting should be asked, if not forced, to see Scott's performance." Although you only see his eyes through that grotesque mask, you sense his every emotion. What Scott does with his body language is spectacular. When he is on the screen you can't take your eyes off him. Trish was adequate as "Beauty." My hunch is that Scott agreed to do the role because his wife wanted to play "Beauty."

On another day, toward the end of the schedule, an assistant director said Mr. Scott wanted to see me immediately in his makeup room. I wondered what the crisis was now. As I entered the makeup room, Scott was sitting in front of his makeup table looking directly at me in the mirror. Next to me stood the director, Fielder Cook. They had obviously had a heated argument. I hadn't a clue as to what the problem was. Scott's beady eyes were fixed on me. He was fuming. He only had a partial section of his prosthesis on and the anger in his voice was equally frightening. Scott crunched his teeth and with a slow hiss said to me, "Get rid of the fucking son-of-a-bitch before I kill him." Scott looked like he could and would.

I said, "What…?"

"Get rid of him." Scott never looked at Cook who was standing two feet away. Cook was ashen-faced. I told Cook to go to his trailer and I would come by and see him. Cook left. Scott was slowly calming down. I said, "I can't fire Cook. Who will take over the directing?" Scott said, "You will. You're the only one around here who knows what the fuck is going on." Thank you, George C. Scott. Nobody directs Scott. He does it his way. All you have to do is point the camera in his direction. I ended up "directing" for about ten days. I also shot additional scenes that I wrote for the European theatrical version.

The reviews were excellent. Hallmark, which released *Beauty and the Beast* on American television, told me that it had received its highest ratings. For my participation, I received the Christopher Award for the Producer of the Best Drama for 1976. That is an honor that the Catholics bestow each year. And I was very proud to receive it. It was the only award I ever received during my entire career.

After *Beauty and the Beast*, I decided to remain in London and treat myself to a long vacation. By this time I had many British friends. I was seeing a great deal of Hermione Baddeley and her constant companion, Lady Assheton-Smith, better known as Lady Joan. Lady Joan was a real

George Hamilton visiting the set.

character. She always had a huge artificial flower pinned to her dress at her shoulder. The flower was so big she could only look in one direction when she turned her head. And she wore the thickest brown makeup. You could claw it off with your fingernails. Lady Joan was a great spirit and loads of fun. She spent her entire fortune on the preservation of the animals in Africa. She would visit Africa regularly. I originally met Lady Joan when we were making *The Unsinkable Molly Brown*. Hermione said she would like me to meet someone very special. We walked to Hermione's stage dressing room. Hermione, with great flair, said, "I'd like you to meet Lady Assheton-Smith," as she opened the dressing room door. Lady Joan was flat on her face on the floor pissed out of her mind. She rolled over and said, "Oh. Hellooo." She then rolled back. Hermione said, "Isn't she a caution?" and shut the dressing room door. Lady Joan was "out" for the rest of the day.

One evening, Hermione gave a "lobster party" at her home on Green Street in London's Mayfair district. The dining room was downstairs on the lower level. On a nearby table, dozens of large cooked lobsters were placed.

All the guests, and there must have been twenty, would take a lobster and go to the dining table and begin eating. I was seated next to Vivien Leigh. Next to Vivien was Kay Medford and next to Kay Medford was my friend Brad Bennett. Although Vivien was fragile looking, she was still a great beauty. We struck up a conversation. It was then that I told her that Elizabeth Taylor had said Vivien was the most beautiful actress in the world.

Kay Medford was a well-known lesbian. I knew Kay from my *BUtterfield 8* days. Kay began to resent Vivien's interest in me. Vivien asked me if I wouldn't mind going upstairs to get her black handbag that she had left in the reception room. I went upstairs and found fur coats, hats and more coats and a dozen or so black handbags. I went back downstairs and asked Vivien to describe the handbag. She described the handbag and I returned upstairs and found it and took it to her. She said, "That's it. Thank you very much indeed." Her handbag was the size of a Gideon's bible. She opened the bag and took out a wrinkled wad of Kleenex tissue. And another wrinkled wad of tissue and yet another wad of tissue. The tissues had jewels wrapped in them. I saw diamond clips, bracelets, a necklace and who knows what else. Vivien was looking for her lipstick. I said, "What are all these jewels doing in your handbag?" She said, "They're mine. I'm afraid to leave them in my flat. They might get stolen." I thought, here she's left her handbag upstairs in the reception room, without an attendant, and anyone could come in and steal all the handbags and the furs and everything else in the room.

Vivien was drinking steadily. Kay was really getting irritated with me. She leaned over Vivien's back and whispered, "Keep your hands off her. I saw her first." I just smiled at Kay. Vivien was aware of Kay's advances. Vivien said to me, "Let's get the fuck out of here." She was pretty smashed by this time. I took Vivien upstairs. I looked back and Kay was glowering at me. Vivien picked out her coat. I helped her with it and we went out into the street. She wanted a cab. I hailed one and helped her get in. She gave me a seductive kiss and was gone. I never saw her again.

Hermione died before Lady Joan. I had lost track of Lady Joan. Years later, when I was in London, I tried to contact her. I had an old address of hers, but I was able to track her down in Fulham in a Catholic convent. I telephoned the convent. Lady Joan had passed away just a few weeks before. The nun said she died a pauper but gave a great deal of pleasure to all those around her. All her millions were spent to save the animals. A very kind Lady.

While in London, I would see Ava Gardner on occasion. It was many years since *Bhowani Junction*. London had been Ava's home for quite a while. She had a flat near the Albert Hall. A few years back, at a cocktail party in her apartment, the conversation went on about all the film stars getting plastic surgery. I said to Ava, "If you had your bags removed, you would look twenty years younger." (Ava didn't have bags, she had suitcases.) She said, "Frank gave me these bags but I made him go bald," she said, speaking of her former husband Frank Sinatra. She laughed. In spite of it, she looked fantastic; she still had her figure and that glorious complexion. When I was working at MGM, I would ask the old-timers who they thought was the most beautiful actress they had ever seen and worked with. Not Garbo, not Lamarr, not Turner, not Taylor—always Ava Gardner. She remained in love with Frank Sinatra and I believe he never stopped loving her. When Ava was making *Mogambo* with Clark Gable and Grace Kelly in Africa, Ava said, "Grace fucked anybody that moved. I didn't touch anyone because I was so much in love with Frank. But I got blamed. Grace was the perennial virgin and I was the 'whore.' It wasn't fair."

When Ava had her stroke, Sinatra sent his private plane to London to take her to the Mayo clinic. I saw Ava shortly before she died in London. She was having a manicure. She was forcing the arm that was affected by the stroke forward so that the manicurist could do her nails. Gradually, the arm would pull back, and she'd shove it forward again. People who knew Ava much better than I said she had a death wish. Her wish was granted soon after I saw her.

I returned to Hollywood. The first call I got from my agent was to go immediately to Dino De Laurentiis' office in Beverly Hills. He was looking for a producer to work on the remake of *King Kong*. De Laurentiis was just moving into his new offices on Canon Drive. I had never met Mr. De Laurentiis before. I got to his office at the designated time. There were movers all over the building. A secretary showed me into his office. De Laurentiis was sitting at a huge desk. Standing behind him was one of the most handsome young men I had ever seen. It was his son Federico (named after Fellini). He looked exactly like his mother, the Italian actress Silvana Mangano. I had once seen Silvana Mangano at the Los Angeles Airport. She was the epitome of Italian aristocracy, so elegant and beautiful. She had a full-length mink coat thrown over her shoulders and a maid and chauffeur hovering over her.

De Laurentiis introduced me to his son. He said his son would help me on the film. I said, "Mr. De Laurentiis, we have to discuss business. I have agents that you must deal with." He said, "Forget the agents. I want you to start now. Do you know many special effects people?" I thought any minute he was going to show me my new office. I said, "Mr. De Laurentiis, I can't start until all the business matters have been resolved." De Laurentiis said, "We don't need to have any business discussions." I said I was sorry and left. That was the end of King Kong and me. Tragically, a few years after that meeting, his son, Federico, was killed in an airplane accident. I understood his mother never got over that loss. She, too, died shortly thereafter.

Chapter 23
The End

Lawrence (Larry) Gordon hired me as the Executive Producer on a movie entitled *The End*. It was my first picture with Burt Reynolds. Burt was also the director. The film also starred Joanne Woodward, Sally Field and Dom DeLuise, and two film veterans, Pat O'Brien and Myrna Loy. This was my second film with Myrna, who played Burt's mother in the film. David Steinberg had a small role. I would soon work with David again.

Burt asked me to see if Jane Withers was available for a small role. Jane Withers was a child actress who was Shirley Temple's nemesis in one of Shirley's films at 20th Century-Fox. I contacted Jane. She didn't have an agent. She asked me to send her the script. I was happy to. In a few days, I heard from her. She said, "I would never consider doing a movie that contained any four-letter words. Sorry." Jane may never work again.

The End was a very funny script. The story was set in Santa Barbara, California about a hypochondriac (Burt) who thinks he has every known disease and is at death's door. We shot all the interiors on a soundstage as well as at several locations in Hollywood before we went to Santa Barbara. We were in Santa Barbara for two weeks. Burt was as good a director as I have ever seen. He's been around a long time. And being an actor first certainly helps. During this film, Sally Field and Burt were lovers in the film as well as in real life. Joanne Woodward played Burt's estranged wife.

When I'm on a location I seldom have dinner with any member of the crew or staff. I figure I spend fourteen to eighteen hours every day on the film and at dinner I just want to relax and not even think of

the film. After we all checked into the hotel I asked the front desk where the best Italian restaurant was in Santa Barbara. I went to the recommended restaurant that evening. It was a typical Italian restaurant—red-checkered tablecloth, Chianti bottle used as a candlestick, and sawdust on the floor. The restaurant appeared to be very popular. There was a large woman with pitch-black hair and small gold earrings. She appeared to be the owner or the manager as she was going from table to table asking the customers how they were enjoying their meals. She came up to me. She said, "You like?" I said, Very much." She said, "You come again." I smiled at her as she walked to the next table. She had a magnificent face. She looked like a real Italian Earth Mother. I had an excellent meal.

One of the scenes we planned to shoot in Santa Barbara was near the opening of the movie. Burt is on a motorcycle—following a funeral procession. He pulls alongside the family car and yells out "What did he die of?" The limousine window rolls down and a man gave Burt the "finger."

The next morning one of the assistant directors said that Burt wanted to see me the minute

I got to the set. I went to him and he said, "Sport, when we shoot the motorcycle scene on Saturday, instead of a man in the family car, I would like a middle-aged woman." I said I just happen to have one lined up. Burt said, "Is it all right if I tell you what I have in mind? After all, I am the director." I said okay, not listening to what he was saying. I had my lady all lined up.

That evening I went to the same restaurant and sat at the same table. My Earth Mother was there. This time I had brought my business card with me. She approached me in the same manner as she had the night before. She recognized me. "I know you like. You come back." I said I had something to discuss with her as I handed her my business card. I said that Burt Reynolds was doing a film in Santa Barbara and would she like to be in it.

"I don't know any Burt Renows," she said. I said that he is a famous actor and director.

"No, I don't know."

"Nevertheless, would you like to be in my movie?"

My Earth Mother said, "Whatta I gotta to do?" I was slightly embarrassed to tell someone's grandmother about the scene with the finger. I figured Burt was the director, that's his problem.

"Burt will tell you when the time comes." I asked her if she had a black dress.

"I nevera weara black."

I asked her if she had a long cross.

"I nevera weara that."

I said not to worry I would arrange all that.

"How mucha money do I getta?"

"Two hundred dollars."

"Two hundred fifty and I do it."

An actress for two minutes and already she is trying to stiff the producer. I took her name and address. I told her if we had no weather problems she would work Saturday morning.

Saturday morning, I sent my limousine to pick up my latest discovery. When she arrived on the set, I beamed with pride. She looked magnificent in her black mantilla and long gold cross. Burt took one look at her and said, "She's perfect. You've done it again. You're the best." Meanwhile, everyone was getting ready to do the motorcycle scene with the funeral cortege. Burt explained to my latest discovery what she was supposed to do in the scene. It was a complicated scene as the camera car had to follow the motorcycle that's following the family car. The action would take them around the block. All was ready. I was standing at the start point. Next to me was a state trooper who was helping with crowd control. Burt took several takes, always returning to the same start point. Burt asked for some pillows to put behind my lady so she was sitting more forward. They started again. The state trooper next to me said, referring to the woman, "Where did you get her?" I said she is my latest discovery. The state trooper said to me, "Your latest discovery happens to be the biggest madam in Santa Barbara County." And here I was embarrassed to tell her about giving Burt the finger.

In the studio, we did a scene with Sam Jaffe, the great character actor. (Remember *Lost Horizon*?) He was playing a dying patient in a hospital. The scene was so real that we cut it out of the final print. After all, this was supposed to be a comedy. Ironically, Sam died soon after. I think it was one of his final performances.

During production, as I got to know Burt better, I asked him during a quiet moment, if he ever took a "prelude." Burt said, "What?" I said, "Did you ever take a prelude?" He gathered some of the crew around him. I knew I must have used the wrong word. Burt said, "Tell them what you just asked me." Hesitantly, I repeated my question. Everyone started to laugh. Obviously, I should have said Quaaludes. What do I know about drugs? Although, I did take a puff of some Columbian "shit" once, in New Orleans.

I got along famously with Burt. He was genuinely a great guy. He had many ups and downs with his career. A great deal of heartbreak and disappointment. If he liked you, he loved you. If you were a friend, you were a friend for life. I think the people that surrounded him took advantage of his kindness and generosity. There were rumors that he was into drugs. In all the films I did with Burt, I never saw that side of him. But I don't know much about drugs. He was loyal to his crew. Some of them unfortunately weren't loyal to him.

Dom DeLuise was a real character and a real comic. He nearly stole the film from Burt as the mad mental patient. People still talk about the climax of the film where DeLuise is chasing Burt along Santa Barbara's seashore.

Myrna Loy was a joy—again. Her part wasn't as large as the role she had in *The April Fools* but she still stood out. She still wanted the black

My first film with Burt.

extras to carry briefcases. It was my second film with Joanne Woodward who is a consummate professional.

Larry Gordon, the producer who initially hired me, became a real friend. He could relate to Burt's character, as Larry is a hypochondriac. (He would never admit to it.) During the production, Burt asked me if I wanted to produce *Hollywood Stuntman*, which was later to be called *Hooper*. I said, "Absolutely."

The End was a fairly successful film, and it was another turning point in my career. It introduced me to Burt Reynolds, Larry Gordon and David Steinberg.

Chapter 24
Hooper

H*ooper* was the most financially successful film I ever produced. It was made in 1978 and I still receive checks from Warner Bros. for it. It is also a film where I made major creative decisions. That was because I knew the director, Hal Needham, and we respected each other. Hal and I began in the business at the same time; he as a stuntman and me as an assistant director. We both were stationed at Fort Bragg, North Carolina during the same time during the Korean "conflict." Hal was a paratrooper with the 82nd Airborne. I was training to be a spy. We never met while at Fort Bragg. I wasn't about to jump out of a plane. Hal made a major impact when his very first directorial effort broke all records. The movie was *Smokey and the Bandit*. Burt Reynolds was Hal's best friend and it was Burt who brought us together.

The story of *Hooper* was about the lives and loves of stuntmen. Burt Reynolds played an aging stuntman, who becomes involved with a young up-and-coming stuntman, played by Jan-Michael Vincent. Every stuntman and stuntwoman in Hollywood worked on the film. The cast included Sally Field, Brian Keith and Robert Klein. Sally and Burt were still lovers. There was a role for an actress to play "Hooper's" wife. (Sally played his girlfriend.) We approached Angie Dickinson to play Burt's wife. Much to my sorrow and, later, hers, she turned down the role. No other actress was approached. We decided to just mention a wife in the dialogue without seeing her.

Working with Hal was a pleasure. Because we respected each other we could discuss the film without getting territorial or defensive over our separate domains. I could discuss the direction and he could discuss the producing. After all, we were partners. The third partner was Larry Gordon who was the Executive Producer. Before the film started, we had many meetings in our offices on the Warner Bros. lot. Our offices were the old school house. One day, Clint Eastwood marched right into Burt's office while Burt and I were having lunch. He was just killing time while they were getting ready on his set. I don't remember what movie Clint was doing. Anyway, Burt and Clint were talking about the possibility of doing a film together one day. After about an hour, Clint left the way he came in. Richard Martin Luther Von Liebegott III, our production coordinator (Liebegott was a permanent fixture on most of my films), came into our office and said, "Who was that workman who just barged into the office?" I said that wasn't a workman that was Clint Eastwood. Mr. Liebegott said, "He should have been announced." Outside of our offices, we heard a female voice cry out, "Where the fuck is my dressing room?" I looked out the window and I saw that the woman yelling all those profanities was our first First Lady—Jane Wyman, the first Mrs. Ronald Reagan. She was shooting *Falcon Crest* at Warner Bros.

The biggest production nightmare was the last scene in the movie. It was a movie within a movie. Our stars were in a red rocket car. The red car was rigged for jet propulsion. This automobile was one of the stars of the film as well. The car is supposed to leap over a chasm that has just been opened by an earthquake. This was to be filmed in Tuscaloosa, Alabama. The reason why Tuscaloosa was selected was that the University of Alabama was going to destroy their married students' quarters. The quarters were built during World War II to accommodate the returning servicemen. The quarters had become obsolete and they were going to make room for new buildings. Hal offered to destroy the area for them. Only in Alabama would they allow a film company to destroy ninety acres. The destruction of that area was to precede the leap over the "earthquake" site.

Hal and I flew to Tuscaloosa with our art director and our special effects man. We checked into a local motel. Hal and I rented separate cars and the next morning we all went to look at the various locations. We met at the proposed demolition site. The area that we were going to blow up didn't look like a small town. It looked exactly like what it was meant to—college living quarters. We decided to build some small buildings, add billboards, etc. to give it more of a small-town look. Our art director did a brilliant job when the time came. Now, we had to resolve the problem of staging an earthquake. Hal and the special effects man found a spot to "make an earthquake." I was not impressed with the effects man. I thought he was a phony. They were discussing the length of the earthquake, where it should start, where it should end, and how deep it should be. It all seemed absurd to me. Finally, I stepped in.

"What are you two talking about? There is no way you can start an earthquake and make it believable. The point of the leap over the chasm created by the earthquake is that our heroes may be jeopardizing their lives. You can't build a big 'hole' unless you can make it look like a mini-Grand Canyon." (This was before all of modern technology. Today, this would not be a problem.)

Hal was noticeably irritated with me. He and the effects man sped off in Hal's car. I took off in mine. On the way to the motel, I crossed a large bridge over a river. I noticed that the traffic coming the opposite way was being diverted. I pulled my car to the side of the highway and got out to look at the bridge more carefully. I ran across the highway. There were state police diverting the oncoming traffic. I asked a state trooper what had happened to the bridge. He said, "A few weeks ago a gasoline truck loaded with petroleum hit the side of one of the girders and the truck exploded, nearly destroying half of the bridge." A light went on. I hurried back to the motel most anxious to see Hal. Hal was anxiously waiting for me to arrive. Almost simultaneously, we said "Bridge." He, too, had seen the bridge. It was decided that the red rocket car would attempt a leap across the bridge over the river and not across an earthquake. That's what makes moviemaking fun. You share thoughts and ideas. The scenes scheduled for Alabama would be shot at the end of the schedule.

The film began at the studio with many local locations. As I said earlier, every stunt person in Hollywood worked on the film at one point or another. And with every stunt imaginable, the only casualty we had when shooting was when a stunt motorcyclist passed a car and grabbed a can of beer from a stunt girl riding in a convertible coming the opposite way. The beer can cut his finger.

One of my main contributions was the end credits. We had shot so much stunt footage that it was impossible to have it all in the body of the film. I had the idea of showing some of the unseen stunt footage run alongside the end credits. So, the film editor, Hal and I chose some stunt shots to be used. As far as I know, *Hooper* was the first film to use this method of running credits with outtakes, something that's pretty common nowadays.

Another major contributor to the movie was our composer, Bill Justis. Again, I worked directly with him. I wanted a theme song to play whenever we saw the red rocket car on the screen. Justis wrote a great theme that was exciting and memorable. Another major contributor to *Hooper* was Bobby Bass, the stunt coordinator. He was a soft-spoken man who was not afraid of anything. Bobby recently passed away. He was Bo Derek's stepfather. He, together with Hal, created many original stunts. It's interesting to note that in all of Hal's films, when a car is turned over or wrecked, you see the driver and occupants get out of the car unscathed. This was a must with Hal. Otherwise, by the end of the film, it would appear that dozens of drivers were "killed." That is not funny.

Tuscaloosa. 1978. The day arrived when we were going to "blow up" the entire "town." We had several camera crews on various specific sites. We also had a camera mounted on a helicopter. I must give Hal all the credit for staging this very difficult sequence. All hell broke loose. It was very exciting to watch. The red rocket car dodged falling buildings, explosions, fires and other cars. Many stuntmen were driving cars, running out of exploding buildings, etc. The slogan of the day was "burn, baby, burn." General havoc. An industrial chimney collapsed just as the red rocket car passed. Thousands of residents were watching from safe vantage points. Not a single person was injured or burned. This scene took several days.

The next order of business was the red rocket car leaping across the river and gorge. That scene took as much preparation as the town being blown up. There was an unknown factor in this scene: where will the red car land? That was not going to be determined by humans—at least not exactly. It was determined by scientific means. Burt and Jan-Michael were in the red car contemplating the leap. After we shot the close-ups, we replaced them with dummies in preparation for the leap. We were preparing for the red car to careen over the gorge, and with any luck, land on the other side of the bridge. We were not certain where the car would land. Heavy rope barriers were strung along the highway to catch the car should it go beyond the anticipated spot. On the opposite side of the gorge facing the camera were hundreds of people standing in the woods watching the activity. I asked one of the assistants to have them clear that area. The red car could just as easily land on them. On the loudspeaker, they were told to please leave the area. It could be dangerous. We had many Alabama state troopers assisting us. They were prepared to stop traffic in all directions once we began shooting. Tension was mounting. I noticed that the people in the woods were still standing there. No one had moved. Once again, over the loudspeaker, they were asked to leave. If they wanted to see the filming, would they please come on this side of the river? Again, no one moved. I called a state trooper over and asked him for his assistance in clearing the wooded area. I did not want anyone hurt or killed. The state trooper said, "Leave it be. They're mountain people. You've asked them to leave twice. Don't mess with them. Only three weeks ago, two niggers were strung up down there under the bridge. Leave it be. Leave it be." I then realized I was in the Deep South. This was 1978—not that long ago.

Everything was set. All the cameras were ready. The traffic in every direction was halted. I crossed my fingers and said a silent prayer. The cameras turned and Hal yelled "Action." The red rocket car flew up and over the bridge and gorge perfectly. It landed about twenty yards further than anticipated. The heavy rope barrier kept the car from crashing beyond the highway. There was a roar of relief and happiness. It was a perfect shot. It couldn't have been more perfect. That scene was the highlight of the film. Speaking of prayer, Hal's elderly mother would always be on the set on the first day of filming. Hal would gather the crew around the camera and Mrs. Needham would say a prayer. She did that on all of Hal's films.

Hooper was on many lists as one of the best films of 1978. It was also Warner Bros.' most financially successful movie of the year. Recently, *Hooper* was listed as one of the six best stunt films ever made.

I didn't see much of David Merrick after *The Great Gatsby*. He had recently had a massive stroke, and he was in bad shape physically. I had heard that Merrick was staying at the Beverly Hills Hotel. Merrick owned two scripts that I was interested in producing. The first was based on Jessamyn West's novel, *The Massacre at Fall Creek*.

The second script is based on a play entitled *Two For The Seesaw* and the subsequent musical *Seesaw*. The film script is a clever idea about a theatrical "bus-and-truck-company." (The cast and crew ride the bus and the equipment and sets are in the truck,) The film script cuts between the musical numbers from *SEESAW* and the drama of the actors going from city to city from *Two For The Seesaw*. By the end of the movie, the audience would have seen musical highlights interspersed with a backstage story.

Arrangements were made with Etan Merrick, David's wife, for me to meet him at 7 p.m. the next night at the Beverly Hills Hotel. My lawyer and I went to his bungalow. I rang the bell and Etan let us in. Etan was attractive as ever. She offered us cocktails. There was a male nurse going in and out of a bedroom. After some polite chitchat, Merrick came out of his room, looking pale and gaunt, and with his toupee askew. He was wearing an expensive suit but he still had the undertaker's look. I introduced my lawyer to Merrick. I could not understand a word Merrick was muttering. The stroke had left him unintelligible. I knew this must have been painful for Merrick. After all, he was a giant on Broadway and he had come to this. I said, "David, I know you are not well so I will get to the point. I am interested in optioning *The Massacre at Fall Creek* and the *Bus and Truck* scripts."

Merrick mumbled something. I looked at my lawyer and together we looked at Etan hoping for a translation. She said, "He said he wants two million dollars for both scripts." As far as I was concerned she could have said ten million dollars. I was dumbfounded. Options can be anywhere from a thousand dollars to fifty thousand dollars but not in the millions. Merrick muttered something else. We looked at Etan. She said, "He said he wanted his name on the screen." I said, "I wouldn't think of not placing your name in the credits."

That was the end of the meeting. I don't know what ever happened to those scripts. They are probably tied up with his estate. They certainly were not produced. I never saw Merrick again. He divorced Etan and married an Oriental lady who was running his empire. Merrick died shortly thereafter.

A proud Uncle showing off his family. Michael, Patricia, Scott, and Richard Moomjian.

Chapter 25
The Next Two

From *Hooper*, I segued into *Smokey and the Bandit II*, again with Hal Needham; the year was 1980. As I mentioned earlier, *Smokey and the Bandit*, Hal's first film as a director, made millions. It was a tremendous hit at the box-office. I was hoping lightning would strike twice. *Smokey II* had the same cast—Burt Reynolds, Jackie Gleason, Sally Field, Jerry Reed and Mike Henry. Dom DeLuise was a welcome addition to the cast. This was to be my third film with Sally Field and my third film with Burt. Burt and Sally were still an item. But I was sensing a cooling off of the relationship.

The film was scheduled to begin shooting in Las Vegas, Nevada, with the interiors shot at Universal Studios. I remember the start date exactly. The Saturday before the Monday start date was my fiftieth birthday. My friends and family had planned a big birthday party for me in Los Angeles. I had been in Las Vegas for nearly a month preparing for the start of the film. Burt, who wasn't required until the second week of filming, called me and said that Sally, her mother and her two sons were coming to Las Vegas that Saturday.

"Would you meet them and give them the royal treatment?"

I said, "Burt, that's my birthday. I'm going home for the day."

"I ask you for a favor once every so often and you turn me down," Burt said. "It's important that you meet Sally."

I knew Burt was annoyed. I didn't want to disappoint him so I said I would be there to meet Sally. I also knew that this must have been very important to Burt otherwise he wouldn't have asked me as he knew it was my fiftieth birthday. He was appreciative. I called home and had them cancel the birthday plans. Work comes first. But I was very disappointed. You don't turn fifty every day.

I made certain that Sally had the best suite in the hotel, and I also made sure Sally's mother was well taken care of. I sent someone to go shopping for some toys for Sally's two sons. I went to the hotel's florist and ordered three gigantic arrangements of flowers wishing Sally "Welcome and Good Luck"—one from Burt, one from Hal and one from me. I made arrangements for the Field entourage to enter the hotel from a side entrance and go to their rooms up the service elevator. You would have thought Elizabeth Taylor was coming. But that was Burt's request.

Saturday arrived and I went to the airport with a limousine and a van to meet Sally and family. The plane was on time. I greeted Sally and introduced myself to Mrs. Field. Sally was like an iceberg. (But she always was—at least to me.) I had porters help us to the vehicles. I rode in the limousine with the party. I was making idle conversation when I said, "You know, Sally, today is my fiftieth birthday."

She said, "No. I didn't know." Such warmth. We got to the hotel and we went up to the rooms. As Sally walked in, she saw the flower arrangements. She walked up to the first arrangement and looked at the card. It was from Burt. She threw it aside. She went to the second arrangement and looked at that card. That one was from me. I was standing three feet from her. She read the card and threw it on the table. She never acknowledged my presence. I thought, you bitch. I could have been with friends and family instead of you. The puzzling thing is that I never had a harsh word with her, nor was there any incident that might explain her chilliness. She was never close to me or really anyone as far as I could see. She just seemed to treat people coldly on general principle. Sally went to the third flower arrangement. She threw Hal's card aside. I later found out that she didn't want to be in the film and that she didn't like Hal Needham's direction. She must have been hell to work with after she won her Oscar for *Norma Rae*.

The first day's shooting was in a small church in Henderson, a suburb of Las Vegas. This was the scene in which Sally was going to marry Junior. There was tension in the air. Sally was on the telephone calling someone. Hal was trying his best to get things moving. Sally wouldn't come out of her trailer dressing room. I was called to the phone. It was Burt calling from Los Angeles. Sally had been on the phone to Burt. "What's going on? What's wrong with Sally?" Burt asked.

The Next One 285

On location with Jackie Gleason in Las Vegas.

"I haven't a clue why Sally refuses to come to the set," I said. Burt asked to speak to Sally. After their conversation, Sally reluctantly came out of her trailer and went into the church and we began shooting. It was a very funny scene where Sally runs out of the church refusing to marry Junior. (I think Junior was the lucky one.)

The next week Burt was with us. Whatever Sally's problem was or whatever her next problem might be, Burt could handle it.

Jackie Gleason was one of the funniest men I had ever met. I thought *The Honeymooners* was one of the great television shows. Jackie would tell stories of his Warner Bros. days. It's hard to believe that Gleason started out in films as a "heavy." His best friends in those days were Humphrey Bogart and his wife at the time, Mayo Methot. They were known as "The Battling Bogarts." Jackie would go to dinner with them often. After dinner and after much drinking, the Bogarts would get into a fight—often a fistfight. She would haul off and sock him and he would haul off and sock her. These weren't slight taps. And these fistfights were always in public places. Jackie said that Mayo's punch was more lethal than Bogart's. Every time Jackie would go out with them, it always ended up in a free-for-all. It was inevitable that they would split up. Jackie Gleason began to do comedy roles and eventually found his niche in show business. He became a popular stand-up comic, did major roles in films and was in one of the most successful television shows in television history. On the set, he liked to reminisce about his early days in Hollywood. When he found out I had worked with Lana Turner, he wanted to hear all about her. He'd say, "Tell me a juicy Lana Turner story." Jackie was a chain smoker and he loved his drink. All he had to do was raise his right arm up and a drink would be in his hand within two minutes. He had a man just for that purpose. But I never saw him drunk. He was a pro through and through.

We eventually finished up in Las Vegas and the company left for Jupiter, Florida—the small town where Burt had a home on the water, a ranch and a summer theater. Many of Burt's films were shot in Florida and several in his hometown. He was loved by all the townspeople. After all, it was Burt who put Jupiter on the map. (Although Perry Como lived there as well.)

Whenever I talked to the Universal executives, they would implore me to have Hal shoot as much of Jackie as possible. The studio considered Jackie "gold." He stole every scene he was in.

So I went to Jackie and picked his brain. Did he have any ideas about another scene involving him? That's about the dumbest question you could ask any actor. Without a pause, he said, "Get me a gas station, six rednecks, my car, and Junior" (played by Mike Henry). I went to Hal and within thirty minutes, the scene was planned. Junior and the Sheriff (Jackie's character) are driving along the highway. The new scene was as follows:

Junior: Daddy, I got to make pee pee.

The sheriff pulls into a gas station. Junior gets out of the car and goes into the men's room. Six rednecks are standing by the gas station entrance. The sheriff is resting on the car's fender waiting for Junior. Junior comes out of the restroom.

Junior: Daddy, Daddy. My zipper is stuck.

The sheriff is exasperated. He bends down and starts to try and pull Junior's zipper up. The rednecks are watching. They begin to start laughing. From their vantage point, it looks like the Sheriff is committing a lewd act. The sheriff looks up and realizes what the rednecks are assuming. Without standing up, he turns his body and walks hunched over to the car.

Sheriff: Get in the car, Junior.
Junior: But Daddy, my zipper is still stuck.
Sheriff: Get in the car, Junior.
The sheriff and Junior get into the police car and start out. The rednecks are still laughing.
Junior: My fly is still open.
Sheriff: Let me tell you something, If you evah embarrass me like that again, I'm gonna get an axe and you're never gonna open your fly again.

It remains one of the funniest scenes in the film. And Jackie thought of it on the spur of the moment. That's genius.

Lily as Ernestine.

Dom DeLuise was equally funny. He played an Italian quack doctor. Burt would crack up at whatever Dom did. There was a lot of clever adlibbing in the movie. The actors would get on a roll and Hal would go along with it. Often, it was better than the written dialogue.

The film finally wrapped.

One of the last things I had to do on the project was to go to Florida with our soundman. Jackie Gleason had had a mild heart attack. We had to get some "wild lines" and looping dialogue from him in his hospital room. I told you Hollywood was a tough place. When the doctors told me it was permissible, we went to Florida with the sound equipment to record him at his hospital bed. Much to my surprise, he was smoking in bed. He didn't look ill. He was still amusing, warm and friendly. After several hours of recording, we finished. Jackie gave me a hug. He was a true professional. I never saw him again.

It was a very successful film but nothing compared to the original *Smokey*. Lightning did not strike twice in this case.

I said that my all-time favorite film to work on was *Cool Hand Luke* and that my most successful film was *Dangerous Liaisons*. But the most miserable film I ever worked on was *The Incredible Shrinking Woman*. I produced that turkey for Universal Studios. The dress designer Joel Schumacher (as in Shoemaker) directed. It's the first time in my entire career that I hated to go to work. There were daily battles. There were hourly battles. It was badly photographed. It was badly written and badly produced. But most importantly it was badly directed. It's the only film I ever worked on—whether as an assistant director or producer—that went over budget by millions. I think that if the studio knew what the budget was going to end up, they would have canceled the project. Lily Tomlin and Charles Grodin starred. Grodin was adequate but not very funny. Lily valiantly tried to make it work. She had her moments but there were not many of them. Rick Baker, who played the gorilla in the movie in a suit that he himself had designed, charged the studio one million dollars for the suit and his services. And he took the gorilla outfit home. Baker is a genius. Just ask him.

I would often be called to the set to arbitrate the latest battle. One day Lily said to me, "I'm tired of your fucking peace-making efforts." Jane Wagner, who was the executive producer and screenwriter, couldn't handle stress. Because she was the executive producer, I made sure she was privy to all the battles that she never saw firsthand as she never went to

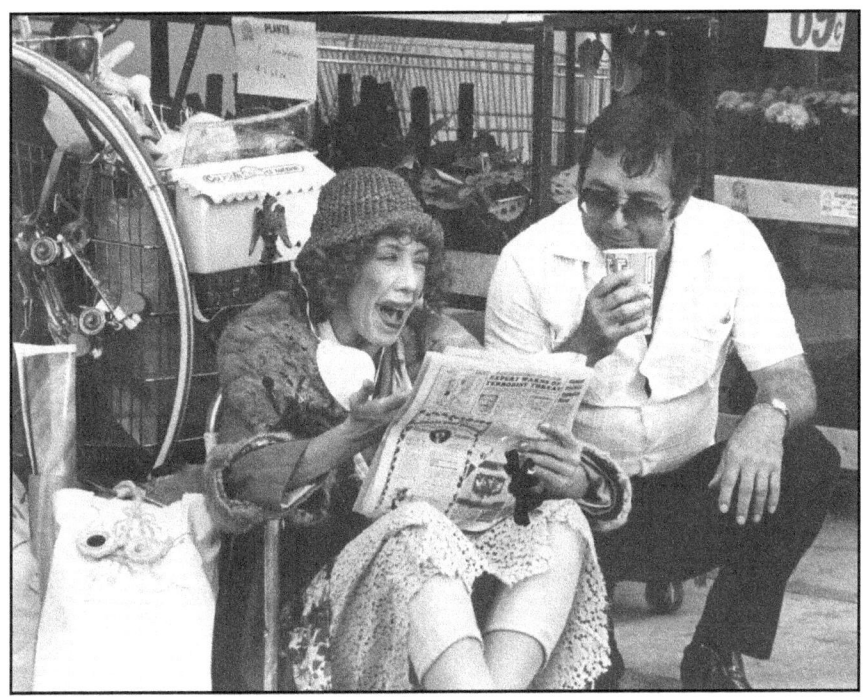

With Lily Tomlin in a cut sequence from *The Incredible Shrinking Woman*.

the set. Why should I be the only one to suffer? When I would go to Jane's office to tell her the latest drama, she would go into the restroom and lock the door. She spent most of the picture in the toilet.

Our publicist Stanley Brossette, who had a wicked sense of humor, came to me and said, "Mr. Moonjean, hasn't anyone told Jane Wagner that the movie is finished shooting?" I said, "Why?" Stanley said, "Well, she's in her office writing a new scene."

There was some pleasure in *Shrinking Woman*. Julie Harding, who ran the Lily Tomlin-Jane Wagner offices, was a gem. She had to have the patience of Job. She also took care of their animals and would often make lunch on a hot plate for some of us. Mr. Liebegott, our coordinator, nicknamed her "Star." She's been Star ever since. She'll be a lifelong friend.

During this disaster, Burt Reynolds was shooting *The Best Little Whorehouse in Texas* on a soundstage across from my office. Burt's co-star was Dolly Parton. I had nothing to do with *Whorehouse*. It just happened to be a coincidence that we were on the same lot. Burt, and more often Dolly, would come into my office and use my telephone. Dolly would pop in and say, "Moonjean, can I use your telephone?" I'd say "Of course. Do you want to be alone?" She'd say "No." This was a regular occurrence. One day, Dolly came into the office saying, "Moonjean, Moonjean. What kind of a name is Moonjean?" I said that I was Armenian. There was a blank look on her face. I said, "I bet you never heard of an Armenian before?" Dolly said, "No, but I have a couple of friends in Texas who are Pollocks!"

Lily Tomlin gave me this photo with her personal caption.

Chapter 26
Paternity and Other Memories

The title was *Buddy Buddy*, but it was confusing when the phones rang in the office. Our production coordinator Mr. Liebegott had a problem with answering the phones, "Good Morning, Buddy, Buddy." It just did not work. So we changed the title to *Paternity*. That title, in my opinion, didn't help the box-office at all. (Titles are very important. When *Road to Perdition* was released, I heard someone say that Perdition is a small town in Wisconsin, which would certainly make it seem less of a must-see film.) Lawrence Gordon and I were the producers of *Paternity*. David Steinberg was the director. The star was Burt Reynolds. It was a Paramount Picture. It was to be made in New York City, with the interiors shot in the studio. The story was about a confirmed bachelor who wants to have a son but not a wife. He is looking for a surrogate mother, and he's willing to pay a considerable amount of money to find the right woman to bear his child. Our offices were the old Howard Hughes offices in the RKO-Desilu Studios—now part of Paramount Studios. (I often wondered what the Howard Hughes' walls would reveal if they could talk.) Charlie Peters wrote the script. At Paramount, two sisters—identical twins—had worked in the secretarial pool for years. It was impossible to tell them apart. One twin was my secretary whom I shared with Charlie. One day, Charlie said, "In the office, she's warm and friendly. When you see her on the lot, she's cold as ice." I don't think ever knew he was talking about 2 different people.

The first order of business was to find the actress to play the surrogate. We had Judy Davis fly in from Australia to be interviewed by Burt, David, Larry and myself. She did not impress us. We then interviewed

Debra Winger. That was a split decision. Larry and David were for. Burt and I were against. I thought Debra Winger was too hard looking for the role. Burt agreed. Guess whose votes carried more weight? We went with Beverly D'Angelo. She was perfect casting. The rest of the cast was Lauren Hutton, Elizabeth Ashley, Paul Dooley, Norman Fell and "my" nun from *The Singing Nun*—Juanita Moore.

We started the film in New York. We had various locations all over Manhattan as well a scene on the Circle Line boat around Manhattan. One afternoon, while filming Burt along Third Avenue, we had three cameras shooting at the same time. I was with one camera shooting down Third Avenue. I looked across the street and saw Greta Garbo walking right toward the camera. I said to the camera operator, "Quick. Start shooting. It's Greta Garbo walking toward us." He looked up at me and said, "Who?" By that time, Garbo realized she was walking into a movie unit; she turned around and went the opposite way. We would have had up-to-date film on the elusive Garbo. I would often see Garbo in that neighborhood. She must have lived nearby. She always wore something unusual which made her stand out. Sydney Guilaroff, who knew her well, would tell me stories of taking her to dinner. She would always select a corner table and sit facing the wall. Guilaroff once said to her that no one recognized her but she seemed to always somehow draw attention to herself.

David Steinberg was fun to work with. He was originally a comedian from Canada. I believe *Paternity* was the first film he directed. We filmed in Madison Square Garden where they let us take over the entire complex. On the last day of shooting in Central Park, I had an idea to shoot a scene not in the script for the ending. I had the wardrobe department get matching jogging suits for three children—ages two, four and six—that matched Beverly and Burt's jogging outfits. I asked casting to get me three girls near those ages and make sure they had long hair. I wanted to make sure they looked like girls—the point being that Burt wanted to have a son and he ended up having three girls. I had a rough time trying to convince David to film it. The actors were already in their jogging sweats. Reluctantly, David agreed to shoot it. I found a path in the park that has a rise. We put the camera on the ground. As the cameras turned, you first saw Burt jogging, holding a little girl, followed by Beverly and the other two little girls. It was a perfect ending to the movie. Someone said at the studio, "Hank is always good at endings." After filming in New York, we returned to Hollywood.

Paternity and Other Memories   293

The worried director is David Steinberg.

The lesser cast members were all excellent. I can't remember any movie I worked on that had so many talented actors. Each and every one of them was perfect. Juanita Moore, as Burt's outspoken maid, was marvelous. They say if you work long enough in Hollywood, you begin repeating the actors you worked with before. Elizabeth Ashley exuded Southern sex and Lauren Hutton was also on the money. But Beverly D'Angelo outshone them all. What a great lady and an excellent actress. But why did she like to lay nude in her dressing room between takes? It was a puzzlement.

Everything went smoothly on the film, but, unfortunately, the film was not a success. Of all the films I produced, *Paternity* was one of my favorites. They say in Hollywood only the productions that are plagued with problems become successful. I don't go along with that theory. If that's the case, *The Incredible Shrinking Woman* should have won ten Academy Awards. I think part of the problem may have been the title as well as the advertising promoting the film. The key ad was a takeoff of Uncle Sam pointing his finger at you asking you to join the army. The Paramount poster had Burt Reynolds pointing his finger at you saying, "He wants *you* to have his baby." I think that may have alienated both the men and the women. The title could have been more provocative. But,

The marvelous Beverly D'Angelo in Central Park.

of course, this is all hindsight. I was always looking for a good reason why the public didn't receive the film better. I'll never know.

Immediately after *Paternity*, Hal Needham married Dani Janssen, the undisputed queen of Beverly Hills' hostesses and the widow of the actor David Janssen. The wedding took place on the back lot of Universal Studios. Nothing Hal or Dani do is ever run-of-the-mill. They had one of the most unusual weddings I ever attended. The theme was the Wild West, and hundreds of guests were spread out all over the studio's western streets. They had a barbecue of ribs, steaks and western-style food, and most of the guests were wearing Western outfits. I wore a pair of Western boots that Burt Reynolds gave me. Since I am short like Burt, the boot had a higher heel on the outside and on the inside. I was beginning to walk like Burt. I felt like I was going to fall forward. The bridal party arrived in a buckboard pulled by two horses. They got off the wagon before a female justice of the peace. The ceremony went on without a hitch. Everyone had a great time.

Angie Dickinson. There's a real treasure. I had met Angie at many parties throughout the years but I really got to know her around this

With Beverly D'Angelo and Paul Dooley on *Paternity* set in New York's Central Park.

period of time in the late seventies. When we would see each other, Angie would say, "Your place or mine?" Angie is one of the sexiest women I ever met. She still is. She can recite the Gettysburg Address and make it sound suggestive and sexy. She has a tremendous sense of humor and a contagious laugh. And she has incredible legs. Everything is perfect with Angie except her hair. She can drive you crazy with her hair obsession. Angie tells a story on herself when she was doing the television show *Police Woman*. She and her co-star Earl Holliman were doing a physical scene— I think it was a gun battle. When the scene ended Angie and Earl said simultaneously, "How's my hair?" It seems Earl worried about his hair too. They couldn't stop laughing.

Through Angie I met Ira and Lenore Gershwin. I really didn't see much of Ira. He wasn't well, and he stayed mostly in his upstairs bedroom. On the rare occasions when Ira came downstairs, he would be immaculately dressed but had nowhere to go. He died shortly after I met him. Ira's wife, Leonore, took a great shining to me. Everybody called her Lee. The Gershwins lived in a fantastic mansion next door to Agnes

Leonore (Lee) Gershwin, Angie Dickinson and me at a Gershwin poker game.

Moorehead. The house contained paintings from all the Masters – Cezanne, Toulouse-Lautrec, Modigliani and many others. There were Henry Moore sculptures in the living room. On the lower level of the mansion, Lee kept George Gershwin's piano—the piano upon which he wrote *Porgy and Bess*.

Friday was poker night at the Gershwins. Lee always insisted that I sit on her right at the poker table. Lee loved to stroke my left arm. She loved my left arm. (Why do people only like certain parts of my body?) I would always make sure I was wearing a short-sleeved shirt so that I would give her full pleasure. I will always be grateful to Angie for introducing the Gershwins to me. Lee was a fascinating character, who had lived a golden life. She was full of Gershwin anecdotes. She knew everyone in the theatrical world. Lee also had a tough side to her personality. Once during a poker game, someone began humming a Gershwin tune. She vehemently said, "You *never* hum Gershwin tunes in this house." Lee enjoyed being eccentric. She'd make absurd statements out of the blue. Once, when I took her to the theater, during the intermission, we stood up to stretch. A very elegant lady came up to Lee and gushed over her. Lee turned her back on her, much to the lady's amazement. After the lady left, Lee whispered to me, "You *never* speak to anyone during intermission. It's rude." During one poker session, someone was continuingly raising Lee. Lee finally said, "I don't know why you bother, I have more money than all of you put together." That is very true. Lee inherited all the Gershwin millions. There are Gershwin music endowments in practically every accredited college in America. The Gershwins, who were immigrants, never forgot their roots. They were forever grateful to America. The poker players were all Hollywood folk: Sam Marx, a producer who discovered Elizabeth Taylor; Alex March, Burt Kennedy and Richard Brooks, who were all directors that I had worked with. Angie and Lee were the only women players. Angie was a consummate poker player. She played like a real pro. I always looked forward to the Friday night sessions. But, alas, other than Angie and myself, all the poker players are now dead. And so went my poker game.

I speak to Angie often, though we seldom see each other. She always has her hands full. She still has a career. Angie lost her devoted sister from Alzheimer's in 2007. She also lost her only child, Nikki Bachrach, the same year. Nikki had many problems. She committed suicide. Angie, naturally, has a tough time coping with this tragedy. However, she is always there for her friends. Angie always remembers my birthday wherever I am. I will always love her. Angie could write six volumes of memoirs about "Everybody." Somehow, I don't think she ever will. She's that kind of a lady.

I was getting ready to produce my fifth picture with Burt Reynolds. It was called *Sharky's Machine*. The year was 1981.

Chapter 27
Sharky's Machine

Sharky's Machine was set in Atlanta, Georgia. The basic storyline was very much like *Laura*, the great Otto Preminger film starring Gene Tierney as Laura. It's about a case of mistaken identity. As in *Laura* our leading lady is assumed dead, until one day she turns up. Casting an unknown is a must. In other words, if you had Glenn Close murdered in the first reel, you know she will return later on. The only exceptions I can think of were Angie Dickinson in *Dressed To Kill* and Janet Leigh in *Psycho*. Both women received top billing and were killed early on in the film—never to be seen again.

Burt Reynolds was to direct as well as star in the film. Our first line of business was to find the leading lady. We asked our casting people to keep on the lookout for a young beautiful unknown girl. We got hundreds of photographs. We interviewed many women.

One day, Burt brought in a *Newsweek* magazine with an article about young actresses. There were photographs of two women—one was Cleo Goldsmith who lived in Italy and the second one was Rachel Ward who was living in England. Both women were brought to Atlanta and Burt and I interviewed them. Rachel won out. Although she had been in a few movies, she wasn't well known to the movie-going public. The remainder of the casting was easy. We contracted Brian Keith, Bernie Casey, Earl Holliman and Henry Silva. We tried to get William Holden for the villain but he refused. His role wasn't big enough. He didn't want to leave home. We got Vittorio Gassman, from Italy, to play that part.

Our offices were in the Hilton Hotel in downtown Atlanta. We shot many scenes in the hotel as well as the office building next door.

Edward Teets was my associate producer and production manager. Mr. Liebegott III was my secretary, Burt's secretary and Edward's secretary *and* the production coordinator. Too much work for one person. I asked him to interview someone to help him in the office. Days would pass. His work was piling up. I finally said to him that if he doesn't get someone in the office soon, I was going to fire him. He said he would have someone in the office Monday morning.

Working hard on the set.

Monday morning I walked into the office and there was our new office worker. After ten minutes, I realized she was the most stupid girl I had ever met. I forgot her name but I'll call her Hortense. When Mr. Liebegott introduced Hortense to Burt, all she could say was "Gosh." Mr. Liebegott didn't want any competition. I designated Hortense to handle Burt's and my personal business. I would dictate several letters on Monday and I was lucky to get them by the following week. Mr. Liebegott had to redo them. Once I asked her to bring me my lunch on a tray. I was too busy and the caterers were next door in the other building. I wasn't there but it was reported to me that Hortense got in line twice— once to get my tray of food and the next time to get her own tray.

Working in Atlanta was a pleasure. We got one hundred percent cooperation. The police were most helpful. Of course, Burt had a home on the outskirts of town and also had an investment in a club in the city, so he was considered a native.

Dar Robinson was one of the top stuntmen in the business. He had to take a fall from the top of a thirty-story building. This stunt took a great deal of calculating. Stunt work requires careful planning. You can't just wing it. You have to take into consideration the wind velocity, the height, etc. A huge eight-foot-high airbag was placed beneath his fall. Should he hit a seam on the airbag, he would more than likely be killed. It seemed that all of Atlanta was there to observe this stunt. It was nerve-racking for me. Fortunately, Dar made a spectacular leap. Sadly, years later, Dar was killed in a motorcycle accident. He was pleasure riding.

Another white-knuckle scene scheduled was a helicopter shot starting from ground level following an elevator up to the top floor of the highest building in Atlanta. It was a night shot. Vittorio Gassman and some ladies of the night were in the elevator. The helicopter was only a few feet from the building. Burt and the camera crew were going to do this shot. Burt doesn't have a scared bone in his body. I have enough for both of us. From my office window, I had a ringside seat of the building and helicopter. For some reason, Sally Field, who was visiting Burt, was in my office. She was knitting or darning something. She showed no concern as to what was about to transpire. I was a basket case. Anything could have happened. The blade of the helicopter could have touched the side of the building. Apparently, my concern showed. Sally, not looking up from whatever she was sewing, said, "Don't worry about Burt, nothing ever happens to him." Gee, I feel much better now. Thank you, Sally.

Jim Nabors on the set of *Stroker Ace*.

Burt made the shot on the first take and I was relieved, but it was a very long night.

The filming went along smoothly. Burt and I had our one and only argument since we first met. One of his ass-kissing friends was getting involved with the movie, which he had nothing to do with. I told this friend to keep his nose out of my business. He went directly to Burt and Burt came directly to me. Burt said to get off his friend's back. I said to Burt, "I don't tell you how to act. Don't you tell me how to produce!" (Didn't I use that line before?) That was the end of it. Nothing else was said. Burt had forgotten about it the next day.

We eventually ended up at the Goldwyn Studios in Los Angeles to do our post-production. On the next stage, Sylvester Stallone was doing post-production on *Rocky 2*. Burt would visit Sylvester's set and vice versa. One day, Stallone came onto our stage.

"I wanna to ask youse guys a question," he said. "I've been asked to do *Rocky 3*. What do ya think?"

Burt said, "With the hit you've had with the first *Rocky*, I'd do *Rocky 4* and *5* and *6* and *23*." Stallone asked me what I thought.

I said, "Only if you kill Talia Shire in this one." Stallone never spoke to me again. I guess I'll never do a Sylvester Stallone movie.

Chapter 28
Another Major Disappointment

Terry and the Pirates was a very popular comic strip when I was a young man. I was on cloud nine when Universal Pictures asked Hal Needham to direct and me to produce the movie. No casting was discussed at this point. In this case, the locations were our top priority. We decided that Hong Kong would suffice since the comic strip was set in China. Shooting in China at that time would have been impossible.

So Hal, Mr. Liebegott and I flew to Hong Kong. This was my first visit. It was 1981, well before the handover to China, and this British Colony was a pleasure to do business in. We checked into the Peninsula Hotel, which had to be one of the best hotels I ever stayed in. We dealt with the Hong Kong film companies. We hired an office staff, which Mr. Liebegott ran with an iron fist. We visited the Raymond Chow Studios in Hong Kong. They were like every other studio in the world. I contacted London to send me an art director to help scout the locations, as this was going to be a British Universal Film.

One of the first things we had to do was to find two Chinese junks, one for our heroes and one for the evil Dragon Lady. I was hoping to get Elizabeth Taylor to play the Dragon Lady but that was far off into the future. First things first.

Hong Kong was a fascinating place; the streets were teeming with tens of thousands of people all day long. It didn't matter if it was ten o'clock in the morning or ten o'clock in the evening or three o'clock in the morning—twenty-four hours of activity. The waters were equally teeming with boats and junks. And amongst the junks were bright-eyed oriental children swimming in that filthy water. Everything, absolutely everything, was floating amongst the children as they swam. They must have had a built-in immunity to whatever diseases you can get from those waters. Chinese production people arranged for us to visit various locations in and around Hong Kong, Kowloon and Macao. I found the entire area fascinating. The Chinese couldn't have been more cooperative. We would go from one area to another taking photographs. At lunchtime, the film commission had made arrangements for us to have lunch at one of the better restaurants along the sea front.

The tables were arranged as if for a banquet. All in all, there were about eight of us. We sat down to enjoy our lunch. The Chinese with us spoke perfect English. The waiters brought the first course. It was a green salad. I remembered about avoiding green salads when in Mexico. I declined the salad. The next course arrived. They were huge prawns that looked great. I asked the waiter, "Are these from Mexico?" He said, "Oh no, these from there." He pointed to the brown water along the waterfront outside the restaurant. I said, "I'm terribly sorry, but I'm allergic to shrimp." The next course arrived. They were the most fabulous-looking lobsters I'd ever seen—one of my favorite foods. I said, "These can't be from Maine, can they?" He said, "Oh no, these from over there." Again, pointing to the filthy water. I wanted to cry. But I thought if nothing else, I would lose weight while in Hong Kong. No such luck: I soon found a Jewish delicatessen.

We continued looking for our key set and we finally decided on an area not too far from the city. The area had been used on a previous Hong Kong production and we were going to combine their sets with ours. Carpenters were hired and we had given them a full go-ahead. I am simplifying all the work that had to be done in preparation for a movie like this; suffice it to say we were at it eighteen hours a day, sometimes more.

Hal and I thought about casting Jackie Chan for the second male lead. Jackie Chan was and still is the most famous star in all Asia. We thought it would give the film a global appeal. Forget it. Hal was told in so many words, and as nicely as possible, don't even think about it. I think we were getting into the realm of the Chinese Mafia. Who needs or wants Jackie Chan? Hal and I decided that it was a bad idea.

Hal and I had been going back and forth to London to begin casting. We tested Sean Connery's son, Jason. He looked too young. We tested many Asians who spoke both English and Chinese. Things were progressing quite well. Many sets were being built. We had secured our junks and it looked like we had better start thinking about the stars and a start date. Mr. Liebegott had everyone under control. His offices were on the sixth floor of the building that housed all our departments.

I had a personal problem with Dani Janssen Needham. She wanted to come to Hong Kong for the shooting with her neurotic dog, Pussy. Hong Kong does not allow any animals into the country. This was a major problem. What to do with Pussy? I thought a submarine would be out of the question. I couldn't get Pussy through China or Macao either. They have the same quarantine restrictions. But before I could solve Dani's Pussy problem, Hal and I had something more serious to worry about. We were summoned to return to the Universal Studios in Hollywood.

"But, Mr. Moonjean, you can't go. A hurricane is on the way," cried Mr. Liebegott. He said it was due to hit any hour. Everyone was battening down all the hatches and the windows were boarded up. The studio insisted we return ASAP. I asked Mr. Liebegott if he could get us on a flight going south to Australia—maybe we could go around the hurricane. How about across Asia? It seems the hurricane was everywhere. But all the planes were taking off on schedule. I said to Hal, "The airplane pilot's life is as valuable to him as ours is to us. If he is going to fly so can we." Mr. Liebegott made all the arrangements. We were to fly to Tokyo and make connecting flights to Los Angeles.

The flight to Tokyo was without incident. After about a two-hour layover, we left for Los Angeles. An hour out of Tokyo, we started to bounce around in the plane like we were on a trampoline. Then we were struck by lightning. The lightning bolt went through the plane along the top of the seats in front of us. The bolt entered from the right side of the plane and across and out of the left side. Talk about white knuckles. I thought, we aren't going to be alive long enough to make *Terry and the Pirates*.

Well, we didn't get to make it, but not because we were killed. A studio executive told us they were shutting down the production. We were not told the reason—at least not the real reason. Maybe it was something to do with the story rights. To this day, neither Hal nor I knew the exact reason. It didn't seem to bother the executives that we had already spent almost two million dollars on the preproduction.

Back in Hong Kong, we had left Mr. Liebegott in his sixth-floor domain. He had refused to have the window next to his desk boarded up. He wanted to see the hurricane. He had the opportunity. The storm hit Hong Kong. It was a miracle that Mr. Liebegott wasn't killed. The rain and wind swept through his offices. He said he could see yachts and junks turned over in the sea. There was much damage. "But, Mr. Moonjean, the only problem I had was my Rolodex got wet. I don't know what I'm going to do." Mr. Liebegott finally wrapped up the offices and came home.

I hope one day some enterprising producer will make *Terry and the Pirates*. It will be one exciting film.

Speaking in London at the British Academy.

Chapter 29
More Disappointments: 1981–1982

After *Sharky's Machine*, I was preparing to produce my sixth film with Burt. Warner Bros. offered *The Bourne Identity*, Robert Ludlum's bestselling novel, to Burt Reynolds to star in and to direct. I had introduced Burt to the director Jack Clayton years ago and they were impressed with each other. Burt and I asked Jack if he would direct *Bourne*. Jack always wanted to do a mystery and he agreed, much to my pleasure.

I left for Europe to begin scouting for locations. The story took place in Switzerland, France and Germany as well as other unidentified countries. I wanted to first determine what studio in what country would be our main headquarters. I knew all the studios in and around London, so I decided to start my investigations in France. I was familiar with the Studios Boulogne in Paris, but I wanted to check out the others. I made arrangements with the French Film Commission to have someone show me the French film studios in and around Paris.

An unshaven production man in a small Renault picked me up at my hotel. I was practically hanging out the window his body odor was so strong. Fortunately, he spoke English. He quickly took me from studio to studio. I took notes on the details of the studio—size and facilities, etc.

The next day, I flew to Munich, Germany. I had made arrangements with the German Film Commission to visit the Bavaria Film Studio. I had heard it was the best studio in all of Europe. A lovely fraulein who spoke perfect English met me at the Munich airport. I had no luggage so we went straight to the car. It was a Mercedes limousine. Fraulein said to me that she had booked a room for me at the Four Seasons Hotel in case I wanted to freshen up. I said it wasn't necessary as I was in Munich just for the day. She asked the chauffeur to go directly to the studio. As we entered the studio, she directed the driver to go to the executive building. As we got in front of the executive building, three well-dressed men were standing at attention. Fraulein introduced me to the three executives one by one. After each introduction, each man clicked his heels and extended his hand. They all spoke perfect English. I was escorted into the building. Fraulein had gone. We went into an office. There were trays of German cakes and desserts. They offered me refreshments. The three executives were in charge of the three main departments of the studio: the laboratories and post-production facilities, the soundstages and all the operating departments and the third, which covered all business matters. I was given pamphlets and plans of the studios, the rates, a detailed list of equipment—everything that I needed. I thought no wonder the Germans took over France so easily during World War II.

One of the executives gave me a tour of the studio. It was like any other studio in the world. It could have been in Hollywood. It was undoubtedly the best studio in Europe. He took me into the property department. On the back wall, there was a German swastika flag hanging from the ceiling. I asked the executive why the flag was hanging there. He said it had been used recently in a television movie and they haven't had a chance to put it away. I saw the amazing submarine that was used in *Das Boot*, a very successful German war film, and probably the best submarine movie ever made. After visiting the various stages and their back lot, I was taken to lunch in the commissary; the other two executives were waiting for us. As we began eating, several department heads came by and introduced themselves to me. I was really impressed with the organization. Nothing was left to my imagination. I decided the Bavaria Studios would be our home base.

While in Munich, I asked if there were furnished apartments available by the month. I was thinking ahead. I was told that the best accommodations for a short period would be in the City of Dachau not too far from Munich. I did not want to live in the city that had one of the worst concentration camps during the war. One would have thought that the Germans would have changed that infamous name.

I flew back to London and had meetings with Clayton. I then decided to go to Portugal. I had been to Portugal several times and I thought it would be a perfect spot for the opening scenes of the movie. Also, I knew that a Portuguese location would have a fresh and different look. Not too many films were made in Portugal. After scouting most of the country, I sent for Clayton. He brought his wife Haya, and our screenwriter. I showed Clayton locations that I thought would work. He liked the Cape just south of Lisbon as a possibility for the opening scenes. Also, he liked the Eiffel elevator in the center of downtown Lisbon. This huge elevator went straight up the side of a mountain to the top street. This Eiffel is the same Eiffel who built the tower in Paris. After many days, we all returned to London. At least, I got the writer to start writing while I was seeing to all the production necessities. I would telephone Burt weekly to give him a progress report. He was most anxious to see a script. So was I. In the meantime, Clayton had spoken to Laurence Olivier, Simone Signoret and John Gielgud about playing cameo roles in the film. The three of them said they would love to be in Jack's movie. That was an exciting thought. Actors respected Jack Clayton and most serious actors wanted a chance to work with him. Meanwhile, I was getting ready to go to Switzerland.

Elizabeth Taylor was in London during this period. She called me to invite me to her fiftieth birthday party. It was on the Saturday before the Sunday that I was to leave for Zurich. I hadn't seen Elizabeth for a while and was looking forward to the party. The party was being held at an "in" nightclub called Legends. Elizabeth had split with Richard Burton during this period. Everybody that Elizabeth knew was invited to this party. Elizabeth, always generous, sent airline tickets to dozens of friends in the States. One of her guests was Peggy Ann Garner. Elizabeth had told me that Peggy was going through a rough time, with marital woes as well as a major drinking problem. Elizabeth asked me to keep an eye on her and make her feel welcomed, as she didn't know too many people. I had Peggy sit at my table. Peggy Ann Garner was one of the brightest natural child actresses in movie history. As far as dramatic roles were concerned, she could run circles around Shirley Temple and Margaret O'Brien. She was brilliant in a movie called *A Tree Grows in Brooklyn*. For that film she won a special juvenile Oscar. A few years earlier, Elizabeth played a small role in *Jane Eyre*. Peggy played Jane, as a child. Joan Fontaine played the adult Jane. After all the years that passed since Elizabeth appeared in *Jane Eyre*, Elizabeth still remained friends with Peggy. The party was a tremendous hit. All the British actors that Elizabeth had worked with or knew were there as well as many friends from all over the world. Peggy was very quiet. She didn't want to dance. I felt sorry for her. Peggy wasn't able to make the transition from child star to adult roles. She became an alcoholic and died at the age of fifty-three of pancreatic cancer. How sad for a young woman with a brilliant future.

There was a story going around about this time, in 1981 or so. I don't know how true it is but it's worth repeating. It seems that Paul Newman was standing at a urinal in a men's room doing his business. A man next to him kept saying, "Aren't you Paul Newman?" Paul ignored him. The man repeated the question. Paul was getting irritated and told the man this wasn't the place to have a conversation. Paul went to the basin to wash his hands. The stranger followed. "Aren't you Paul Newman?" Exasperated, Paul said, "Yes." The stranger said, "Do you know Peggy Ann Garner?" Paul said he didn't know her but knew of her. The stranger said, "Well, I fucked her maid." It is said that everybody has fifteen minutes of fame once in his or her lifetime.

Back to Elizabeth Taylor's birthday party. Suddenly, there was a commotion. Richard Burton had arrived. He wasn't invited and Elizabeth was visibly upset. Burton, as usual, was feeling no pain. Burton sat at Elizabeth's table.

I was getting bored. I'd had a busy week and I was tired. I was leaving for Zurich early in the morning. I kissed Peggy and walked toward Elizabeth to wish her happy birthday and say good night. As I approached her, she got up and came toward me. She said, "Let's dance." Elizabeth was wearing a white pants suit with lots of frills. We started to jitterbug. The frills were flying all about her. Cameras were snapping away as we danced.

The next morning at the airport, I went to the newsstand. Every newspaper had a front-page photograph of Elizabeth and me jitterbugging. For some reason, they featured Elizabeth and showed only the back of my head. I was identified as a producer named Hank Noonjean and Hank Noojean, and many with the correct spelling of my name. Not used to celebrity, it was a strange feeling to see my name and picture on every paper being read by people around me. I boarded the plane and took off for Zurich. Much work lay ahead.

Zurich was freezing. A representative of the Swiss Film Board met me at the airport. She was very attractive. She was going to help me find several locations—mainly a hotel and a bank. The bank was very important to the project. I found a bank that had an "open" elevator, which is a slowly moving, never-stopping open lift that you step in as it goes by. I was very surprised that I was allowed in the inner vaults. I would have thought the security would be extreme. I must have an honest face. After finding several possibilities, I told my contact that I would return with the director and screenwriter in a few weeks. I called Clayton and asked him to meet me in Munich. We would scout Munich and then go on to Switzerland. Clayton, Mrs. Clayton and the screenwriter met me in Munich. As Clayton left the airport and headed to his waiting car, he looked around and said, "The last time I was here, I was dropping bombs." Haya Clayton, who is a Sabra Jew, was quite uncomfortable being in Germany at first. After several days in Munich she said to me, "I hate to admit it but I find Munich charming and very cosmopolitan." I took them all to the Bavaria Studios and Clayton was impressed with the facilities.

That night I called Burt from my hotel. He wanted to know about the status of the script. I said the script was not ready to be seen. Burt insisted on seeing what we had accomplished thus far. I discussed it with Clayton. Clayton said for me to send him a copy of the script whatever condition it was in. I said I thought that would be a mistake. Either Clayton or I should be with Burt when he reads the script. There were too many "holes." Nevertheless, much against my will, I sent the script via Lufthansa Airlines. He would have the script the next day.

The next morning we drove to Vienna, which was not that far from Munich. We stopped at the "salt mines." These were the famous caves between Munich and Vienna in which Adolf Hitler hid all the stolen treasures of Europe. Jack, the writer and I decided to go into the caves with some other tourists. We were given a black hat and a black poncho because of the soot and dirt in the caves. We straddled a small train. Just like the Toonerville Trolley, we went through long caves going lower and lower into the earth straddling this miniature train. The train stopped and we all got off. The interior of the cave was huge. It looked as large as the Hollywood Bowl. There were stairs leading down to the next level. There was also a slick wooden shaft that you could actually straddle to slide down to the lower level. It is rather difficult to describe this slide. It wasn't the concave curved type of a children's slide. This was a thick, solid-looking piece of wood shaped like a large upside down "U." It was very smooth and must have been used for decades. Everybody straddled the slide and we all held onto each other, and slid backwards, like children sliding down a banister. At the bottom, there was another slide and stairs leading to a deeper cave. We repeated the slide. When we reached the bottom, there was the little trolley train to take us back to the top. It was all fascinating. To think, that at one time, these caves were filled with valuable paintings and statuary looted from all over Europe.

We also visited Berchtesgaden, the mountaintop retreat where Hitler and his mistress, Eva Braun, spent time together. It had fantastic views of Austria and Germany. After getting stills of the various possible locations, we returned to Munich and the next day flew to Zurich. Clayton liked the locations I found. He and the writer spent a lot of time in the bank. After three days in Zurich, I made arrangements for us to take the mountain train from Zurich to Geneva. I thought it might inspire the writer or Clayton to shoot a scene or two on the train. It was a fantastic trip going through the snow and mountains. It was certainly better than flying to Geneva. After spending approximately a week in Geneva, we returned to London.

Upon my return, there was a phone message from Burt. I guessed what it would be about. I reluctantly returned his phone call. Burt had received the script and hated it. I said he was not being fair. I had told him it wasn't ready to be seen and that he had insisted on jumping the gun. He wouldn't listen to reason. He wanted me to return to Hollywood immediately. He had found another project he wanted to do. This was going to be difficult for me to pass on to Jack Clayton. But he, like most people in the industry, knew how to accept a disappointment. It wasn't his first and certainly not his last.

I returned to the studio and immediately wrote letters to all my European contacts telling them about the cancellation. They were difficult letters to write. I was extremely disappointed. I tried to analyze why Burt turned down the project. It wasn't the script. That was just an excuse. Every script ever written always needs work even when you are in the midst of shooting. I think a lot had to do with the fear of working in a foreign location with a foreign director and actors of the caliber of Olivier, Gielgud and Signoret. Also, Burt would not have been able to take his regular crew to Europe. I thought that would be an asset. Burt was always loyal to the people who worked on his films. Many of them became complacent and Burt had no challenges. That's now history.

Recently, there was a television version of *The Bourne Identity*. I did not see it. Universal Studios released a theatrical version of the film in 2002 to mixed reviews. The movie that Burt chose to direct and star instead was called *Stick*. It was set in Florida. Burt asked me to read the script. It was the same old crap that he had been doing. I said to him that you see better made-for-television films on television every night. I said I didn't want to produce it. Besides, there was already a Universal producer on the project. That was a small point that Burt neglected to mention. And it caused me a great deal of embarrassment with the Universal executives. I couldn't have produced the film even if I wanted to. Burt was disappointed with me. He was going through a bad time with his health and personal life. He was saying that "everyone" was leaving him. That was not the case with me. Burt eventually understood the situation. We are still friends. Burt is one of the most loyal persons I know. All the crew loved him. Sometimes it's better to be a bastard. Many of his "friends" took advantage of his loyalty and turned on him when the chips were down. I never worked with him again.

Burt made *Stick* with Candice Bergen and it was not well received.

At Winston Churchill's grave marker outside of London. One of my heroes.

Chapter 30
Stealing Home – 1987

Stealing Home was an original script written by Steven Kampmann and Will Aldis. They were also going to direct. That was bad news at the outset. Two chiefs on one project. It's not a good idea. Thom Mount, who I knew when he was an executive at Universal Studios, and I were going to produce. It was going to be a Columbia picture. The story was about a young man growing up and following his dream of becoming a baseball player. The entire film was going to be made in the Philadelphia area, where Kampmann grew up, with some other locations at the New Jersey shore. Kampmann neglected to tell us that story was autobiographical. We interviewed dozens and dozens of actors. Kampmann kept rejecting them. Finally, it dawned on us that he was searching for look-alikes of the people he had known and written about. It would have been much easier if he had just given us photos initially.

The studio was concerned that Kampmann and Aldis had no experience directing and insisted that they go to Sundance to study directing. You probably can tell at this stage that disaster was pending. How do you learn directing in two weeks? Jodie Foster, Blair Brown, Jonathan Silverman and William McNamara were the stars. Mark Harmon played the lead. The Columbia executives did not want Harmon in the movie. They didn't think he was strong enough for the role. We all disagreed. We all wanted Harmon in the movie. After many arguments and discussions, we came to a standoff. In the end, Columbia passed on the project and Warner Bros. agreed to produce the film.

William McNamara was the grandson of Robert McNamara, the Secretary of Defense under the Kennedy administration. This was McNamara's best role to date. McNamara played Harmon as a younger man.

The Mount Company had an accountant who was "different." She was a walking computer. She did the work of three people. No one was better at her job. I don't recall her name but let's call her Maisie. Maisie was a character. She had the worst taste in clothes. When you walked on the lot with her, heads turned. Her hair was yet another story; every week her hair color would change—blue or red or green or a combination of all the colors. It wasn't unusual to see Maisie wearing yellow and green slacks with red polka dots with a zebra-striped blouse. Maisie was a free soul and most probably had a screw loose. She had a great sense of humor but more importantly she was the best at what she did.

Halloween was Maisie's favorite holiday. She looked forward to going to a Halloween party with the same friends every year. This was her day because she would often win first prize. This particular year she said she had the most fantastic costume ever. She wouldn't tell anyone in the office what the costume was. She would show photographs later. She was counting the days to Halloween.

Halloween arrived. As fate would have it, there was a crisis in the office; something to do with a report that had to be turned in before the end of the day. Maisie dove right into it. She worked on the report until after 7 p.m.

Unfortunately, she did not have time to go home and change into her costume. Oh well, it would keep until the next year. She went directly to the party, which was in full progress. She was there for five minutes when she was told that she had been awarded second prize for the best costume —in her everyday attire.

My godson and grandnephew, Scott Moomjian, was a production assistant on the film. He worked very hard, was well liked and I was very proud of him. I thought maybe he would follow in my footsteps. However, he became a successful lawyer, married and produced two handsome sons.

Jodie Foster is a great talent. She's an actress through and through. This was a very small role for her. I was surprised she accepted it but was pleased she did. Jodie is very laid back and extremely intelligent. The entire crew adored her. Jodie knew everyone on the crew by his or her first name. In my experiences in the film world, I found that the more famous and successful the stars were, the easier they were to work with. Jodie was a perfect example of this.

Kampmann and Aldis had written a scene that I kidded them about from the moment I read the script. The scene, as written, would have taken a minor miracle to shoot but was more than likely completely impossible. The scene is as follows:

EXT. SEASMOKE—NIGHT
A cloud passes over the moon. A night bird flies and its cry is heard. The bird swoops over a dead fish lying on the sand. We stay on the fish as night turns into day. Hope bends down into frame and peers at the fish with keen curiosity.

Long after the film was completed, I received a framed script page from Kampmann and Aldis. The inscription read, "Dear Hank. As far as we're concerned, there will always be one missing scene from *Stealing Home*. Will & Steven."

Stealing Home was not a successful film. It should have been. The script was excellent. The two directors from the beginning were adequate, but, as the film progressed, they became complacent. Many an ego has destroyed many a movie.

With Jodie Foster at the New Jersey shore.

Chapter 31
Dangerous Liaisons – 1988

Bernie Brillstein, the head of Lorimar Productions, asked me if I would like to produce *Les liaisons dangereuses*. Christopher Hampton based his successful play on a French novel written by in the eighteenth century author, Choderlos de Laclos, and he adapted the play into an amazing movie script. In my forty years in the film business, having read thousands of scripts, I never read a script as brilliant and powerful. After I finished it, I immediately called Christopher Hampton to tell him that his script would win an Academy Award. He didn't want to hear about it. His words were captivating. I would tell friends that when they were viewing the film, not to look away or get distracted. You must listen to every word. I accepted the assignment. I could hardly wait.

I flew to London to meet the director, Stephen Frears. He was an odd character. I liked him immediately. He always looked like he just got out of bed. As always, the first order of business was securing the locations. Many Hollywood films were then being shot in the Eastern bloc cities, such as Prague and Budapest. Research told me that Prague wasn't suitable but Budapest was a possibility.

Frears and our production designer, Stuart Craig, met me in Budapest. I had gone earlier to check out the studios. There were two studios in Budapest—one in central Budapest that was antiquated and a more modern studio on the outskirts of the city. Neither studio was suitable. But like most Europeans, when you ask a pertinent question, everyone says, "Yes."

"Can you provide plasterers?"

"Yes."

"Do you have actors who can speak proper English?"
"Yes."
"Are there palatial homes in and around the countryside?"
"Yes."

The reason for going to Budapest was to save money. I was beginning to have my doubts. The three of us went from one end of Hungary to the other end looking for grand homes. There were many large homes but every one of them was a rusty-brown color. Craig said we could paint them. I said, "No way." After about ten days in Hungary, I decided that the film should be made in Paris. That's where the story is set and that's where it should be made. I received an okay from Brillstein.

I had worked with a well-respected production woman named Suzanne Wiesenfeld. We had worked together as production assistants many years ago on *Fanny*. I was pleased she was available. Suzanne knew every inch of Paris and knew the top crews. She and her staff found each and every location with the assistance of Craig. Frears was pleased with what had been selected. Craig went to work with the French crew.

Frears and I returned to London to begin the casting. John Malkovich was already set to play the male lead—Vicomte de Valmont. The female lead was up for grabs. The first choice for the role of Madame de Merteuil

Uma Thurman, Michelle Pfeiffer, Glenn Close, John Malkovich and Mildred Natwick in the only scene where they all appear together.

was Glenn Close. She knew the play and thought the role was a challenge. Close said she did not know Malkovich and before she made a commitment, she wanted to meet him. Arrangements were made for Frears and Malkovich to go to New York City. Close met with Malkovich. The meeting went well. She agreed to play the part.

The second female lead was the part of Madame de Tourvel. It was down to Angelica Huston and Michelle Pfeiffer. I knew Angelica and I was hoping it would be her, but Michelle Pfeiffer got the part. Two newcomers, Uma Thurman and Keanu Reeves, played the other parts. Veterans Swoosie Kurtz and Mildred Natwick played the two remaining principal roles.

James Acheson was the wardrobe designer. Frenchman Philippe Rousselot was our cameraman. After many weeks of preparation, we all congregated in Paris. Everyone but Glenn Close. She had recently had a baby and didn't want to work until her body "got back into shape." This request cost the production an enormous amount of money, for reasons I'll explain later.

My early MGM training came in handy. I insisted that all wardrobe, all hairstyles and all makeup be tested before production began. The makeup was most important. We wanted to be sure that we adhered to the period as much as possible. In the pre-revolutionary days, the French aristocracy wore heavy white powder makeup, most probably to cover up smallpox and syphilitic scars. We tested Michelle Pfeiffer with the white makeup. It's not easy to make Michelle look unattractive, but the white makeup looked horrible. It was immediately decided to forego the white look.

We were fortunate to find all our locations only an hour's drive from downtown Paris. In most cases the film would be shot on actual locations. We worked out of a small studio in Joinville, a village outside of Paris. It was the oldest studio in Paris. Shortly after *Les liaisons dangereuses*, the studio was demolished to make room for new apartments.

I had my hands full with Uma Thurman. (Lucky me.) She was only seventeen years old but going on thirty. She had been emancipated, an American formality in which the courts mandate that an underage teenager's parents are no longer legally responsible for the child. I took an immediate fatherly interest in this tall beauty. She wanted to take an apartment on the left bank. I said, "Definitely not!" I wanted her in the hotel with the crew and some of the actors. Uma was extremely intelligent, spoke fluent French and was wise far beyond her years. I didn't want her to get involved with that "left bank crowd." Uma even had her agents call me. I wouldn't give in. She decided to play her records loudly in hopes she would be asked to leave the hotel. That didn't work either. She finally gave in. I adored her. I knew that one day she would be an important actress. I used to call her "Ums." I knew she liked me, even though I gave her a bad time. Uma said, "Only you and my brother can call me 'Ums.'"

Keanu Reeves was another story. I don't think he knew where he was or what he was doing. He didn't even know what *I* was doing. He asked me, "What does a producer do?" I had it written in his contract he was not to ride a motorcycle until he finished his role. Not too many years ago, Keanu had been in a serious motorcycle accident. He has a hole in his stomach that you can almost put your fist in. The only time I saw Stephen Frears upset was at Keanu. It was a scene where Keanu is supposed to have tears running down his face. He couldn't cry. They tried everything. Finally, tears came. I think it was because he was so embarrassed. But, unlike Uma, I thought Keanu's acting days were almost over. How could I be so wrong? He'll be making *Matrix* films for a long time and laughing all the way to the bank.

I'd never been on a film with so many actors with such unusual names. Often I would say, "Swoosie, do you give Uma to Keanu in marriage?" or something like that. The film ran smoothly, thanks to Frears being so well organized and thanks to Suzanne for having such a great crew. Mr. Liebegott was given a small trailer that opened out on one side like a hot dog concession. When the trailer reached the location, they would raise the side and hook it to the top. One morning someone in the art department painted a sign saying "HOT DOGS – CANDY – HAMBURGERS" and attached it to the side of the trailer. Mr. Liebegott could not understand why people kept stopping and ask for candy. It was the first film that I worked on where we had a fax machine. What a great invention. With the fax machine I seldom was awakened by a telephone call from California at some early hour.

The script was structured in such a way that the characters played by Glenn Close and Michelle Pfeiffer are in only one scene together. And because of Close's unavailability at the start, we shot Pfeiffer's scenes first. Both actresses had scenes on the same locations. But because Close wasn't

A recent photograph, in Paris, with Liza Minnelli.

available we had to return to the same location a second time. That meant "striking" the location, removing all our props and bringing them back a second time. Everything had to be repeated, which I said cost an enormous amount, the kind of waste of time and money that drives producers crazy. Pfeiffer's last scene to be filmed was the first scene that Close was in—the only time they are on the screen together.

The scene was staged in the music room of Madame de Rosemonde's residence. Close and Pfeiffer never speak to each other. They just pass one another in the music room as they are about to be entertained by a castrato. The singer who played the castrato was actually a castrato that we brought from Rome. For those who have never heard of a castrato, it is a man who has had his testicles removed so that he will not lose the high-pitched, soprano voice of a male child before his voice breaks. Believe it or not, this mutilation is still done in Brazil, which is where our castrato had his operation. His speaking voice was also very high. When he first arrived many of the crew members snickered when he spoke. I must confess, so did I. After hearing him sing and getting to know him, I realized this moment was the high point of his entire life. He had finally "made it." He was in an important film. And this film will remain his contribution to the world. During the day's filming, he would ingratiate himself with the entire company. When we were not shooting, he sang for the extras. Both Frears and I posed for a photograph with him. He seemed to be a fulfilled, happy man.

One evening, I had taken Frears and some of the actors to L'Orangerie, a swank restaurant on Ile St. Louis. Michelle's date was the actor Michael Keaton. I thought he was a great guy. I enjoyed his company. All of a sudden I heard a scream and looked up to see Liza Minnelli. She ran up to me and gave me a big hug and kiss. I hadn't seen Liza in years. Tears filled her eyes. I said, "You better not cry." She said she wanted me to meet someone. I went to her table where she was dining with Charles Aznavour, the famous French singer. I began speaking to him in Armenian. Liza and he were amazed. Liza did not know that Aznavour and I were both Armenians. And we were definitely not "Pollocks." Liza said, "You bring back happy memories." Tears began running down her cheeks. Liza is a terrific woman who has had a rough life. She worshipped her father as well as her mother, Judy Garland. And her life has been complicated since the day she was born. But when she saw me, she must have remembered my early days with her parents. They both worshipped her.

During shooting one day, Glenne Headly, who was John Malkovich's wife at the time, was visiting the set. She was an actor as well. She stood by the camera and me. As the camera rolled, John entered the room and made a deep bow to Glenn Close. Frears said, "Cut." Headly said, in front of the entire crew, "That looked like shit." No one on the set remarked upon or reacted to Headly's remark.

The Fourth of July was upon us. I had a party for all the Americans on the film. I invited Glenn, her daughter's nanny, Michelle, Swoosie, Uma and Mr. Liebegott. Malkovich had gone to Marseilles. My nephew Richard, his wife Patricia and their youngest son Steven came from San Francisco. They brought hot dogs, hot dog rolls and some Fourth of July paraphernalia. I ordered two pumpkin pies from a local bakery. I had to explain how to make it. I remember they charged me forty dollars per pie. Richard and I decorated my apartment. My place on Ile St. Louis had to be the greatest apartment I have ever seen. It was like a MGM set. It had five bedrooms and was on the top floor of the building. From the roof, I could see all of Paris, a 360-degree view.

The bathroom alone could hold at least twenty people and the bathtub could easily accommodate six people—twelve if they are very friendly. It had a huge walk-in fireplace and the kitchen had all the modern conveniences. My next-door neighbor was Madame Pompidou, the widow of the French president. It had a very narrow elevator that really only held one person—two if they were very close. Patricia had brought some American CDs such as John Philip Sousa and other American patriotic music. The party was a success and we were all glad and proud to be Americans. The hot dogs were sensational. The pumpkin pies were awful.

We were having discussions about changing the title of *Les Liaisons Dangereuses*. In Europe, we could stay with the French title but we felt that we had to change it for the English-speaking countries. Obviously, the English translation *Dangerous Liaisons* would do but I was trying to be more commercial with a more provocative title. Since the original book by de Laclos was comprised of only letters, I thought a good title would be *The French Letters*. I was told that in Britain a "French letter" was a condom. So I figured the film would have been a major hit in Great Britain. It was in any case.

Bastille Day came on a Friday. A good friend of mine from California, Jerry Wilhelm, was visiting. I thought since it was a long weekend, we could go to Vienna to celebrate Jerry's birthday. I asked Mr. Liebegott to call a friend in London and get the name and address of a contact in Vienna. Liebegott got all the information and typed it on a piece of paper: Dr. Harris, Sickness Center, and a street address.

Jerry and I arrived in Vienna and we checked into the Imperial Hotel. A young bellhop showed us to our rooms. I knew that the Imperial Hotel was where Hitler always stayed when he was in Vienna. I asked the bellhop which room Hitler occupied when he stayed in Vienna. The bellhop asked, "Who?" I said, "Adolf Hitler." The bellhop said he never heard of Hitler. How quickly they forget.

The next morning Jerry and I went out to look for the Sickness Center. We asked directions to the address that Mr. Liebegott gave us. We came upon this building and we asked where the Sickness Center was. No one knew what we were talking about. We kept looking around. We discovered that the "Sickness" center was a "Fitness" center. Mr. Liebegott was losing it. Mr. Harris was not a doctor either. When I got back to Paris I asked him where he got the "Doctor" from. He said, "Mr. Moonjean, a Sickness Center is always run by a doctor."

The Vienna Opera House is dark during the summer but they have tours. So Jerry and I took the tour. We were with an English-speaking tour group. The German lady guide spoke perfect English. The guide would say, "This staircase was bombed during the war but the left side of the staircase is the original." We would walk along and the guide would say, "This hallway up to that door is the original, the other end of it was bombed during the war." We continued to the backstage area. The guide would say to the two-dozen or more of us—mostly Americans, "The backstage area was completely bombed during the war—completely destroyed." The tour lasted about an hour. And every comment had to do with the partial bombing of the opera house. When the tour ended, the guide asked if there were any questions. I was the only one with a question. I said, "You keep saying this was bombed and that was bombed. Who did the bombing?" The guide said, "The Americans." Jerry looked at me and said, "You had to ask?" The Americans in the group glared at me.

Back in Paris. The *Dangerous Liaisons* rushes were sensational. I knew the film was going to be a success. I was very proud to be part of it. Every aspect was perfect. The actors were perfect. The costumes were perfect. The locations were perfect. Stephen Frears never stopped surprising me. He refused to go to the rushes. He said he left that to his film editor. He was wearing a pair of sneakers that were about to fall apart. He wore them all the time. I finally told the wardrobe man to go out and buy Frears a pair of sneakers before he fell and broke his neck.

We filmed on one location, which was a picture-perfect farm just outside of Paris. The owner of the property spoke English. When she discovered I was an American, she came up to me and said, "I love Americans." She said the Americans had saved her farm and her country. She pointed to a distant hill and said, "That's where the American tanks came over the hill and down this gully." I found what she said very touching.

We were filming in the village of Versailles—not the Palace. (For some reason, we were not allowed to film in the Palace.) I was sitting on the steps of this manor watching the filming. A local Frenchman came up to me and said, "Do you know who used to live in this house?" I said that I had no idea. He said that it was the house where Madame DuBarry lived. There was an underground passageway that led to the Palace, which wasn't that far away. He continued, "When they guillotined Madame

Being presented by Princess Diana at the World Premiere in London. That's screenwriter Christopher Hampton next to me and Stephen Frears next to him.

DuBarry in the village square, the townspeople brought her severed head and threw it just where you are sitting." During the French Revolution, they dragged all the aristocrats out of the Palace of Versailles and took them into the village and began guillotining them in the town square. As a matter of fact, all the characters in *Dangerous Liaisons*, supposedly based on real people, were guillotined.

We also filmed in the small opera house in Versailles. According to our research, everyone stood on the main floor during a performance. There were no chairs. The aristocracy sat in the boxes. It was also interesting that when someone who had brought shame to their name entered the opera house, the audience would start booing and hissing. We reproduced that in the movie.

The final scenes with Glenn Close were fantastic. The scene where she gets hysterical upon hearing of Valmont's death was done in one take. The last scene is of Glenn sitting in front of a mirror (which, in fact, is the camera) removing her makeup very slowly. Philippe Rousselot, our cameraman, sat on the floor with a dimmer. Gradually, as Glenn removes her makeup, Philippe slowly dimmed the lights. The end shows

Princess Diana being presented to Uma Thurman, the brilliant actor John Malkovich and Glenn Close.

Glenn's face as skeletal. That, too, was done in one take. The only scene shot that was not in the final print was Glenn's head being lopped off by the guillotine.

The world premiere of *Dangerous Liaisons* was in London, and it was there that Stephen Frears, Christopher Hampton, John Malkovich, Glenn Close, Michelle Pfeiffer, Uma Thurman and I were presented to Princess Diana.

Oscar nominations. I received my first and only Academy Award nomination as producer of the Best Picture, Glenn Close was nominated

The late Mildred Natwick in her final film role.

as Best Actress, Michelle Pfeiffer was nominated as Best Supporting Actress, James Acheson was nominated for Best Costumes, Christopher Hampton was nominated for Best Screenplay, and Stuart Craig was nominated for Best Production Designer. I was amazed and disappointed that Stephen Frears and Philippe Rousselot were not nominated. It's always puzzling when a Best Picture nomination doesn't naturally receive a Best Director nod, as if a Best Picture directed itself.

A week before the Oscars, Rosemary and Danny Thomas had a party at Chasen's Restaurant to honor some princess from the Middle East who was a close friend of the Thomases. Angie Dickinson was my date; or, rather, I was her date. Other guests were Shirley Jones, her husband Marty Ingels, Casey Kasem and his wife, and Red Buttons and his wife. We were having drinks and hors d'oeuvres. Red Buttons said, "How about a joke, Marty?" Marty started and it went around to Red. Next, was Angie. She said, "I can't tell jokes. You go ahead, Hank." I started out, "Did you hear the one about Pia Zadora…?" Red quickly leaned over and said, "Shhh," rolling his eyes to the left. I looked over and twenty feet away sat Pia Zadora. Pia looked straight at me and said, "*That's* an old joke."

At the end of a long day.

I don't think I was ever so embarrassed. I know I was never that embarrassed. Everything went very quiet. I said to Angie that I must go to Pia and apologize. I had never met her. I excused myself and walked to her table. Pia was looking straight up at me—she was not smiling. I said, "Miss Zadora, I am extremely embarrassed. Please accept my apology." She said, "I would like you to meet my husband." I shook his limp hand. A child was with them. Her husband wasn't smiling either. I had heard he was with the Israeli Mafia. God, I'm going to be killed before I receive my Oscar. I returned to my table. Angie gave me a kiss. I needed that.

Now for the joke that I never finished. Pia Zadora was appearing in the title role of *Anne Frank* in a Toronto theater. Toward the end of the first act, when Nazi soldiers enter looking for Anne Frank, someone in the audience yelled out, "She's in the attic."

The morning that the Oscar nominations were announced, I received a phone call around 8 a.m. from my Aunt Mary in Boston. She proudly told me that I had been nominated for an Academy Award, which was the first I'd heard of it. I was pleased. But, in all modesty, I knew the picture would be nominated. I knew that when I first read the script.

Oscar Night, 1988. I had been to many Oscar ceremonies but this was the first time I was a nominee. What an exciting evening. Angie Dickinson was my date. She looked beautiful in a white gown and her hair was (I thought) perfect. We had to get to the Shrine Auditorium by 3 p.m. There was great fanfare before the actual event. Pictures were taken of all the arrivals. Angie and I spoke to Army Archerd before entering the Shrine. There was a great deal of hugging and kissing. I wasn't nervous at all. I knew I wasn't going to win, so that made it easier. Angie knew everyone. She stopped and talked to each and every person. Then she went into the ladies room. I waited and waited. There was an announcement telling everybody to take their seats. (After a certain time, no one is allowed to enter the auditorium.) The women in their gorgeous gowns were piling out of the ladies room. No Angie. Here, I am on the most important evening of my career and I'm going to miss the ceremonies. Finally, Angie came out. I'm sure she was the last one out. We raced to our seats. Angie's hair was giving her problems. So what's new? I sat between Angie and Carrie Fisher in the first row of the auditorium. (I could have been on the stage in less than a minute if called.) Mike Nichols and Diane Sawyer sat behind us.

I think the Oscar presentation that year was the worst one ever produced. That was also the consensus of everyone who attended. It started out with Snow White and Rob Lowe, and went downhill thereafter. Carrie was resting her head on my shoulder throughout most of the show. As each winner was announced, I was getting excited. Stuart Craig won. James Acheson won. Christopher Hampton won. We were on a roll. I thought if either Michelle Pfeiffer or Glenn Close wins, it would be a sweep. I was beginning to think of what I should say in my acceptance speech. Then, Michelle Pfeiffer didn't win and neither did Glenn Close. I stopped thinking of an acceptance speech. However, I was still proud to have been a nominee and had been so close to winning.

The film that won best picture was *Rain Man*. I think years from now *Dangerous Liaisons* will be remembered and *Rain Man* will be forgotten. Maybe I am prejudiced. I received many telegrams telling me I was cheated. I received a telegram from Marty Ingels with just one word: "WRONG."

Chapter 32
The Wind Down

The years have whizzed by since I produced *Dangerous Liaisons* in 1988. It has been years since I have seen Elizabeth Taylor. The last time was at Elizabeth's sixtieth birthday celebration at Disneyland, where I met her last husband, Larry Fortensky. The only husband that I had not met or knew was Senator John Warner. I once asked Elizabeth why she left the senator. Elizabeth said, "Have you ever had tea with a bunch of senators' wives?" I guess Elizabeth was bored to death. The Disneyland party was exceptional. Thousands of guests attended the party, which was held in a small section of the theme park. I sat with Alice Faye. Alice had long since retired and moved to Palm Springs. Alice knew that I was a friend of Betty Grable's. Alice got on the subject of a recent tell-all book written on Betty Grable. She said there should be a law against writing such a book when the person is not alive. A person should have the right to refute the charges or insinuations.

All of Elizabeth's guests received gifts. The rides were open to all. The food concessions were open as well. Elizabeth's generosity was overwhelming. I didn't get to say much to Elizabeth that evening. Other friends and all the photographers mobbed her. She pulled me to her side and said to Fortensky, "And this is my friend..." and she used a term of endearment, which Elizabeth has called me since the *Raintree County* days. That remains my secret. I shook Fortensky's hand and I gave Elizabeth a peck on her cheek and that was it. Later, we all gathered around a large stage and a group photograph was taken.

When Elizabeth appeared in the play *The Little Foxes* in Los Angeles in 1981, I said I would like to arrange a Sunday brunch for her.

(Sunday the theater was dark.) I asked her to give me a guest list. I wanted to make sure that everyone there was an acquaintance of Elizabeth's. The next week, her secretary sent me a list of two-hundred-plus people. I called her and said I couldn't handle that many people—cut it down to fifty, please. I had the brunch catered. I made several Armenian dishes that I knew Elizabeth enjoyed. I had parking attendants and a full staff of help including bartenders. Tables were arranged around the swimming pool. Everything was running smoothly and on schedule.

Suddenly, over the radio came the news that Natalie Wood had drowned the night before in Catalina. I was shocked and felt sad. Natalie was a very special person. And I knew this was the end of Elizabeth attending the brunch. I immediately called Elizabeth. She had heard the bad news. She said, "We should go over to R.J.'s immediately." R.J. was Natalie's sometimes husband. I said, "I can't. I have all these people coming for brunch. I don't even know who most of them are. Your secretary made all the calls." Gradually, some of the guests started coming. I had called Rock Hudson and a few others that I knew from the guest list. But most of the guests were from *The Little Foxes* company. The only one I recognized was Sada Thompson, who co-starred with Elizabeth in the play. One of the servers kept calling Sada "Sadie." He knew *Sadie* Thompson but he didn't know Sada Thompson. Needless to say, the brunch was a disaster. Some guests ate and left. Many of them just turned around and went home. I didn't go see R.J. because I didn't know him that well and I didn't really like him. It was Natalie who was a friend. It was a sad day when Hollywood lost Natalie Wood.

As I said, I haven't seen Elizabeth in years. When Chen Sam, Elizabeth's fantastic publicist, was alive, I was able to speak to Elizabeth often on the telephone. Whenever Chen came to Los Angeles from her apartment in New York City, she would make sure that I spoke to Elizabeth. After Chen's death, I never was able to get through to Elizabeth. Either she was upset with me for some unknown reason and refused to speak, or her many male secretaries wouldn't put me through. I gave up trying.

Prior to Elizabeth's sixtieth birthday party, we would occasionally see each other. Once, Chen arranged to have a small party at La Cage Aux Folles, a nightclub on La Cienega Boulevard that had a drag show. The party consisted of Elizabeth, Rock Hudson, Chen, Brad and myself and several other friends of Chen's. Rock was very drunk. When Rock was sober he was the sweetest person you would want to meet. "Sweet" is not the usual adjective to use when describing a man, but Rock was sweet as well as kind and thoughtful and amusing. Rock was often my bridge partner. He was an exceptional bridge player. But when Rock had been drinking or was out-and-out drunk, he was mean and belligerent. He was a Jekyll and Hyde. The poor guy must have been suffering for a long time.

Our small group was practically seated on the stage. This was a typical drag show. All the "girls" would imitate and lip-sync to a recording of some famous personality. They had the usual drags—Marlene Dietrich, Judy Garland, Carol Channing, and Barbra Streisand. This night they had a Julie Andrews. The Julie Andrews drag was unbelievable. "She" looked exactly like Andrews. She moved like Andrews. "Elizabeth Taylor" followed Andrews. The club knew that Elizabeth would be attending. "Elizabeth" came on stage as Cleopatra. "She" was not a bad copy

Celebrating Debbie's birthday, 1989.
(Debbie's six-months younger than Elizabeth)

On the set of *These Old Broads*, a television production.

but no one can ever look like the real Elizabeth Taylor. The fake Elizabeth started doing her routine about the filming of *Cleopatra* and, then, she got into the personal life of Elizabeth and her numerous husbands. I could see Elizabeth blistering. Elizabeth is a terrific sport. She would laugh the hardest if the act were in good taste. Elizabeth stood up and said, "We are *not* amused." And thus ended the party.

On another occasion, I took Elizabeth to UCLA to see Martha Graham and her troupe. We sat in the front row when someone came up to us and asked us if we would like to go backstage. We saw the entire production from the wings. As we were leaving, we were mobbed by autograph seekers.

I mentioned early on that Debbie Reynolds was the hardest-working actress I knew. Today, she is still working very hard. She does her one-woman show all over the country. She goes from city to city for a one-or-two-day gig. She is always on the go. She even squeezes in an occasional guest appearance on a television show. She will die on stage one day. That is her wish. In 2002, the Savannah Film Festival honored Debbie with a Lifetime Achievement Award in Film.

Debbie has had bad luck with her three husbands. Enough has been said about Eddie Fisher. Debbie's second husband, Harry Karl, the millionaire shoe salesman, lost his fortune and business to gambling and along the way gambled away nearly all of Debbie's personal assets. Karl died leaving personal debts amounting to hundreds of thousands of dollars that Debbie systematically paid off. Debbie's third husband was another winner. He was an architect or a land developer or who knows what and as soon as he married Debbie, he quit his profession and became Debbie's agent. Debbie didn't need an agent, she needed a husband. Debbie bought a small hotel off the Las Vegas Strip. She spent whatever money she had to renovate and upgrade the hotel, and she set up her Movie Star Museum in the hotel. After a couple of years, lo and behold, husband number three left with some of the hotel's assets. Debbie had to file bankruptcy. I hope Debbie never marries again. She once said to me, "Three strikes and you're out."

When my phone rings around 3 a.m., I know it's Debbie. She's somewhere on the road tired and lonely and can't sleep. So she calls a friend. "Hello, Hankala??? This is Debala. Did I awaken you?"

"No, Debbie, I was laying here waiting for your call. Why would I be asleep at three in the morning?" We would talk for quite a while

Eva Marie Saint after receiving The Lifetime Achievement Award in Savannah.

about nothing. When Debbie is in town (and that isn't too often), she'll call and say, "You put on the pasta and I'll put on my wig and I'll be right over."

Debbie is a very special person to me. She is the first MGM actress that I met way back in 1954. Her devotion and friendship has never altered. When you are a friend of Debbie's, it's usually for life. Recently, Debbie gave me a color photograph of Elizabeth and her on the set of that awful *These Old Broads* television movie made in 2001. Debbie is resting her head on the shoulder of Elizabeth. Debbie said, "Put this picture in your book. No one will believe it."

I still see Eva Marie Saint and Jeffrey Hayden. I see Hal Needham and Burt Reynolds every so often. I've lost touch with David Steinberg. I still see Angie Dickinson and Dani Janssen. My only contact with Paul Newman is when I use "Newman's Own" spaghetti sauce.

Several years ago, I sat next to Paul on an airplane. Paul said to me, "I've done more movies with you than I have with Joanne." It's probably true.

Gone are many of my friends: Lana Turner, Rita Hayworth, Jackie Gleason, Bette Davis, Montgomery Clift, Edward G. Robinson, Cyd Charisse, Agnes Moorehead, Elizabeth Hartman, Jo Van Fleet, Susan Hayward, Paulette Goddard, Marlene Dietrich, Laurence Harvey, Hermione Baddeley, Charles Boyer, Myrna Loy, Anthony Perkins, Maurice Chevalier, Jack Clayton, David Merrick, Henry Koster, Pandro S. Berman, Lewis Milestone, Kay Kendall, Richard Harris, Mildred Natwick, Leon Shamroy, Joe Ruttenberg, Betty Field, Mildred Dunnock, George Cukor, Barry Fitzgerald, Elvis Presley, Judy Garland, Frank Sinatra, Gregory Peck, Richard Brooks, Katharine Hepburn, and many, many more. But that's the way things go. There must be one hell of a "stock company" in heaven.

Sadly, in the spring of 2008, my production coordinator, Richard Liebegott passed away. Richard, in the 40-plus years I knew him, never called me "Hank". It was always Mr. Moonjean. I miss Richard, his humor and his friendship.

My career has been filled with laughs and excitement. I often say that I would not change one second of one minute of one hour of one day of my entire career. It's been a fun life.

As a small boy, I dreamed of working in films. Movies were my pleasure, my education and my dreams. Not too many young people know what they want to do for the rest of their life. I knew exactly what I wanted to do. And it came so easily. As I said earlier, I think God had His hand on my shoulder. And when I look back, no two days were ever the same. Another director, another cast, another script and many more good times and laughs. And yet another new day.

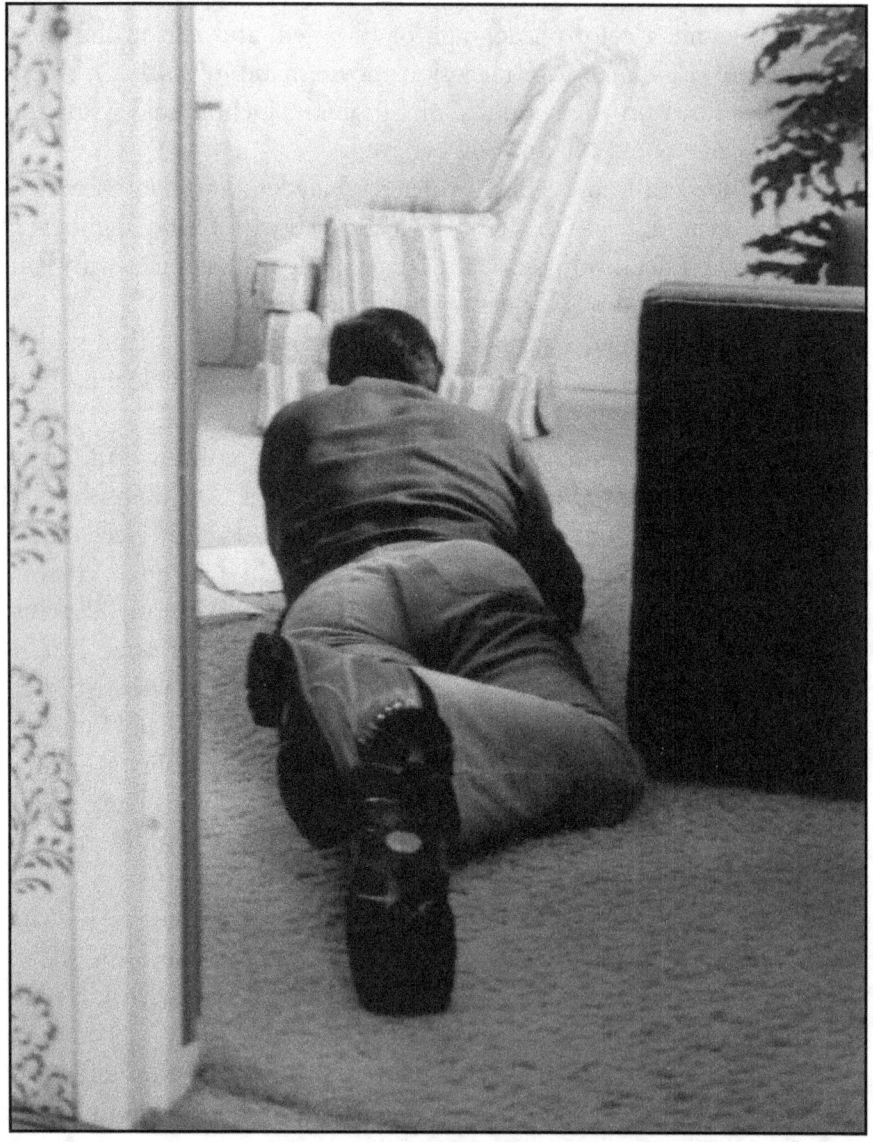

"THE END"

Postscript

During Hollywood's "Golden Era", MGM's top star, Joan Crawford, married her second husband, Franchot Tone, for a spell. (How can you seriously say, Franchot, I love you.) Nevertheless, for a couple of short years, Joan Crawford was known as…Joan Tone.

Filmography

2nd Assistant Director – Uncredited (All MGM films, unless otherwise indicated)

• (Indicates on production anywhere from 2 days to 2 weeks)

1954 -

•*Bhowani Junction*
Producer: Pandro S. Berman
Director: George Cukor

Cast:
Ava Gardner
Stewart Granger
Bill Travers

1955 -

• *Blackboard Jungle*
Producer: Pandro S. Berman
Director: Richard Brooks

Cast:
Glenn Ford
Anne Francis
Sidney Poitier

• *The Prodigal*
Producer: Charles Schnee
Director: Richard Thorpe

Cast:
Lana Turner
Edmund Purdom

• *Moonfleet*
Producer: John Houseman
Director: Fritz Lang

Cast:
Stewart Granger
Joan Greenwood
Viveca Lindfors
Liliane Montevecchi

• *It's Always Fair Weather* (Dance Unit Only)
Producer: Arthur Freed
Directors: Stanley Donen, Gene Kelly

Cast:
Gene Kelly
Cyd Charisse
Dolores Gray
Dan Dailey

• *Love Me or Leave Me*
Producer: Joe Pasternak
Director: Charles Vidor

Cast:
Doris Day

James Cagney
Cameron Mitchell

Oklahoma! (Todd-AO) (Dance Unit Only)
Choreographer: Agnes de Mille

• *The Tender Trap*
Producer: Lawrence Weingarten
Director: Charles Walters

Cast:
Frank Sinatra
Debbie Reynolds
Celeste Holm

• *Interrupted Melody*
Producer: Jack Cummings
Director: Curtis Bernhardt

Cast:
Eleanor Parker
Glenn Ford
Roger Moore

• *I'll Cry Tomorrow*
Producer: Lawrence Weingarten
Director: Daniel Mann

Cast:
Susan Hayward
Richard Conte
Jo Van Fleet
Eddie Albert

• *The Cobweb*
Producer: John Houseman
Director: Vincente Minnelli

Cast:
Richard Widmark
Lauren Bacall
Charles Boyer
Lillian Gish
Susan Strasberg

• *The Last Hunt*
Producer: Dore Schary
Director: Richard Brooks

Cast:
Robert Taylor
Stewart Granger
Anne Bancroft (Debra Paget)

• *Ransom!*
Producer: Nicholas Nayfack
Director: Alex Segal

Cast:
Glenn Ford
Donna Reed

Kismet
Producer: Arthur Freed
Director: Vincente Minnelli

Cast:
Howard Keel
Ann Blyth

Dolores Gray
Vic Damone
Monty Woolley

1956 -

•*The Swan*
Producer: Dore Schary
Director: Charles Vidor

Cast:
Grace Kelly
Louis Jourdan
Alec Guinness

Lust For Life (Culver City shooting only)
Producer: John Houseman
Director: Vincente Minnelli

Cast:
Kirk Douglas
Anthony Quinn
Pamela Brown
Jill Bennett

The Catered Affair
Producer: Sam Zimbalist
Director: Richard Brooks

Cast:
Bette Davis
Debbie Reynolds
Ernest Borgnine
Barry Fitzgerald

• *These Wilder Years*
Producer: Jules Schermer
Director: Roy Rowland

Cast:
Barbara Stanwyck
James Cagney

• *Tea and Sympathy*
Producer: Pandro S. Berman
Director: Vincente Minnelli

Cast:
Deborah Kerr
John Kerr

• *The Opposite Sex*
Producer: Joe Pasternak
Director: David Miller

Cast:
June Allyson
Ann Sheridan
Joan Collins
Ann Miller
Agnes Moorehead

• *Forbidden Planet*
Producer: Nicholas Nayfack
Director: Fred M. Wilcox

Cast:
Walter Pidgeon
Anne Francis
Leslie Nielsen

•*Somebody Up There Likes Me*
Producer: Charles Schnee
Director: Robert Wise

Cast:
Paul Newman
Pier Angeli
Sal Mineo

•*High Society*
Producer: Sol C. Siegel
Director: Charles Walters

Cast:
Bing Crosby
Grace Kelly
Frank Sinatra
Celeste Holm
John Lund

•*The Teahouse of the August Moon*
Producer: Jack Cummings
Director: Daniel Mann

Cast:
Marlon Brando
Glenn Ford
Eddie Albert

1957 –

•*Designing Woman*
Producer: Dore Schary
Director: Vincente Minnelli

Cast:
Gregory Peck
Lauren Bacall
Dolores Gray

Until They Sail
Producer: Charles Schnee
Director: Robert Wise

Cast:
Paul Newman
Jean Simmons
Joan Fontaine
Sandra Dee
Piper Laurie

Raintree County
Producer: David Lewis
Director: Edward Dmytryk

Cast:
Elizabeth Taylor
Montgomery Clift
Eva Marie Saint
Lee Marvin

•*Jailhouse Rock* (Dance Unit Only)
Producer: Pandro S. Berman
Director: Richard Thorpe

Cast:
Elvis Presley

Something of Value
Producer: Pandro S. Berman
Director: Richard Brooks

Cast:
Rock Hudson
Sidney Poitier
Dana Wynter

Les Girls
Producer: Sol C. Siegel
Director: George Cukor

Cast:
Gene Kelly
Mitzi Gaynor
Kay Kendall
Taina Elg

The Seventh Sin
Producer: David Lewis
Directors Ronald Neame, Vincente Minnelli

Cast:
Eleanor Parker
Jean-Pierre Aumont
Françoise Rosay
Bill Travers

1958 –

•*Cat on a Hot Tin Roof*
Producer: Lawrence Weingarten
Director: Richard Brooks

Cast:
Elizabeth Taylor
Paul Newman
Burl Ives
Judith Anderson

•*South Pacific* (20th Century-Fox) (Dance Unit Only)
Choreographer: Leroy Prinz

•*Some Came Running*
Producer: Sol C. Siegel
Director: Vincente Minnelli

Cast:
Frank Sinatra
Shirley MacLaine
Dean Martin

Gigi (Paris Location Only)
Producer Arthur Freed
Director: Vincente Minnelli

Cast:
Leslie Caron
Louis Jourdan
Maurice Chevalier

The Diary of Anne Frank (20th Century-Fox)
(2nd Unit Amsterdam, Holland location only)
Producer: George Stevens
Director: George Stevens Jr.

1959 –

• *The Wreck of the Mary Deare*
Producer: Julian Blaustein
Director: Michael Anderson

Cast:
Gary Cooper
Charlton Heston

• *Green Mansions*
Producer Edmund Grainger
Director: Mel Ferrer

Cast:
Audrey Hepburn
Anthony Perkins
Lee J. Cobb

• *Cimarron*
Producer: Edmund Grainger
Director: Anthony Mann

Cast:
Glenn Ford
Maria Schell
Anne Baxter

•*Home from the Hill*
Producer: Edmund Grainger
Director: Vincente Minnelli

Cast:
Eleanor Parker
Robert Mitchum
George Peppard
George Hamilton

1959 –

Tall Story (Warner Bros.) (As 1st Assistant Director)
Producer: Joshua Logan
Director: Joshua Logan

Cast:
Anthony Perkins
Jane Fonda
Anne Jackson
Marc Connelly

Never So Few (As 1st Assistant Director, uncredited)
Producer: Edmund Grainger
Director: John Sturges

Cast:
Frank Sinatra
Gina Lollobrigida
Steve McQueen

1960 –

BUtterfield 8 (As 1st Assistant Director)
Producer: Pandro S. Berman
Director: Daniel Mann

Cast:
Elizabeth Taylor
Laurence Harvey
Eddie Fisher
Dina Merrill

1961 –

Fanny (Warner Bros.) (As Assistant Director; Paris Location only, uncredited)
Producer: Joshua Logan
Director: Joshua Logan

Cast:
Leslie Caron
Charles Boyer
Maurice Chevalier
Horst Buchholz

The Four Horsemen of the Apocalypse (As 1st Assistant Director, uncredited; Paris Second Unit Only)
Producer: Julian Blaustein
Director: Vincente Minnelli

1962 –

How The West Was Won (As 2nd Unit Director, uncredited)
Producer: Bernard Smith
Directors: John Ford, Henry Hathaway and George Marshall

Sweet Bird of Youth
(As 1st Assistant Director)
Producer: Pandro S. Berman
Director: Richard Brooks

Cast:
Paul Newman
Geraldine Page
Ed Begley
Mildred Dunnock

Mutiny On The Bounty (As 1st Assistant Director, uncredited)
Producer: Aaron Rosenberg
Directors: Sir Carol Reed, Lewis Milestone

Cast:
Marlon Brando
Trevor Howard
Richard Harris
Tarita

1963 –

Drums of Africa (As 1st Assistant Director)
Producer: Al Zimbalist
Director: James Clark

Cast:
Frankie Avalon

Mariette Hartley
Lloyd Bochner

The Prize (As 1st Assistant Director)
Producer: Pandro S. Berman
Director: Richard Brooks

Cast:
Paul Newman
Edward G. Robinson
Elke Sommer
Diane Baker

1964 –

•*Kissin' Cousins* (As 1st Assistant Director, uncredited)
Producer: Sam Katzman
Director: Gene Nelson

Cast:
Elvis Presley
Pamela Austin

•*Viva Las Vegas* (As 1st Assistant Director)
Producer: Jack Cummings
Director: George Sidney

Cast:
Elvis Presley
Ann-Margret

The Unsinkable Molly Brown (As 1st Assistant Director)
Producer: Lawrence Weingarten
Director: Charles Walters

Cast:
Debbie Reynolds
Harve Presnell
Hermione Baddeley
Ed Begley

1965 –

A Patch of Blue (As 1st Assistant Director)
Producer: Pandro S. Berman
Director: Guy Green

Cast:
Sidney Poitier
Shelley Winters
Elizabeth Hartman
Wallace Ford

The Money Trap (As 1st Assistant Director)
Producer: Max Youngstein
Director: Burt Kennedy

Cast:
Glenn Ford
Rita Hayworth
Ricardo Montalban
Elke Sommer
Joseph Cotten

•*Harum Scarum* (As 1st Assistant Director, uncredited)
Producer: Sam Katzman
Director: Gene Nelson

Cast:
Elvis Presley
Mary Ann Mobley

1966 –

The Singing Nun (As 1st Associate Producer/1st Assistant Director)

Producers: John Beck, Hayes Goetz
Director: Henry Koster

Cast:
Debbie Reynolds
Greer Garson
Agnes Moorehead
Ed Sullivan
Ricardo Montalban

The Dangerous Days of Kiowa Jones (As Associate Producer)
Producer: Max Youngstein
Director: Alex March

Cast:
Robert Horton
Diane Baker
Sal Mineo

1967 –

Cool Hand Luke (Warner Bros.) (As 1st Assistant Director)
Producer: Gordon Carroll
Director: Stuart Rosenberg

Cast:
Paul Newman
George Kennedy
Jo Van Fleet

Spinout (As Associate Producer)
Producer: Joe Pasternak
Director: Norman Taurog

Cast:
Elvis Presley
Shelley Fabares
Diane McBain

Welcome to Hard Times (As Associate Producer)
Producer: Max Youngstein
Director: Burt Kennedy

Cast:
Henry Fonda
Janice Rule
Aldo Ray

1968 –

The Odd Couple (Paramount) (As 1st Assistant Director)
Producer: Howard W. Koch
Director: Gene Saks

Cast:
Jack Lemmon
Walter Matthau

The Secret Life of an American Wife (20th Century-Fox)
  (As Associate Producer/1st Assistant Director
Producer/Director: George Axelrod

Cast:
Walter Matthau
Anne Jackson
Patrick O'Neal

1969 –

WUSA (Paramount) (As Associate Producer/1st Assistant Director)
Producer: John Foreman
Director: Stuart Rosenberg

Cast:
Paul Newman
Joanne Woodward
Anthony Perkins
Laurence Harvey

The April Fools (National General) (As 1st Assistant Director)
Producer: Gordon Carroll
Director: Stuart Rosenberg

Cast:
Jack Lemmon
Catherine Deneuve
Myrna Loy
Charles Boyer

1970 –

Move (20th Century-Fox) (1st Assistant Director)
Producer: Pandro S. Berman
Director: Stuart Rosenberg

Cast:
Elliott Gould
Paula Prentiss
Genevieve Waite

1973 –

Child's Play (Paramount) (As Associate Producer)
Producer: David Merrick
Director: Sidney Lumet

Cast:
James Mason
Robert Preston
Beau Bridges

1974 –

The Great Gatsby (Paramount) (As Associate Producer)
Producer: David Merrick
Director: Jack Clayton

Cast:
Robert Redford
Mia Farrow
Lois Chiles
Karen Black

1975 –

The Fortune (Columbia) (As Associate Producer)
Producers: Mike Nichols, Don Devlin
Director: Mike Nichols

Cast:
Jack Nicholson
Warren Beatty
Stockard Channing

1976 –

Beauty and the Beast (Hemdale) (As Producer)
Director: Fielder Cook

Cast:
George C. Scott
Trish Van Devere
Virginia McKenna

1978 –

The End (United Artists) (As Executive Producer)
Producer: Lawrence Gordon
Director: Burt Reynolds

Cast:
Burt Reynolds
Sally Field
Joanne Woodward
Dom DeLuise

Hooper (Warner Bros.) (As Producer)
Director: Hal Needham

Cast:
Burt Reynolds
Sally Field
Jan-Michael Vincent
Brian Keith

1980 –

Smokey and the Bandit II (Universal) (As Producer)
Director: Hal Needham

Cast:
Burt Reynolds
Sally Field
Jackie Gleason
Dom DeLuise

1981 –

Paternity (Paramount) (As Producer)
Director: David Steinberg

Cast:
Burt Reynolds
Beverly D'Angelo
Lauren Hutton
Elizabeth Ashley

Sharky's Machine (Warner Bros.) (As Producer)
Director: Burt Reynolds

Cast:
Burt Reynolds
Rachel Ward
Vittorio Gassman
Brian Keith

1982 –

The Incredible Shrinking Woman (Universal) (as Producer)
Director: Joel Schumacher

Cast:
Lily Tomlin
Charles Grodin

1983 –

Stroker Ace (Universal) (As Producer)
Director: Hal Needham

Cast:
Burt Reynolds
Jim Nabors
Loni Anderson

1987 –

Stealing Home (Warner Bros.) (As Producer)
Directors: Steven Kampmann, Will Aldis

Cast:
Jodie Foster
Mark Harmon
Blair Brown

1988 –

Dangerous Liaisons (Warner Bros.) (As Producer)
Director: Stephen Frears

Cast:
Glenn Close
John Malkovich
Michelle Pfeiffer
Swoosie Kurtz
Mildred Natwick

Index

2001: A Space Odyssey	93	Axelrod, George	210, 211, 363
		Aznavour, Charles	326
Abel, Walter	42		
Abrams, Bob	122, 132	Bacall, Lauren	5, 124, 348,
Acevedo, Del	275		352
Acheson, James	323, 331, 333	Bachrach, Nikki	297
Albert, Eddie	196, 347, 351	Baddeley, Hermione	102, 165, 167,
Aldis, Will	317, 367		169, 266, 341,
Aldredge, Theoni V.	238, 252		360
Allen, Gracie	18	Bailey, Pearl	191, 193
Allyson, June	350	Baker, Diane	151, 156, 359, 361
Alonso, John	260	Baker, Joe Don	207
Anderson, Judith	79, 354	Baker, Rick	288
Anderson, Loni	367	Ball, Lucille	67
Angeli, Pier	20, 351	Bancroft, Anne	77, 196, 348
Anna Karenina	129	Bankhead, Tallulah	87
Antonio, Lou	207	*Barry Lyndon*	249
April Fools, The	211, 215, 216,	Bass, Bobby	279, 280
	274, 363	Baxter, Anne	89, 355
Archerd, Army	251, 333	Beaton, Cecil	70
Arden, Eve	67	*Beauty And The Beast*	265, 266, 267,
Armstrong, Louis	86		268, 269, 375
Arnaz, Desi	19	*Been There, Done That*	125
Arrington, Maggie	i	*Being There*	178, 179
Arthur, Beatrice	210	*Bells Are Ringing*	103
Ashley, Elizabeth	292, 293, 366	*Ben Hur*	80, 135
Assheton - Smith,		Bennet, Jill	64, 349
Lady Joan	266, 267	Bennett, Brad	i, 32, 153, 159,
Auchincloss, Janet	239		268, 336
Aumont, Jean-Pierre	75, 353	Berenson, Berry	95
Avanlon, Frankie	162, 358	Bergen, Candice	224, 236, 315

Bergerac, Jacques 70
Berle, Milton 18, 163
Berman, Pandro S. 67, 77, 85, 97, 98, 99, 114, 115, 116, 117, 151, 152, 153, 155, 173, 174, 175, 222, 224, 341, 345, 350, 352, 353, 357, 358, 359, 360, 364
Best Little Whorehouse In Texas, The 289
Bhowani Junction 7, 269, 345
Black, Karen 239, 364
Blackboard Jungle, The 345
Blanch, Lesley 5
Blyth, Ann 18, 55, 56, 59, 348
Bochner, Lloyd 162, 359
Bogart Slept Here 263
Bogart, Humphrey 285
Booth, Margaret 85
Borgnine, Ernest 13, 14, 349
Borzage, Lew 197
Bourne Identity, The 309, 314
Box, John 237, 238, 245
Boyd, Stephen 107, 121
Boyer, Charles 96, 109, 213, 214, 341, 348, 357, 363
Brandon, Marlon 47, 58, 138, 139, 141, 228, 351, 358
Bridges, Beau 229, 233, 364
Brillstein, Bernie 321, 322
Brooks, Mel 78
Brooks, Richard 13, 79, 114, 117, 154, 297, 341, 345, 348, 349, 353, 354, 358, 359
Brossette, Stanley 55, 289
Brown, Blair 317, 367
Brown, Joe E. 89
Brown, Pamela 64, 65, 66, 349
Buchholtz, Horst 109, 357
Buddy Buddy 291
Bundle Of Joy 98
Burns, George 18
Burns, Lillian 83
Burton, Maria 122

Burton, Richard 121, 127, 129, 130, 131, 179, 188, 197, 312
Burton, Sybil 129
BUtterfield 8 91, 93, 94, 95, 96, 97, 98, 99, 100, 101, 102, 103, 104, 105, 106, 196, 268, 357
Buttons, Red 331
Cagney, James 15, 347, 350
Callow, Ridgeway (Reggie) 10, 38, 41, 135, 136, 148
Capote, Truman 236
Cardiff, Jack 71
Caron, Leslie 109, 354, 357
Carroll, Diahann 175
Carroll, Gordon 199, 362, 363
Carson, Jack 79, 115, 119
Casey, Bernie 299
Cass, Mama 259, 260, 261
Cat On A Hot Tin Roof 40, 79, 80, 115, 117, 119, 129, 354
Catered Affair, The 13, 14, 15, 349
Cavell, Marc 202
Chan, Jackie 306
Channing, Stockard 260, 262, 263, 265
Chaplin, Charlie 129, 250
Chaplin, Oona 129
Chayevsky, Paddy 13, 128
Chevalier, Maurice 70, 109, 341, 354, 357
Child's Play 227, 228, 232, 364
Children's Hour, The 98
Chiles, Lois 236, 240, 264
Christie, Julie 262
Chucky 227
Clayton, Jack 233, 235, 236, 237, 239, 242, 243, 244, 245, 246, 249, 251, 253, 309, 310, 311, 313, 314, 341, 364

Index

Cleopatra   38, 103, 107, 108, 121, 123, 125, 127, 128, 129, 131, 132, 133, 138, 157, 183, 337, 339
Clift, Montgomery   29, 30, 36, 40, 47, 49. 341, 352
Close, Glenn   94, 299, 322, 323, 324, 326, 329, 330, 334, 368
Cobweb, The   8, 348
Coccinelle   23
Cohen, Norman   238, 239, 241, 242, 244, 265
Cole, Jack   58, 59
Collins, Joan   67, 350
Connelly, Marc   93, 356
Connery, Jason   306
Constant Nymph, The   27
Cook, Fielder   265, 266
Cook, Joe   5
Cool Hand Luke   199, 201, 202, 203, 204, 205, 206, 207, 288, 362
Cooley, Isabel   38
Coppola, Francis Ford   236
Cotten, Joseph   181, 185, 360
Craig, Stuart   321, 323
Crawford, Joan   52, 84, 343
Crosby, Betty   88, 199, 200, 206, 207, 211, 217, 219
Crosby, Bing   3, 19, 351
Crosby, Floyd   98
Crowning Glory: Reflections Of Hollywood's Favorite Confidant   52
Cukor, George   5, 6, 7, 19, 25, 181, 341, 345, 353

D'Angelo, Beverly   292, 293, 294, 295, 366
Daily Variety   251, 262
Damone, Vic   55, 59, 349
Dandridge, Dorothy   191, 193

Dangerous Liaisons   1, 210, 280, 288, 321, 323, 325, 327, 328, 329, 330, 331, 332, 333, 334, 335, 361, 368
Daniel, William   152
Darrieux, Danielle   52
Das Boot   310
Davis, Bette   13, 14, 15, 16, 17, 77, 341, 349
Davis, Sammy Jr.   80
David-Gough, Annabel   251
De Havilland, Olivia   26, 27
De Laurentiis, Dino   279
De Mille, Agnes   8, 347
De Niro, Robert   237, 263
Dean, James   20, 53
Dee, Sandra   21, 22, 352
De'lon, Alain   124
DeLuise, Dom   271, 274, 283, 284, 365, 366
DeLynn, Alan   229, 230
Deneuve, Catherine   211, 212, 213, 214, 215, 216, 363
Derek, Bo   280
Dern, Bruce   239, 240
Designing Women   9, 10, 55, 352
Devlin, Dean   261
Devlin, Don   259, 261, 265
Diana, Princess Of Wales   1, 247, 329, 330
Diary Of Anne Frank, The   70, 71, 355
Dickinson, Angie   i, 277, 294, 295, 296, 297, 299, 331, 341
Dietrich, Marlene   3, 214, 337, 341
Dmytryk, Edward   29, 34, 43, 47, 49, 352
Dooley, Paul   292, 295
Dorleac, Françoise   225
Douglas, Kirk   63, 64, 65, 66, 237, 238, 239, 240, 349
Dr. Zhivago   237

Dressed To Kill	299	Fitzgerald, Barry	13, 341, 349
Drums Of Africa	358	*Five Finger Exercise*	103
Duchess of Windsor	22, 23	Flanagan, Agnes	214
Duel	255	Fogler, Gertrude	83
Duke Of Windsor	22, 23, 24, 25	Fonda, Jane	91, 93, 94, 95, 96, 98, 104, 105, 356
Duke, Dorris	240, 241, 242		
Dulles, Josh Foster	131		
Dunaway, Faye	236	Fontaine, Joan	21, 22, 23, 25, 26, 27, 133, 311, 352
Duncan, Margie	165, 189		
Dunnock, Mildred	98, 99, 100, 101, 115, 196, 341, 358		
		Fontanne, Lynn	22
		Ford, Glenn	9, 10, 11, 89, 180, 181, 184, 185, 345, 347, 348, 351, 355, 360
Duquette, Tony	55. 56		
Durbin, Deanna	72		
East Of Eden	53	Ford, John	163, 196, 197, 198, 358
Eastman, Carol	259		
Eastwood, Clint	278	Ford, Wallace	173, 360
Edens, Roger	85, 165, 166	Foreman, John	219, 221, 222, 363
Elg, Taina	19, 353		
Elmer Gantry	115	Forensky, Larry	335
End, The	271, 272, 273, 274, 275, 365	*Fortune, The*	259, 262, 263, 365
Erhardt, Tom	i	Foster, Jodie	317, 318, 319, 367
Esposito, Joe	179		
Evans, Robert	227, 236	*Four Horsemen Of The Apocalypse, The*	111, 357
Fabulous Redhead, The	32, 188	Francis, Anne	96, 345, 350
Fanny	109, 322, 357	Frank, Otto	71
Farrow, Mia	236, 240, 250, 364	Frawley, William	86
Fath, Jacques	22	Frears, Stephen	321, 324, 328, 329, 330, 331, 368
Faye, Alice	87, 88, 335		
Fell, Norman	292		
Ferrer, Mel	21, 355	Freed, Arthur	70, 85, 346, 348, 354
Field, Betty	98, 196, 197, 198, 235, 341		
		French Letters, The	327
Field, Sally	271, 277, 283, 284, 285, 301, 365, 366	Frings, Kurt	46
		Gammon, James	207
Fields, Verna	255, 256	Garbo, Greta	6, 75, 85, 152, 269, 292
Finch, Peter	107, 121, 243		
Fisher, Carrie	189, 224, 233	Garden, Mary	11
Fisher, Eddie	13, 18, 79, 80, 98, 121, 122, 123, 124, 125, 126, 127, 130, 131, 132, 339, 357	Gardner, Stewart	5
		Garland, Judy	57, 58, 216, 218, 326, 337, 341
		Garner, Peggy Ann	311, 312
		Gaslight	84

Gassman, Vittorio 292, 301, 367
Gaynor, Mitzi 19, 353
Gennaro, Peter 165, 166, 171
Gershwin, Ira 32, 295
Gershwin, Leonore 32, 295, 296
Gibson, Mel 9
Gielgud, John 311, 314
Gigi 69, 70, 111, 354
Gilbert, Jody 262
Gilda 184
Gingold, Hermione 169
Gleason, Jackie 283, 285, 288, 341, 366
Goddard, Paulette 3, 249, 250, 251, 252, 341
Golden Earrings 3
Goldsmith, Cleo 299
Gone With the Wind 27, 29, 43, 260
Good Earth, The 84
Goodbye Mr. Chips 68
Gordon, Lawrence (Larry) 256, 271, 275, 277, 291, 365
Gould, Elliot 222, 364
Grable, Betty 87, 88, 335
Granger, Stewart 5, 7, 8, 78, 345, 346, 348
Grant, Cary 78, 79
Gray, Dolores 9, 55, 56. 58, 67, 346, 349, 352
Great Gatsby, The 227, 233, 235, 237, 239, 241, 243, 245, 247, 249, 251, 252, 253, 281, 364
Great Nick, The 239
Green Mansions 20, 124, 355
Green, Guy 173, 175, 360
Greenwillow 103
Greenwood, Joan 8, 346
Griffen, Arvid (Griff) 53
Griffith, Hugh 135, 142, 146, 147, 149
Grodin, Charles 288, 367

Guilaroff, Sydney 51, 52, 99, 107, 114, 116, 183, 214, 292
Guinness, Alec 10, 349
Gypsy 102

Haack, Morton 166
Hall, Conrad 199
Hall Of Mirrors 219
Hamilton, George 8, 267, 356
Hampton, Christopher 321, 329, 330, 331, 333
Hanley, Richard (Dick) 107, 108, 121, 122, 123, 130, 132
Harareet, Haya 80, 239, 240, 242, 311, 313
Harding, Julie 289
Harmon, Joy 200, 205
Harmon, Mark 317, 367
Harris, Richard 134, 135, 143, 341, 358
Harrison, Joan 96
Harrison, Rex 121, 125
Hartley, Mariette 162, 163, 359
Hartman, Elizabeth 173, 175, 176, 341, 360
Harvey, Laurence 98, 102, 169, 219, 222, 341, 357, 363
Hathaway, Henry 163, 358
Hayden, Jeffrey 46, 341
Hayes, Rosalind 38
Hayward, Susan 51, 53, 202, 341, 347
Hayworth, Rita 23, 181, 182, 183, 184, 185, 341, 360
Headly, Glenne 326
Heckart, Eileen 174
Heiress, The 27
Henry, Mike 283, 286
Hepburn, Audrey 20, 124, 125, 355
Hepburn, Katharine 67, 181, 182, 183, 341
Hereford, Kathryn 99, 222

High Society	19, 20, 48, 86, 351	*It's Always Fair Weather*	8, 346
Hilton, Barron	33, 203	Ives, Burl	79, 115, 354
Hilton, Marilyn Hawley	33	Jackson, Anne	91, 93, 210, 356, 363
Hilton, Nicky	33		
Hit the Deck	8	Jaffe, Sam	274
Hitchcock, Alfred	78, 96, 196	*Jailhouse Rock*	78, 352
Holliman, Earl	295, 299	James, Cliff	207
Hollywood Stuntman	275	James, Harry	87
Hollywood, Ken	86	*Jane Eyre*	311
Holm, Celeste	13, 19, 347, 351	Janssen, Dani	294, 307, 341
		Jaws	255, 256, 257
Holman, Libby	40	Johansson, Ingemar	103, 104
Home from the Hill	8, 356	Jourdan, Louis	10, 349, 354
Hooper	275, 277, 278, 279, 280, 281, 283, 366	Kadish, Ben	71, 109
		Kalassian, Mary	18, 211, 333
Hope, Bob	3	Kahn, Aga	22, 23
Hopper, Dennis	199	Kampmann, Steven	317, 319, 367
Hopper, Hedda	116, 154	Kaplan, William	69, 111
Houseman, John	63, 346, 348, 349	Karl, Harry	339
		Karnilova, Maria	165, 171
How The West Was Won	163, 358	Kassem, Casey	331
How To Marry A Millionaire	88, 124	Kaufman, Millard	34, 49
Howard, Irene	170	Kaye, Nora	226
Howard, Trevor	135, 136, 140, 146, 148, 249, 358	Keaton, Diane	230
		Keaton, Michael	326
		Keel, Howard	55, 60, 348
Hudson, Rock	69, 336, 353	Keith, Brian	277, 299, 366, 367
Humphrey, Hubert	214, 285		
Hunt, Martita	165, 166, 167, 168, 169, 170, 171	Kelley, Bob	33
		Kelly, Gene	19, 346, 353
Hurok, Sol	225	Kelly, Grace	10, 19, 52, 269, 349, 351
Huston, Angelica	323		
Hutton, Betty	3	Kelly, Orry	114
Hutton, Lauren	292, 293, 366	Kendall, Kay	19, 341, 353
Hyams, Peter	224, 225, 226	Kennedy, Burt	181, 182, 184, 185, 297, 360, 362
I Love Lucy	86, 87		
I'll Cry Tomorrow	51, 53, 97, 202, 347	Kennedy, George	199, 202, 205, 362
Incredible Shrinking Woman, The	288, 289, 293, 367	Kerr, Deborah	19, 350
		Kershner, Irvin	131, 179
		Khan, Aga	22, 23
Independence Day	261	Khan, Aly	22, 23
Ingels, Marty	331, 334	*King Kong*	269, 270
Interrupted Melody	10, 11, 347	*King Solomon's Mines*	162

Index 375

Kismet	55, 56, 57, 58, 60, 61, 63, 348
Klein, Robert	277
Koch, Howard W.	209, 362
Kosinski, Jerzy	179
Koster, Henry	72, 188, 191, 192, 194, 196, 341, 361
Kubrick, Stanley	93
Kurtz, Swoosie	323, 368
Lambrinos, Vassili	167
Lamkin, Marguerite	39, 40
Lanchester, Elsa	169
Lansbury, Angela	167
Last Hunt, The	78, 348
Laura	299
Laurie, Piper	21, 22, 352
Lawford, Peter	213, 215
Lawrence, Marjorie	10, 11, 12
Lawrence Of Arabia	237
Leachman, Cloris	222
Lederer, Charles	139, 141
Lee, Anna	159, 196
Lee, Bernard	265
Lee, John	122, 130
Leeds, Andrea	67
Lehman, Ernest	151, 179
Leigh, Vivien	124, 268
Leighton, Margaret	196
Lemmon, Jack	163, 209, 211, 212, 215, 216, 363
Les Girls	19, 353
Les Liaisons Dangereuses	321, 323, 327
Letter From An Unknown Woman, A	27
Lewis, David	40, 352
Lewis, Jerry	18, 129
Liberace	38
Little Foxes, The	335, 336
Little Night Music, A	103
Lockwood, Gary	93
Logan, Joshua	86, 92, 93, 228, 356, 357
Logan, Lesley	i
Logan, Nedda Harrigan	94, 103
Lollobrigida, Gina	80, 81, 82, 83, 356
Loren, Sophia	69
Lost Horizon	247, 274
Love Me or Leave Me	8, 346
Lowe, Rob	333
Loy, Myrna	212, 213, 214, 217, 271, 274, 341, 363
Luck Of Ginger Coffey, The	131
Lucy Show, The	77
Lumet, Sidney	228, 232, 364
Lunt, Alfred	22
Lupino, Ida	96
Lust For Life	63, 64, 65, 349
Lyon, Sue	196
MacLaine, Shirley	98, 165, 354
Magnani, Anna	14
Malkovich, John	322, 323, 326, 330, 368
Mamoulian, Rouben	107, 121
Mangano, Silvana	269
Mankiewicz, Joseph	107, 121, 128, 129, 132
Mann, Daniel	97, 347, 351, 357
March, Alex	297, 361
Marie Antoinette	52
Marshall, Frank	257
Marshall, George	163, 358
Martin, Dean	47, 354
Martin, Mary	103
Martin, Strother	199, 206, 224
Marty	13
Marvin, Lee	44, 224, 352
Marx, Groucho	18, 19
Marx, Sam	297
Mash	207
Mason, James	228, 233, 364
Massacre At Fall Creek, The	281, 282
Massey, Raymond	163
Matrix, The	324
Matthau, Walter	209, 210, 363
Maugham, Somerset	22
Maxwell, Elsa	22

McDaniel, Hattie 27
McDowall, Roddy 34, 127
McGarry, William (Bill) 76
McGill, Moyna 167
McGraw, Ali 227
McKenna, Virginia 265, 365
McNamara, William 317, 318
McQueen, Steve 80, 236, 356
Medford, Kay 98, 102, 268
Merman, Ethel 32, 56, 102
Merrick, David 227, 228, 229, 230, 231, 233, 235, 236, 237, 238, 239, 240, 243, 249, 250, 252, 253, 281, 282, 341, 364
Merrick, Etan 231, 240, 281, 282
Merrill, Dina 98, 103, 357
Merrill, Gary 15
Methot, Mayo 285
Michel, Keith 64
Midler, Bette 259
Milestone, Lewis 142, 143, 147, 148, 341, 358
Milland, Ray 3
Miller, Ann 67, 350
Minnelli, Liza 57, 325, 326
Minnelli, Vincente 8, 9, 20, 55, 56, 63, 75, 111, 112, 348, 349, 350, 352, 353, 354, 356, 357
Miracle Worker, The 78
Mitchum, Robert 8, 356
Mogambo 269
Money Trap, The 181, 183, 185, 360
Monroe, Marilyn 23, 88, 102, 214, 215
Montalban, Ricardo 181, 185, 188, 256, 360, 361
Montevecchi, Liliane 8, 346
Moomjain, Cary 16
Moomjiam, Steven 326
Moomjian, John 16
Moomjian, Mary 16, 17
Moomjian, Patricia 20, 282, 326
Moomjian, Peris 16, 18,
Moomjian, Richard 20, 282, 326
Moomjian, Ruth 16
Moomjian, Scott 282
Moonfleet 8, 346
Moore, Juanita 191, 193, 292, 293
Moore, Roger 10, 347
Moorehead, Agnes 29, 32, 35, 42, 67, 89, 182, 188, 190, 247, 295, 296, 341, 350, 361
Morey, Edward 195, 196
Morgan, Michele 46
Morley, Ruth 230, 231
Mount, Thom 317
Move 222, 364
Mrs. Miniver 191
Mutiny On The Bounty 84, 135, 136, 137, 138, 139, 140, 141, 142, 143, 144, 145, 146, 147, 148, 358
My Fair Lady 40

Nabors, Jim 302, 367
Natwick, Mildred 322, 323, 331, 341, 368
Neal, Patricia 196
Needham, Hal 277, 283, 284, 294, 305, 307, 341, 366, 367
Neptune's Daughter 69
Network 13
Never So Few 80, 81, 211, 356
Newman, Arthur 199
Newman, Paul 21, 22, 79, 114, 117, 118, 151, 152, 153, 157, 161, 162, 199, 200, 201, 204, 206, 219, 222, 224, 312, 351, 352, 354, 358, 359, 362, 363

Nichols, Mike	177, 179, 180, 188, 189, 249, 251, 259, 260, 262, 263, 333, 365	Peckinpah, Sam	193
		Peppard, George	8, 356
		Perkins, Anthony	20, 21, 91, 92, 95, 97, 102, 219, 220, 341, 355, 356, 363
Nicholson, Jack	84, 237, 259, 262, 263. 365	Peters, Charlie	291
Niles, Mary Ann	165, 171	*Peyton Place*	249
Niven, David	96	Pfeiffer, Michelle	322, 323, 324, 325, 330, 331, 334, 368
Norma Rae	284		
North By Northwest	78		
Novak, Kim	33	*Philadelphia Story, The*	84, 183
		Philippe	139, 140, 142, 143, 144, 145, 146, 323, 329, 331
O'Brian, Pat	271		
O'Neal, Patrick	210, 363		
O'Neal, Ryan	249		
O'Sullivan, Maureen	249, 250	Picasso, Pablo	22
Odd Couple, The	210, 362	Pidgeon, Walter	83, 350
Oklahoma	8, 347	Pierson, Frank R.	199
Oliver, Susan	98, 99	Plunkett, Walter	43, 66
Olivier, Laurence	311	*Pocket Money*	44, 224
On The Waterfront	31	Poitier, Sidney	173, 175, 177, 345, 353, 360
Onassis, Aristotle	22		
Onassis, Jacqueline Kennedy	239, 240	*Porgy And Bess*	193, 296
Opposite Sex, The	67, 350	Porter Cole	19
		Powell, Eleanor	83
Page, Geraldine	114, 115, 116, 117, 118, 119, 358	Powell, Jane	5
		Powell, William	214, 235
		Prentiss, Paula	222, 223, 364
Paget, Debra	78, 348	Presley, Elvis	178, 179, 341, 353, 359, 361, 362
Pan, Hermes	125, 185		
Parker, Colonel	178		
Paker, Eleanor	8, 10, 11, 12, 75, 76, 77, 96, 347, 353, 356	Presnell, Harve	165, 168, 169, 360
		Preston, Robert	229, 232, 233, 364
Parsons, Louella	116		
Parton, Dolly	289, 290	Previn, Andre	85, 240, 253
Pasternak, Joe	72, 346, 350, 362	Princess Yasmin	23
		Prinz, Leroy	86, 354
Patch Of Blue	173, 176, 177, 360	*Prize, The*	151, 153, 155, 156, 157, 159, 161, 162, 163, 359
Paternity	291, 292, 293, 294, 295, 297, 366		
		Prodigal, The	53, 61, 346
Patterson, Floyd	103, 104	*Psycho*	299
Pearce, Donn	199, 206	Purdom, Edmund	53, 54, 346
Peck, Gregory	9, 341, 352	*Purple Noon*	124

Queen Elizabeth	247	Romberg, Sigmund	32
Quinn, Anthony	63, 65, 349	Roosevelt, Eleanor	72, 73
		Rosay, Françoise	75, 77, 353
Radziwell, Princess Lee	240	Rose, Helen	9, 52, 99, 166
Rain Man	334	Rosenberg, Aaron	135, 358
Rainier, Prince of Monaco	19	Rosenberg, Ruby	135
Raintree County	29, 30, 31, 32, 33, 34, 35, 36, 37, 39, 40, 41, 43, 44, 45, 47, 49, 79, 163, 335, 352	Rosenberg, Stuart	163, 199, 211, 219, 224, 362, 363, 364
		Ross, Herbert	224, 226
		Rousselot, Philippe	323, 329, 331
		Russo, Rene	9
Ransohoff, Martin	85	Ruttenberg, Joseph	99, 104, 341
Ransom	9, 348		
Rebecca	27, 252	Saint, Eva Marie	29, 31, 39, 49, 124, 340, 341, 352
Redford, Robert	237, 239, 240, 244, 246, 248, 252, 253, 364		
		Saks, Gene	209, 210, 362
Redgrave, Sir Michael	68	Sam, Chen	336, 337
Reed, Donna	19, 348	Sanders, George	75, 77
Reed, Jerry	283	Sawyer, Diane	333
Reed, Sir Carol	135, 142, 358	Saxon, Mary Barron	203
Reeves, Keanu	2, 323, 324	Schary, Dore	8, 11, 46, 348, 349, 352
Remarque, Erich Maria	250		
Render, Rudy	169	Schell, Maria	89, 121, 122, 345
Reynolds, Debbie	13, 52, 79, 80, 98, 165, 171, 186, 188, 194, 339, 347, 349, 360, 361		
		Scheuer, Stanley	156
		Scott, George C.	265, 266, 365
		Scott, Randolph	115
Reynolds, Lynn	223	*Secret Life Of An American Wife, The*	210, 363
Rhodes, Marie	137		
Rhodes, Phil	137	*Seesaw*	281
Rich, Elisa	189	Segal, Alex	8, 9, 348
Rich, Young And Pretty	52	Sellers, Peter	179
Richardson, Tony	68	*Separate Tables*	68
Riddle, Nelson	262	*Seven Women*	196
Road To Perdition	291	*Seventh Sin, The*	75, 76, 353
Robinson, Dar	301	Shamroy, Leon	210, 211, 341
Robinson, Edward G.	151, 154, 161, 341, 359	*Sharky's Machine*	297, 299, 301, 303, 309, 366
		Shaw, Peter	166
Robinson, Julie	58	Shearer, Norma	52
Robson, Flora	196	Shepherd, Cybill	236
Robson, Mark	151, 152, 157	Sheridan, Ann	67, 350
Rocky 2	303	Sherwood, Madeliene	79, 115, 116, 119
Rocky 3	303		
Rogers, Ginger	66, 70		
Rogers, Wayne	204, 207, 224	Shire, Talia	303

Signoret, Simone	311, 314	*Sunset Boulevard*	129, 182
Silva, Henry	299	Surtees, Robert	135
Silverman, Jonathan	317	*Swan, The*	10, 19, 349
Simmons, Jean	21, 22, 352	Swanson, Gloria	129, 182
Simon, Neil	209, 210, 311	*Sweet Bird Of Youth*	114, 117, 119, 165, 358
Simone, Lela	85		
Sinatra, Frank	13, 19, 80, 81, 82, 211, 269, 341, 347, 351, 354, 356	Sylbert, Richard	260, 261
		T. R. Baskin	224, 226
Singing Nun, The	188, 191, 193, 195, 196, 292, 361	*Tall Story*	91, 92, 93, 94, 95, 96, 97, 98, 99, 100, 101, 102, 103, 104, 105, 356
Slocombe, Douglas	237, 238, 239, 240, 245	Tarita	139, 140, 141, 358
Smith, Scottie Fitzgerald	236	Taylor, Elizabeth	19, 30, 33, 35, 52, 79, 97, 98, 100, 117, 121, 122, 127, 130, 138, 196, 204, 214, 268, 284, 297, 305, 311, 312, 335, 339, 352, 354, 357
Smokey And The Bandit	277, 283		
Smokey And The Bandit II	283, 366		
Snake Pitt, The	27		
Somebody Up There Likes Me	20, 351		
Sommer, Elke	151, 154, 161, 181, 185 359, 360		
South Pacific	86, 91, 354		
Spielberg, Steven	255, 256, 257	Taylor, Robert	19, 83, 84, 348
Spinout	178, 362	Taylor, Sara	132
Stage Door	67, 197	*Tea And Sympathy*	350
Stallone, Sylvester	303	Teets, Edward	300
Stanton, Harry Dean	207	*Tender Trap, The*	347
Stanwyck, Barbara	350	*Terry And The Pirates*	307
Stark, Ray	263	Thalberg, Irving	6, 52, 84, 85
Stealing Home	317, 318, 319, 367	Thau, Benny	96, 194, 195
		These Old Broads	338, 341
Stein, Mike	114, 115, 117	*Thin Man, The*	214
Steinberg, David	271, 275, 291, 292, 293, 341, 366	Thomas, Danny	331
		Thomas, Rosemary	331
		Thompson, Kay	85
Sterke, Jeanette	64	Thompson, Marshall	133
Stevens, George Jr.	70, 355	Thompson, Sada	336
Stick	315	Thorpe, Richard	53, 54, 346, 352
Stompanato, Johnny	54	Thurman, Uma	322, 323, 330
Stone, Robert	219	*Tin Pan Alley*	87
Streisand, Barbara	222, 337	Todd, Liza	121, 122, 123
Strickling, Howard	55, 81, 181	Todd, Mike	34, 35, 40, 79, 80, 107, 347
Strohm, Walter	4, 5, 6, 7, 135, 147		
Stroker Ace	302, 367	Tomlin, Lily	18, 288, 289, 290, 367

Index 379

Tone, Franchot	343	Webb, Bobby	138
Torchia, Emily	55, 154	Weingarten, Lawrence	165, 347, 354, 360
Torn, Rip	115, 116		
Trader Horn	5, 162	Weld, Tuesday	236
Travers, Bill	75, 345, 353	*West Side Story*	103
Tree Grows In Brooklyn, A	311	West, Mae	43, 69
Turkel, Ann	236	*Who's Afraid Of Virginia Woolf*	179
Turner, Lana	53, 54, 55, 61, 269, 286, 341, 346	Wiesenfeld, Suzanne	322
		Wilder Shores of Love, The	5, 6, 7
		Wilding, Michael	30, 35
Tuttle, William	88, 115, 183	Wilhelm, Jerry	327
Twist Of The Key	96	Williams, Edy	210
Two For The Seesaw	97, 281	Williams, Esther	83, 84
Tyson, Cicely	191	Williams, Tennessee	114, 115, 117, 210
Unsinkable Molly Brown, The	13, 165, 168, 267, 360	Wilson, Scott	239
		Winchell, Walter	116, 117
		Winger, Debra	292
Until They Sail	21	Winters, Shelley	173, 174, 176, 178, 360
		Wise, Robert	21, 351, 352
Van Devere, Trish	265, 365	Withers, Jane	271
Van Fleet, Jo	53, 199, 200, 202, 203, 341, 347, 362	*Women, The*	67, 144, 333
		Wood, Natalie	336
		Woodward, Joanne	94, 219, 220, 221, 271, 275, 363, 365
Vanni, Don	59, 60, 61		
Vidal, Gore	13		
Vincent, Jan Michael	277, 366	Woodward, Morgan	207
Vintage, The	46	Woolley, Monty	55, 349
Virgin Queen, The	14	*Wusa*	222, 363
Vivian Vance	86	Wyman, Jane	278
Vogel, Bob	56		
Von Liebgott, Richard Martin Luther III	278	Young Lions, The	47
		Youngerman, Joe	7
Wagner, Jane	288, 289	Zadora, Pia	331, 332, 333
Waite, Genevieve	364	Zanuck, Darryl F.	87, 88
Waite, Ralph	201, 207		
Wallach, Eli	93, 94, 210		
Wallerstein, Rowe	170, 197		
Walston, Ray	91, 93		
Walters, Charles	70, 165, 167, 168, 169, 171, 347, 351, 360		
Ward, Rachel	299, 367		
Waterson, Sam	239		
Wayne, John	96		

They say there's nothing like a good book...

We think that says quite a lot!

BearManorMedia

P O Box 71426 • Albany, GA 31708
Phone: 760-709-9696 • Fax: 814-690-1559
Book orders over $99 always receive FREE US SHIPPING!
Visit our webpage at www.bearmanormedia.com
for more great deals!

www.ingramcontent.com/pod-product-compliance
Lightning Source LLC
Chambersburg PA
CBHW051625230426
43669CB00013B/2186